What People Are Saying About
Test-Driven Development for Embedded C

In this much-needed book, Agile methods expert James Grenning concisely demonstrates why and how to apply Test-Driven Development in embedded software development. Coming from a purely embedded background, I was myself skeptical about TDD initially. But with this book by my side, I'm ready to plunge right in and certain I can apply TDD even to device drivers and other challenging low-level code.

➤ **Michael Barr**
   Author of *Programming Embedded Systems: With C and GNU Development Tools* and *Embedded C Coding Standard*, Netrino, Inc.

"Test-Driven Development cannot work for us! We work in C, and Test-Driven Development requires an object-oriented language such as Java!" I frequently hear statements such as these when coaching teams in TDD in C. I've always pointed them to the work of James Grenning, such as the article "Embedded TDD Cycle." James is a true pioneer in applying Agile development techniques to embedded product development. I was really excited when he told me he was going to write this book because I felt it would definitively help the embedded Agile community forward. It took James more than two years, but the result, this book, was worth waiting for. This is a good and useful book that every embedded developer should read.

➤ **Bas Vodde**
   Author of *Scaling Lean and Agile Development* and *Practices for Scaling Lean and Agile Development*, Odd-e, Singapore

I have been preaching and teaching TDD in C for years, and finally there is a book I can recommend to fellow C programmers who want to learn more about modern programming techniques.

➤ **Olve Maudal**
   C programmer, Cisco Systems

This book is a practical guide that sheds light on how to apply Agile development practices in the world of embedded software. You'll soon be writing tests that help you pinpoint problems early and avoid hours tearing your hair out trying to figure out what's going on. From my experience writing code for robotics, telemetry, and telecommunications products, I can heartily recommend reading this book; it's a great way to learn how you can apply Test-Driven Development for embedded C.

➤ **Rachel Davies**
   Author of *Agile Coaching*, Agile Experience Limited

Test-Driven Development for Embedded C is the first book I would recommend to both C and C++ developers wanting to learn TDD, whether or not their target is an embedded platform. It's just that good.

➤ **C. Keith Ray**
   Agile coach/trainer, Industrial Logic, Inc.

This book is targeting the embedded-programmer-on-the-street and hits its target. It is neither spoon-fed baby talk nor useless theory-spin. In clear and simple prose, James shows working geeks each of the TDD concepts and their C implementations. Any C programmer can benefit from working through this book.

➤ **Michael "GeePaw" Hill**
   Senior TDD coach, Anarchy Creek Software

Test-Driven Development for Embedded C

James W. Grenning

The Pragmatic Bookshelf

Dallas, Texas • Raleigh, North Carolina

Many of the designations used by manufacturers and sellers to distinguish their products are claimed as trademarks. Where those designations appear in this book, and The Pragmatic Programmers, LLC was aware of a trademark claim, the designations have been printed in initial capital letters or in all capitals. The Pragmatic Starter Kit, The Pragmatic Programmer, Pragmatic Programming, Pragmatic Bookshelf, PragProg and the linking *g* device are trademarks of The Pragmatic Programmers, LLC.

Every precaution was taken in the preparation of this book. However, the publisher assumes no responsibility for errors or omissions, or for damages that may result from the use of information (including program listings) contained herein.

Our Pragmatic courses, workshops, and other products can help you and your team create better software and have more fun. For more information, as well as the latest Pragmatic titles, please visit us at *http://pragprog.com*.

The team that produced this book includes:

Jacquelyn Carter (editor)
Potomac Indexing, LLC (indexer)
Kim Wimpsett (copyeditor)
David Kelly (typesetter)
Janet Furlow (producer)
Juliet Benda (rights)
Ellie Callahan (support)

Copyright © 2011 James W. Grenning.
All rights reserved.

No part of this publication may be reproduced, stored in a retrieval system, or transmitted, in any form, or by any means, electronic, mechanical, photocopying, recording, or otherwise, without the prior consent of the publisher.

Printed in the United States of America.
ISBN-13: 978-1-934356-62-3
Printed on acid-free paper.
Book version: P3.0—September 2014

In dedication to my dad, for giving me a good compass, and my loving wife Marilee for helping me not lose it.

Contents

Foreword by Jack Ganssle xiii

Foreword by Robert C. Martin xv

Acknowledgments xix

Preface xxi

1. **Test-Driven Development** 1
   1.1 Why Do We Need TDD?   2
   1.2 What Is Test-Driven Development?   4
   1.3 Physics of TDD   5
   1.4 The TDD Microcycle   6
   1.5 TDD Benefits   8
   1.6 Benefits for Embedded   10

Part I — Getting Started

2. **Test-Driving Tools and Conventions** 13
   2.1 What Is a Unit Test Harness?   13
   2.2 Unity: A C-Only Test Harness   14
   2.3 CppUTest: A C++ Unit Test Harness   21
   2.4 Unit Tests Can Crash   24
   2.5 The Four-Phase Test Pattern   25
   2.6 Where Are We?   25

3. **Starting a C Module** 27
   3.1 Elements of a Testable C Module   27
   3.2 What Does an LED Driver Do?   29
   3.3 Write a Test List   29
   3.4 Writing the First Test   31
   3.5 Test-Drive the Interface Before the Internals   36

	3.6	Incremental Progress	42
	3.7	Test-Driven Developer State Machine	45
	3.8	Tests Are FIRST	46
	3.9	Where Are We?	47

4. Testing Your Way to Done 49
	4.1	Grow the Solution from Simple Beginnings	49
	4.2	Keep the Code Clean—Refactor as You Go	64
	4.3	Repeat Until Done	67
	4.4	Take a Step Back Before Claiming Done	73
	4.5	Where Are We?	74

5. Embedded TDD Strategy 77
	5.1	The Target Hardware Bottleneck	77
	5.2	Benefits of Dual-Targeting	78
	5.3	Risks of Dual-Target Testing	79
	5.4	The Embedded TDD Cycle	80
	5.5	Dual-Target Incompatibilities	83
	5.6	Testing with Hardware	88
	5.7	Slow Down to Go Fast	91
	5.8	Where Are We?	91

6. Yeah, but... 93
	6.1	We Don't Have Time	93
	6.2	Why Not Write Tests After the Code?	97
	6.3	We'll Have to Maintain the Tests	97
	6.4	Unit Tests Don't Find All the Bugs	98
	6.5	We Have a Long Build Time	98
	6.6	We Have Existing Code	99
	6.7	We Have Constrained Memory	99
	6.8	We Have to Interact with Hardware	100
	6.9	Why a C++ Test Harness for Testing C?	101
	6.10	Where Are We?	102

Part II — Testing Modules with Collaborators

7. Introducing Test Doubles 107
	7.1	Collaborators	107
	7.2	Breaking Dependencies	108
	7.3	When to Use a Test Double	112

	7.4	Faking It in C, What's Next	113
	7.5	Where Are We?	116
8.	**Spying on the Production Code**		**117**
	8.1	Light Scheduler Test List	118
	8.2	Dependencies on Hardware and OS	118
	8.3	Link-Time Substitution	119
	8.4	Spying on the Code Under Test	120
	8.5	Controlling the Clock	126
	8.6	Make It Work for None, Then One	127
	8.7	Make It Work for Many	140
	8.8	Where Are We?	145
9.	**Runtime-Bound Test Doubles**		**147**
	9.1	Testing Randomness	147
	9.2	Faking with a Function Pointer	149
	9.3	Surgically Inserted Spy	152
	9.4	Verifying Output with a Spy	156
	9.5	Where Are We?	160
10.	**The Mock Object**		**163**
	10.1	Flash Driver	163
	10.2	MockIO	171
	10.3	Test-Driving the Driver	174
	10.4	Simulating a Device Timeout	178
	10.5	Is It Worth It?	180
	10.6	Mocking with CppUMock	180
	10.7	Generating Mocks	183
	10.8	Where Are We?	185

Part III — Design and Continuous Improvement

11.	**SOLID, Flexible, and Testable Designs**		**189**
	11.1	SOLID Design Principles	190
	11.2	SOLID C Design Models	193
	11.3	Evolving Requirements and a Problem Design	195
	11.4	Improving the Design with Dynamic Interface	203
	11.5	More Flexibility with Per-Type Dynamic Interface	210
	11.6	How Much Design Is Enough?	214
	11.7	Where Are We?	216

12. Refactoring 219
12.1 Two Values of Software 219
12.2 Three Critical Skills 220
12.3 Code Smells and How to Improve Them 222
12.4 Transforming the Code 232
12.5 But What About Performance and Size? 249
12.6 Where Are We? 252

13. Adding Tests to Legacy Code 253
13.1 Legacy Code Change Policy 253
13.2 Boy Scout Principle 254
13.3 Legacy Change Algorithm 255
13.4 Test Points 257
13.5 Two-Stage struct Initialization 260
13.6 Crash to Pass 263
13.7 Characterization Tests 268
13.8 Learning Tests for Third-Party Code 271
13.9 Test-Driven Bug Fixes 274
13.10 Add Strategic Tests 274
13.11 Where Are We? 274

14. Test Patterns and Antipatterns 277
14.1 Ramble-on Test Antipattern 277
14.2 Copy-Paste-Tweak-Repeat Antipattern 279
14.3 Sore Thumb Test Cases Antipattern 280
14.4 Duplication Between Test Groups Antipattern 282
14.5 Test Disrespect Antipattern 283
14.6 Behavior-Driven Development Test Pattern 283
14.7 Where Are We? 284

15. Closing Thoughts 285

Part IV — Appendixes

A1. Development System Test Environment 291
A1.1 Development System Tool Chain 291
A1.2 Full Test Build makefile 293
A1.3 Smaller Test Builds 294

A2.	**Unity Quick Reference**	**297**
	A2.1 Unity Test File	297
	A2.2 Unity Test main	299
	A2.3 Unity TEST Condition Checks	299
	A2.4 Command-Line Options	300
	A2.5 Unity in Your Target	300
A3.	**CppUTest Quick Reference**	**303**
	A3.1 The CppUTest Test File	303
	A3.2 Test Main	304
	A3.3 TEST Condition Checks	304
	A3.4 Test Execution Order	305
	A3.5 Scripts to Create Starter Files	305
	A3.6 CppUTest in Your Target	306
	A3.7 Convert CppUTest Tests to Unity	307
A4.	**LedDriver After Getting Started**	**309**
	A4.1 LedDriver First Few Tests in Unity	309
	A4.2 LedDriver First Few Tests in CppUTest	310
	A4.3 LedDriver Early Interface	310
	A4.4 LedDriver Skeletal Implementation	311
A5.	**Example OS Isolation Layer**	**313**
	A5.1 Test Cases to Assure Substitutable Behavior	314
	A5.2 POSIX Implementation	315
	A5.3 Micrium RTOS Implementation	317
	A5.4 Win32 Implementation	319
	A5.5 Burden the Layer, Not the Application	320
A6.	**Bibliography**	**321**
	Index	**323**

Foreword by Jack Ganssle

Test-Driven Development for Embedded C is hands-down the best book on the subject. This is an amiable, readable book with an easy style that is fairly code-centric, taking the reader from the essence of TDD through mastery using detailed examples. It's a welcome addition to the genre because the book is completely C-focused, unlike so many others, and is specifically for those of us writing firmware.

James skips no steps and leads one through the gritty details but always keeps the discussion grounded so one is not left confused by the particulars. The discussion is laced with homey advice and great insight. He's not reluctant to draw on the wisdom of others, which gives the book a sense of completeness.

The early phases of a TDD project are mundane to the point of seeming pointlessness. One writes tests to ensure that the most elemental of things work correctly. Why bother checking to see that what is essentially a simple write works correctly? I've tossed a couple of books on the floor in disgust at this seeming waste of time, but James warns the gentle reader to adopt patience, with a promise, later fulfilled, that he'll show how the process is a gestalt that yields great code.

TDD does mean one is buried in the details of a particular method or a particular test, and the path ahead can be obscured by the tests at hand. If you're a TDD cynic or novice, be sure to read the entire book before forming any judgments so you can see how the details morph into a complete system accompanied by a stable of tests.

Better than any book I've read on the subject, *Test-Driven Development for Embedded C* lays out the essential contrast between TDD and the more conventional write-a-lot-of-code-and-start-debugging style for working. With the latter technique, we're feeding chili dogs to our ulcers as the bugs stem from work we did long ago and are correspondingly hard to find. TDD, on the other hand, means today's bug is a result of work one did ten minutes ago. They're exposed, like ecdysiast Gypsy Rose Lee's, uh, assets. A test fails? Well, the bug must be in the last thing you did.

One of TDD's core strengths is the testing of boundary conditions. My file of embedded disasters reeks of expensive failures caused by code that failed because of overflows, off-by-one errors, and the like. TDD—or, at least James' approach to it—means getting the "happy" path working and tested and then writing tests to ensure each and every boundary condition is also tested. Conventional unit testing is rarely so extensive and effective.

Embedded TDD revolves around creating a test harness, which is a software package that allows a programmer to express how production code should behave. James delves into both Unity and CppUTest in detail. (Despite its name, the latter supports both C++ and C). Each test invokes creation and teardown routines to set up and remove the proper environment, like, for instance, initializing a buffer and then checking for buffer overflows. I found that very cool.

Test-Driven Development for Embedded C is an active-voice work packed with practical advice and useful aphorisms, such as "refactor on green" (get the code working first, and when the tests pass, then you can improve the code if necessary). Above all, the book stresses having fun while doing development. And that's why most of us got into this field in the first place.

Jack Ganssle

Foreword by Robert C. Martin

You've picked up this book because you are an embedded software engineer. You don't live in the programmer's world of multicores, terabytes, and gigaflops. You live in the *engineer's* world of hard limits and physical constraint and of microseconds, milliwatts, and kilobytes. You probably use C more than C++ because you *know* the code the C compiler will generate. You probably write assembler when necessary because sometimes even the C compiler is too profligate.

So, what are you doing looking at a book about Test-Driven Development? You don't live in the kind of spendthrift environment where programmers piddle around with fads like that. Come on, TDD is for Java programmers and Ruby programmers. TDD code runs in interpreted languages and virtual machines. It's not for the kind of code that runs on *real metal*, is it?

James Grenning and I cut our teeth on embedded software in the late 70s and early 80s. We worked together programming 8085 assembler on telephone test systems that were installed in racks in telephone central offices. We spent many an evening in central offices sitting on concrete floors with oscilloscopes, logic analyzers, and prom burners. We had 32KB of RAM and 32KB of ROM in which to work our miracles. And boy, what miracles we worked!

James and I were the first to introduce C into the embedded systems at our company. We had to fight the battles against those hardware engineers who claimed "C is too slow." We wrote the drivers, the monitors, and the task switchers that allowed our systems run in a 16-bit address space split between RAM and ROM. It took several years, but in the end, we saw all the newer embedded systems at our company written in C.

After those heady days in the 70s and 80s, James and I parted company. I wandered off into the realms of IT and product-ware, where resources flow like wine at an Italian wedding. But James had a special love for the embedded world, so for the past thirty+ years James Grenning has been writing code in embedded environments such as digital telephone switches, high-speed photocopiers, radio controllers, cell phones, and the like.

James and I joined forces again in the late 90s. He and I consulted at Xerox on the embedded C++ software running on 68000s in Xerox's high-end digital printers. James was also consulting at a well-known cell phone company on its communications subsystems.

As accomplished as James is as an embedded software engineer, he is also an accomplished software craftsman. He cares deeply about the code he writes and the products he produces. He also cares about his industry. His goal has always been to improve the state-of-the-art in embedded development.

When the first XP Immersion took place in 1999, James was there. When the Agile Manifesto was conceived in Snowbird in 2001, James was there and was one of the original signatories. James was determined to find a way to introduce the embedded industry to the values and techniques of Agile software development.

So, for the past decade, James has participated in the Agile community and worked to find a way to integrate the best ideas of Agile software development with embedded software development. He has introduced TDD to many embedded shops and helped their engineers write better, more reliable, embedded code.

This book is the result of all that hard work. This book is the integration of Agile and embedded. Actually, this book has the wrong title. It should be *Crafting Embedded Systems in C* because although this book talks a lot about TDD, it talks about an awful lot more than that! This book provides a very complete and highly professional approach to engineering high-quality embedded software in C, quickly and reliably. I think this book is destined to become the bible of embedded software engineering.

Yes, you *can* do TDD in the embedded world. Not only that, you should! In these pages, James will show you how to use TDD economically, efficiently, and profitably. He'll show you the tricks and techniques, the disciplines, and the processes. And, he'll show you the code!

Get ready to read a lot of code. This book is chock-full of code. And it's code written by a craftsman with a lot to teach. As you read through this book and all the code within it, James will teach you about testing, design principles, refactoring, code smells, legacy code management, design patterns, test patterns, and much more.

And, on top of that, the code is almost entirely written in C and is 100 percent applicable to the constrained development and execution environments of embedded systems.

So, if you are a pragmatic embedded engineer who lives in the real world and codes close to the metal, then, yes, this book is for you. You've picked it up and read this far. Now finish what you started and read the rest of it.

Robert C. Martin (Uncle Bob)
October 2010

Acknowledgments

To my reviewers—Michael Barr, Sriram Chadalavad, Rachel Davies, Ian Dees, Jack Ganssle, Anders Hedberg, Kevlin Henney, Olve Maudal, Timo Punkka, Mark VanderVoord, and Bas Vodde—thank you for the time, effort, constructive comments, and challenges. Let me add a special thank you to Timo Punkka, my fine Finnish friend, for going above and beyond. I'll also add specific thanks to Olve Maudal who nitpicked the code; it's much improved because of his suggestions. Thanks, Bas Vodde, for the extremely careful reads, excellent suggestions, and blunt feedback, as well as your efforts on CppUTest. And speaking of test harnesses, thanks to the developers of the Unity test harness: Mark VanderVoord, Greg Williams, and Mike Karlesky.

Thank you, Bob Martin and Jack Ganssle, for writing the forewords to my book. Bob, also thank you for the years as my colleague and mentor who helped me establish a solid foundation to be able to write this book. Jack, thanks for listening to a guy who thinks he has part of the answer for the quality problems that plague the embedded software industry. I appreciate how you have helped me expose these ideas to the community.

I'd like to thank my clients for giving me the opportunity to teach TDD for embedded C and C++. They helped me learn the important questions and develop (I hope) articulate and convincing answers to the challenges of applying TDD to embedded C. Thanks for giving me the opportunity to teach and learn in your organizations.

Thanks to Gerard Meszaros for checking my work on test doubles. Thanks to Mike "GeePaw" Hill for a careful read and many useful comments. Thank you, Randy Coulman, Nancy Van Schooenderwoert, and Ron Morsicato for contributing stories. Thanks to Jean Labrosse and Matt Gordon of Micrium for donating hardware to my effort and for the µC/OS-III example code. Dan Saks, thanks for your expert help with some C language questions. Thank you, Hidetake Uwano, Masahide Nakamura, Akito Monden, and Ken-ichi Matsumoto for the use of the eye-movement graphs.

Thanks to software development heros and pioneers Brian Kernighan, Donald Knuth, Martin Fowler, Joe Newcomer, Michael Feathers, Kent Beck, and others already mentioned for letting me quote you in my book.

Many problems, small and large, were found by the readers of my beta book. Thank you, Kenny Wickstrom, Keith Ray, Nathan Itskovitch, Kenrick Chien, Charles Manning, David Wright, Mark Taube, Dave Kellogg, Alex Rodriguez, Dave Rooney, Nick Barendt, Jake Goulding, Mark Dodgson, Michael Chock, Thomas Eriksson, John Ratke, Florin Iucha, Donghee Park, Hans Peter Jepsen, Michael Weller, Kenelm McKinney, Edward Barnard, Lluis Gesa Boté, Paul Swingle, Andrew Johnson, and any of you I missed. You were very generous with your time and efforts, which allowed me to weed out problems as the book evolved.

Thanks to the Pragmatic Programmers, Andy and Dave, for giving me the opportunity to work with you. I probably would not have even thought to bring my book to the Pragmatic Bookshelf if not for a chance meeting with Ken Pugh and a walk through Valley Forge. Thanks for the suggestion, Ken.

Writing is a challenge. So, I must give Jackie Carter, my editor, a big thank you. She helped me go from not being able to string two coherent pages together to writing this book. You really helped, as did a few others, in the effort to learn to write. Thanks, Mike Cohn, for suggesting Stephen Wilbers' book, *Keys to Great Writing [Wil00]*. It helped me get the most out of every word. Thanks to my sister-in-law Debbie Cepla, a fifth-grade schoolteacher; she showed me where semicolons go and where they don't. Thanks to Jeff Langr for suggesting I read all my words out loud so I could hear what I wrote. This was good advice, but too often I still read what I thought I wrote. That leads me to thank Vikki, the text-to-speech voice on my Mac, for brutally reading every word to [deleted: to] me.

Finally, I want to thank my loving wife, Marilee, and family for encouraging me and generously giving me the time to write this book. She even selflessly asked what my next book would be.

Preface

I was first exposed to Test-Driven Development at the first Extreme Programming Immersion[1] in 1999. At the time, I was working on a team creating an embedded communications system. We had just begun extracting use cases from the project's requirements document when I took a week away from the client to attend Immersion. It changed my professional life. I had discovered Test-Driven Development (among other things).

As with many embedded development efforts, having a product release held up by software development was not new. But we couldn't start, because the hardware and OS were not decided on or ready. Each day added to the overall schedule. We were set up, again, because the target hardware bottleneck choked progress to a slow drip. What could we do but meet, talk, argue, dream, and document the software we might write? As it turns out, plenty.

Every embedded developer has experienced the target hardware bottleneck. Often the hardware is developed alongside the software and unavailable for much of the development cycle. If that's not bad enough, both the hardware and the software have bugs, and it's not always clear where they are. For others, the target hardware is so expensive that there's no way for each developer to have their own target system, ready when they are. Developers have to wait, and waiting is expensive.

After a week of immersion in Extreme Programming, the big a-ha hit me! We can do more than document and wait. We can take action. Test-Driven Development was the key to making meaningful progress on the code before hardware and throughout the development cycle.

In the years following that a-ha, I learned TDD and taught TDD in C, C++, Java, and C#. I've dabbled in several other languages as well. I found that I was nearly the only voice working to bring TDD to embedded developers. I needed to write this book.

---

1. XP Immersion is an Object Mentor training course.

Who Is This Book For?

Although the word *test* is in the title, this book isn't written for software testers; I wrote the book for you, the embedded software developer. You probably thought TDD was for someone else. All the books were written in Java or high-level dynamic languages. Conference talks and papers were targeted at web apps or desktop applications. Those talking about TDD wrote code in a foreign language; they spoke about foreign problems. Your concerns were never mentioned or considered.

My mission with this book is to bring you some of the great ideas in software development refined over the past ten years. I wrote this book with examples that will look familiar to you, in your language. The ideas will challenge you. They will help you build better software and free you from the long hours of "test and fix."

Although the primary audience for the book is embedded C programmers, any C programmer can learn TDD from this book. The examples are all from the embedded space, but that does not change the lessons. My style of C is rather object oriented, so you C++ programmers could also learn a lot about TDD from this book.

How to Read This Book

The book is meant to be read from beginning to end, although you don't have to read the whole book to get started with TDD. You will be able to start once you finish the first full example, the LED driver. Let me describe the three major parts of the book.

After a short introduction to TDD, we spend the first part of the book looking at a couple open source test harnesses. Then we go test by test developing our first module. Usually after seeing TDD, developers often have a lot of questions. So, rather than letting them linger, I spend a couple chapters answering some of the questions I've been asked over the past ten years about TDD and TDD applied to embedded systems development.

In the middle part of the book, we get into the techniques needed to test code that interacts with other modules in the system. We'll go through examples where we stub out the dependencies of the code under test. I'll introduce the concept of a *test double* and a *mock object*, both important to being able to thoroughly test-drive your code. This part of the book will arm you with the tools you will need to develop code in the more complex world of interacting modules.

The final part of the book has four important chapters. First we will look at important design principles that can help guide you to better code. We'll look at some advanced techniques in C programming to build testable and flexible designs. Then we'll get into *refactoring*, the practice of improving existing code. After that, we'll look at some of the problems you already have in your *legacy code* base and how you can safely get tests around them that start to improve the existing code that you have invested so much in already. We'll conclude with a few guidelines on writing and maintaining tests.

If you are already experienced in TDD and are now just starting to test-drive C, you can skim the first part of the book. (If you discover that I'm doing TDD in a way that is not familiar to you, maybe you'd better go back to the beginning.) The meat of the book for an experienced TDD programmer just applying TDD to C is in the second and third parts.

If you are more of a beginner at TDD, work through the book from start to finish. Code the examples as you go. Do some of the activities suggested in the *Put the Knowledge to Work* sections at the end of each chapter. After the first and second parts, you will have a good toolkit to apply to your projects.

If you are relatively new at C or not using all of C, you might find Chapter 11, *SOLID, Flexible, and Testable Designs*, on page 189 challenging. If it's too much, come back to it in a few months after getting TDD in C experience.

The Code in This Book

There is a lot of code in this book. You can't understand TDD in detail without a lot of code. Read the code and program along with me to get the most out of this book.

In Appendix 1, *Development System Test Environment*, on page 291, you can find some help on getting a host development system test environment. Look at code/README.txt in the code download for instructions on building the book's example code. If you have the electronic copy of this book, you can click the filename above the code snippet, and the containing file will download for your perusal.

As the book progresses, the code evolves. Some of the evolutions are small, with older versions kept within the same file but compiled using #if 0 ... #endif directives. Other code evolutions are larger, requiring part of one chapter's code to be cloned and evolved in a new directory hierarchy. In the later part of the book, you will notice the evolving code/t0, code/t1, code/t2, and code/t3 directories.

It's likely I did not use your coding style. But I did make considerable effort to present a consistent code style. The C code compiles under an ANSI-compatible compiler—I used GCC.

I use two test harnesses in the book, Unity and CppUTest. Both are included in the book's code download. Unity is a C-only test harness and used in the beginning part of the book. CppUTest is written in C++ but intended for both C and C++. There are many C programmers around the world using CppUTest. The C++ is hidden in macros. The CppUTest-based tests look almost identical to the Unity tests. I'll make my case why I use a C++ compiler for the later examples before we make the transition. As you learn more about TDD and test harnesses, you will be able to decide for yourself which test harness best suits your product development needs.

Thanks for picking up *Test-Driven Development for Embedded C!* I hope you find it helpful in your own quest to creating great software.

About the Cover

That's a bee, not a bug. It keeps the system clean and well structured.

Online Resources

Here are some of the online resources you may appreciate:

Home page for this book . . . . http://www.pragprog.com/titles/jgade
Get book updates, discuss, report errata, and download the book's code.

Book code on James' github account . . . . https://github.com/jwgrenning
Get the latest version of the book's code and other example code.

CppUTest.org . . . . http://www.cpputest.org
Find documentation, discussions about CppUTest and the latest version.

Unity . . . . http://unity.sourceforge.net
Visit the home of Unity.

Author's Website . . . . http://www.jamesgrenning.com
Get up-to-date information about the book, TDD, and Agile for embedded from my blog, as well as find links to other related material.

Debugging is twice as hard as writing the code in the first place. Therefore, if you write the code as cleverly as possible, you are, by definition, not smart enough to debug it.
➤ Brian Kernighan

CHAPTER 1

Test-Driven Development

We've all done it—written a bunch of code and then toiled to make it work. Build it and then fix it. Testing was something we did after the code was done. It was always an afterthought, but it was the only way we knew.

We would spend about half our time in the unpredictable activity affectionately called *debugging*. Debugging would show up in our schedules under the disguise of test and integration. It was always a source of risk and uncertainty. Fixing one bug might lead to another and sometimes to a cascade of other bugs. We'd keep statistics to help predict how much time would be needed to get the bugs out. We would watch for the knee of the curve, the trend that showed we finally started to fix more bugs than were introduced and reported. The knee showed that we were almost done—but we never really knew whether there was another killer bug hiding in a dark corner of the code.

QA started to write regression test suites so they could quickly find new problems, rather than letting them lay in wait only to be discovered in the mad rush at the bottom of the waterfall. But we still got surprised; a small mistake could take days, weeks, or months to find. Some were never found.

Some insightful people saw the potential; they saw that short cycles led to fewer problems. They saw that aggressive test automation saved time and effort. Tedious and error-prone work did not have to be repeated. Tests could be run without the great expense incurred when mobilizing a small army of manual testers. Side effects were detected quickly; debug sessions were avoided. One root cause of schedule variability was isolated, and more predictable schedules emerged.

Jack Ganssle, a well-known embedded guru, suggests, in *Fabric of Development*, on page 2, that integration and test are the fabric of development. Well, they aren't—at least not yet, not in any widespread fashion—but they

> **Fabric of Development**
>
> "The only reasonable way to build an embedded system is to start integrating today. The biggest schedule killers are unknowns; only testing and running code and hardware will reveal the existence of these unknowns. Test and integration are no longer individual milestones; they are the very fabric of development."
>
> —From *The Art of Designing Embedded Systems [Gan00]*, by Jack Ganssle

need to be. Test-Driven Development is one way, an effective way, to weave testing into the fabric of software development. It's Kevlar for your code.[1]

There's a lot to applying TDD to embedded C, and that's what this book is about. In this chapter, you will get the 10,000-foot view of TDD. After that, you'll apply TDD to a simple C module. Of course, that will lead to questions, which we'll address in the following chapters. Before we begin, let's look at a famous bug that could have been prevented by applying TDD.

1.1 Why Do We Need TDD?

Test-Driven Development might have helped to avoid an embarrassing bug, the *Zune bug*. The Zune is the Microsoft product that competes with the iPod. On December 31, 2008, the Zune became a brick for a day. What was special about December 31, 2008? It's New Year's Eve and the last day of a leap year, the first leap year that the 30G Zune would experience.

Many people looked into the Zune bug and narrowed the problem down to this function in the clock driver. Although this is not the actual driver code, it does suffer from exactly the same bug:[2]

```c
src/zune/RtcTime.c
static void SetYearAndDayOfYear(RtcTime * time)
{
    int days = time->daysSince1980;
    int year = STARTING_YEAR;
    while (days > 365)
    {
        if (IsLeapYear(year))
        {
            if (days > 366)
            {
                days -= 366;
```

---

1. Kevlar is a registered trademark of DuPont.
2. The actual Zune code could not be used because of copyright concerns. Zune is a registered trademark of Microsoft Corporation.

```
                year += 1;
            }
        }
        else
        {
            days -= 365;
            year += 1;
        }
    }

    time->dayOfYear = days;
    time->year = year;
}
```

Many code-reading pundits reviewed this code and came to the same wrong conclusion that I did. We focused in on the boolean expression (days > 366). The last day of leap year is the 366th day of the year, and that case is not handled correctly. On the last day of leap year, this code enters an infinite loop! I decided to write some tests for SetYearAndDayOfYear() to see whether changing boolean to (days >= 366) fixes the problem, as about 90 percent of the Zune bug bloggers predicted.

After getting this code into the test harness, I wrote the test case that would have saved many New Year's Eve parties:

```
tests/zune/RtcTimeTest.cpp
TEST(RtcTime, 2008_12_31_last_day_of_leap_year)
{
    int yearStart = daysSince1980ForYear(2008);
    rtcTime = RtcTime_Create(yearStart+366);
    assertDate(2008, 12, 31, Wednesday);
}
```

Just like the Zune, the test goes into an infinite loop. After killing the test process, I apply the popular fix based on reviews by thousands of programmers. To my surprise, the test fails, because SetYearAndDayOfYear() determines that it is January 0, 2009. New Year's Eve parties have their music but still a bug; it's now visible and easily fixable.

With that one test, the Zune bug could have been prevented. The code review by the masses got it close, but still the correct behavior eluded most reviewers. I am not knocking code reviews; they are essential. But running the code is the only way to know for sure.

You wonder, how would we know to write that one test? We could just write tests where the bugs are. The problem is we don't know where the bugs are; they can be anywhere. So, that means we have to write tests for everything, at least everything that can break. It's mind-boggling to imagine all the tests that are needed. But don't worry. You don't need a test for every day of every year; you just need a test for every day that matters. This book is about writing those tests. This book will help you learn what tests to write, it will help you learn to write the tests, and it will help you prevent problems like the Zune bug in your product.

Finally, let's get around to answering "Why do we need TDD?" We need TDD because we're human and we make mistakes. Computer programming is a very complex activity. Among other reasons, TDD is needed to systematically get our code working as intended and to produce the automated test cases that keep the code working.

1.2 What Is Test-Driven Development?

Test-Driven Development is a technique for building software incrementally. Simply put, no production code is written without first writing a failing unit test. Tests are small. Tests are automated. Test-driving is logical. Instead of diving into the production code, leaving testing for later, the TDD practitioner expresses the desired behavior of the code in a test. The test fails. Only then do they write the code, making the test pass.

Test automation is key to TDD. Each step of the way, new automated unit tests are written, followed immediately by code satisfying those tests. As the production code grows, so does a suite of unit tests, which is an asset as valuable as the production code itself. With every code change, the test suite runs, checking the new code's function but also checking all existing code for compatibility with the latest change.

Software is fragile. Just about any change can have unintended consequences. When tests are manual, we can't afford to run all the tests that are needed to catch unintended consequences. The cost of retest is too high, so we rerun the manual tests we think are needed. Sometimes we're not too lucky and defects are created and go undetected. In TDD, the tests help detect the unintended consequences, so when changes are made, prior behavior is not compromised.

Test-Driven Development is not a testing technique, although you do write a lot of valuable automated tests. It is a way to solve programming problems. It helps software developers make good design decisions. Tests provide a clear warning when the solution takes a wrong path or breaks some forgotten constraint. Tests capture the production code's desired behavior.

TDD is fun! It's like a game where you navigate a maze of technical decisions that lead to highly robust software while avoiding the quagmire of long debug sessions. With each test there is a renewed sense of accomplishment and clear progress toward the goal. Automated tests record assumptions, capture decisions, and free the mind to focus on the next challenge.

1.3 Physics of TDD

To see how Test-Driven Development is different, let's compare it to the traditional way of programming, something I call *Debug-Later Programming*. In DLP, code is designed and written; when the code is "done," it is tested. Interestingly, that definition of *done* fails to include about half the software development effort.

It's natural to make mistakes during design and coding—we're only human. Therein lies the problem with Debug-Later Programming; the feedback revealing those mistakes may take days, weeks, or months to get back to you, the developer. The feedback is too late to help you learn from your mistakes. It won't help you avoid the mistake the next time.

With the late feedback, other changes may be piled on broken code so that there is often no clear root cause. Some code might depend on the buggy behavior. With no clear cause and effect, your only recourse is a bug hunt. This inherently unpredictable activity can destroy the most carefully crafted plans. Sure, you can plan time for bug fixing, but do you ever plan enough? You can't estimate reliably because of unknowable unknowns.

Looking at Figure 1, *Physics of Debug-Later Programming*, on page 6, when the time to discover a bug (T_d) increases, the time to find a defect's root cause (T_{find}) also increases, often dramatically. For some bugs, the time to fix the bug (T_{fix}) is often not impacted by T_d. But if the mistake is compounded by other code building on top of a wrong assumption, T_{fix} may increase dramatically as well. Some bugs lay undetected or unfound for years.

Now take a look at Figure 2, *Physics of Test-Driven Development*, on page 7. When the time to discover a bug (T_d) approaches zero, the time to find the bug (T_{find}) also approaches zero. A code problem, just introduced, is often obvious. When it is not obvious, the developer can get back to a working system by simply undoing the last change. $T_{find} + T_{fix}$ is as low as it can get, given that things can only get worse as time clouds the programmer's memory and as more code depends on the earlier mistake.

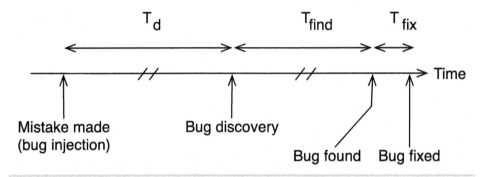

Figure 1— Physics of Debug-Later Programming

In comparison, TDD provides feedback immediately! Immediate notification of mistakes prevents bugs. If a bug lives for less than a few minutes, is it really a bug? No, it's a prevented bug. TDD is defect prevention. DLP institutionalizes waste.

1.4 The TDD Microcycle

I'll start by telling you what TDD is not. It is not spending an hour, a day, or a week writing masses of test code, followed by writing reams of production code.

TDD is writing one small test, followed by writing just enough production code to make that one test pass, while breaking no existing test. TDD makes you decide what you want before you build it. It provides feedback that everything is working to your current expectations.

At the core of TDD is a repeating cycle of small steps known as the TDD microcycle. Each pass through the cycle provides feedback answering the question, does the new and old code behave as expected? The feedback feels good. Progress is concrete. Progress is measurable. Mistakes are obvious.

The steps of the TDD cycle in the following list are based on Kent Beck's description in his book *Test-Driven Development [Bec02]*:

1. Add a small test.
2. Run all the tests and see the new one fail, maybe not even compile.
3. Make the small changes needed to pass the test.
4. Run all the tests and see the new one pass.
5. Refactor to remove duplication and improve expressiveness.

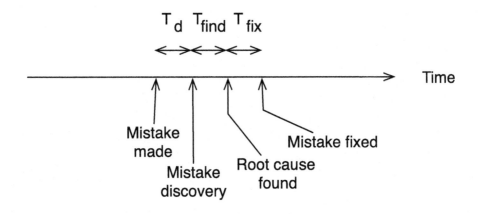

Figure 2— Physics of Test-Driven Development

Each spin through the TDD cycle is designed to take a few seconds up to a few minutes. New tests and code are added incrementally with immediate feedback showing that the code just written actually does what it is supposed to do. You grow the code envisioned in your mind from simple roots to its full and more complex behavior.

As you progress, not only do you learn the solution, but you also build up your knowledge of the problem being solved. Tests form a concrete statement of detailed requirements. As you work incrementally, the test and production code capture the problem definition and its solution. Knowledge is captured in a nonvolatile form.

With every change, run the tests. The tests show you when the new code works; they also warn when a change has unintended consequences. In a sense, the code screams when you break it!

When a test passes, it feels good; it is concrete progress. Sometimes it's a cause for celebration! Sometimes a little, sometimes a lot.

Keep Code Clean and Expressive

Passing tests show correct behavior. The code has to work. But there's more to software than correct behavior. Code has to be kept clean and well structured, showing professional pride in workmanship and an investment in future ease of modification. Cleaning up code has a name, and it's the last step of the repeating microcycle. It's called *refactoring*. In Martin Fowler's book *Refactoring: Improving the Design of Existing Code [FBBO99]*, he describes refactoring like this: refactoring is the activity of changing a program's structure without changing its behavior. The purpose is to make less work by creating code that is easy to understand, easy to evolve, and easy to maintain by others and ourselves.

Small messes are easy to create. Unfortunately, they are also easy to ignore. The mess will never be easier to clean up than right after—ahem—*you* make it. Clean the mess while it's fresh. "All tests passing" gives an opportunity to refactor. Refactoring is discussed and demonstrated throughout this book, and we'll focus on it in Chapter 12, *Refactoring*, on page 219.

TDD helps get code working in the first place, but the bigger payoff is in the future, where it supports future developers in understanding the code and keeping it working. Code can be (almost) fearlessly changed.

Test code and TDD are first about supporting the writer of the code, getting the code to behave. Looking further out, it's really about the reader, because the tests describe what we are building and then communicate it to the reader.

You will hear TDD practitioners call the rhythm embodied by the microcycle *Red-Green-Refactor*. To learn why, see *Red-Green-Refactor and Pavlov's Programmer*, on page 9.

1.5 TDD Benefits

Just as with any skill, such as playing pool or skiing black diamonds,[3] TDD skills take time to develop. Many developers have adopted it and would not go back to Debug-Later Programming. Here are some of the benefits TDD practitioners report:

Fewer bugs
:   Small and large logic errors, which can have grave consequences in the field, are found quickly during TDD. Defects are prevented.

Less debug time
:   Having fewer bugs means less debug time. That's only logical, Mr. Spock.

Fewer side effect defects
:   Tests capture assumptions, constraints, and illustrate representative usage. When new code violates a constraint or assumption, the tests holler.

---

3. Black diamond ski runs are really steep.

> ### Red-Green-Refactor and Pavlov's Programmer
>
>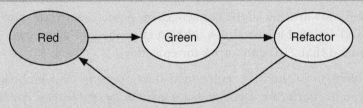
>
> The rhythm of TDD is referred to as *Red-Green-Refactor*. Red-Green-Refactor comes from the Java world, where TDD practitioners use a unit test harness called JUnit that provides a graphical test result representation as a progress bar. A failing unit test turns the test progress bar red. The green bar is JUnit's way of saying all tests passing. Initially, new tests fail, resulting in an expected red bar and a feeling of being in control. Getting the new test to pass, without breaking any other test, results in a green bar. When expected, the green bar leaves you feeling good. When green happens and you expected red, something is wrong—maybe your test case or maybe just your expectation.
>
> With all tests passing, it is safe to refactor. An unexpected red bar during refactoring means behavior was not preserved, a mistake was detected, or a bug was prevented. Green is only a few undo operations away and a safe place to try to refactor from again.

Documentation that does not lie
: Well-structured tests become a form of executable and unambiguous documentation. A working example is worth 1,000 words.

Peace of mind
: Having thoroughly tested code with a comprehensive regression test suite gives confidence. TDD developers report better sleep patterns and fewer interrupted weekends.

Improved design
: A good design is a testable design. Long functions, tight coupling, and complex conditionals all lead to more complex and less testable code. The developer gets an early warning of design problems if tests cannot be written for the envisioned code change. TDD is a code-rot radar.

Progress monitor
: The tests keep track of exactly what is working and how much work is done. It gives you another thing to estimate and a good definition of *done*.

Fun and rewarding
: TDD is instant gratification for developers. Every time you code, you get something done, and you know it works.

1.6 Benefits for Embedded

Embedded software has all the challenges of "regular" software, such as poor quality and unreliable schedules, but adds challenges of its own. But this doesn't mean that TDD can't work for embedded.

The problem most cited by embedded developers is that embedded code depends on the hardware. Dependencies are a huge problem for nonembedded code too. Thankfully, there are solutions for managing dependencies. In principle, there is no difference between a dependency on a hardware device and one on a database.

There are challenges that embedded developers face, and we'll explore how to use TDD to your advantage. The embedded developer can expect the same benefits described in the previous section that nonembedded developers enjoy, plus a few bonus benefits specific to embedded:

- Reduce risk by verifying production code, independent of hardware, before hardware is ready or when hardware is expensive and scarce.
- Reduce the number of long target compile, link, and upload cycles that are executed by removing bugs on the development system.
- Reduce debug time on the target hardware where problems are more difficult to find and fix.
- Isolate hardware/software interaction issues by modeling hardware interactions in the tests.
- Improve software design through the decoupling of modules from each other and the hardware. Testable code is, by necessity, modular.

The next part of the book is dedicated to getting you started with TDD. After a TDD programming example in the next couple chapters, we'll talk more about some of the additional techniques needed for doing TDD for embedded software in Chapter 5, *Embedded TDD Strategy*, on page 77.

Part I

Getting Started

Don't use manual procedures.
> ➤ *Andrew Hunt and Dave Thomas*

CHAPTER 2

Test-Driving Tools and Conventions

I rarely get bored, but following a manual procedure is boring, error-prone, tedious...take your pick. Defining one is not so bad; at least there is something creative there. But repeating it time and time again, that's another story.

Automation is much more fun. You still have to define the procedure, but you define it so a computer can do the grunt work. It is repeatable. It frees your mind so you can focus on the creative work, knowing that the procedure, once established, can run itself. TDD relies on test automation.

We don't get into TDD in this chapter, but we do look at example unit tests using two unit test harnesses. Along the way, we will also discuss some of the common terminology of automated unit testing.

We run the test cases natively on the development system, not on a target platform. We'll talk about when to run tests on the target system in Chapter 5, *Embedded TDD Strategy*, on page 77.

2.1 What Is a Unit Test Harness?

A unit test harness is a software package that allows a programmer to express how production code should behave. A unit test harness's job is to provide these capabilities:

- A common language to express test cases
- A common language to express expected results
- Access to the features of the production code programming language
- A place to collect the unit test cases for the project, system, or subsystem
- A mechanism to run the test cases, either in full or in partial batches
- A concise report of the test suite success or failure
- A detailed report of any test failures

The unit test frameworks used in this book are both popular for testing embedded C and for open source, and they are easy to use. Both the test harnesses are descendants of the xUnit family of unit test harnesses.[1]

First we'll employ Unity, a C-only test harness. Later in the book we will use CppUTest, a unit test harness written in C++ but not requiring C++ knowledge to use. You'll find that the bulk of the lessons in this book can be applied using any test harness.

Here are a few terms that will come in handy while reading this book:

- *Code under test* is just like it sounds; it is the code being tested.
- *Production code* is code that is (or will be) part of the released product.
- *Test code* is code that is used for testing the production code and is not part of the released product.
- A *test case* is test code that describes the behavior of code under test. It establishes the preconditions and checks that significant post conditions are met.
- A *test fixture* is code that provides the proper environment for a series of test cases that exercise the code under test. A test fixture will assist in establishing a common setup and environment for exercising the production code.

To take the mystery out of these terms, let's look at a few tests for something we've all used: sprintf(). For this first example, sprintf() is the *code under test*; it is *production code.*

sprintf() is good for a first example because it is a stand-alone function, which is the most straightforward kind of function to test. The output of a stand-alone function is fully determined by the parameters passed immediately to the function. There are no visible external interactions and no stored state to get in the way. Each call to the function is independent of all previous calls.

2.2 Unity: A C-Only Test Harness

Unity is a straightforward, small unit test harness. It is comprised of just a few files. Let's get familiar with Unity and unit tests by looking at a couple example unit test cases. If you are a long-time Unity user, you'll notice some

---

1. If your company has a policy forbidding open source in your product, the test harness code does not go into the product. It is used only for the test build and may not violate your policy.

additional macros that are helpful when you are not using Unity's scripts to generate a test runner.

sprintf() Test Cases in Unity

A test should be short and focused. Think of it as an experiment that silently does its work when it passes but makes some noise when it fails. This test checks that sprintf() handles a format spec with no format operations.

unity/stdio/SprintfTest.c
```
TEST(sprintf, NoFormatOperations)
{
    char output[5];

    TEST_ASSERT_EQUAL(3, sprintf(output, "hey"));
    TEST_ASSERT_EQUAL_STRING("hey", output);
}
```

The TEST() macro defines a function that is called when all tests are run. The first parameter is the name of a group of tests. The second parameter is the name of the test. We'll look at TEST() in more detail later in the chapter.

The TEST_ASSERT_EQUAL() macro compares two integers. sprintf() should report that it formatted a string of length three, and if it does, the TEST_ASSERT_EQUAL() check succeeds. As is the case with most unit test harnesses, the first parameter is the expected value.

TEST_ASSERT_EQUAL_STRING() compares two null-terminated strings. This statement declares that output should contain the string "hey". Following convention, the first parameter is the expected value.

If either of the checked conditions is not met, the test will fail. The checks are performed in order, and the TEST() will terminate on the first failure.

Notice that TEST_ASSERT_EQUAL_STRING() could pass by accident; if the output just happened to hold the string "hey", the test would pass without sprintf() doing a thing. Yes, this is unlikely, but we better improve the test and initialize the output to the empty string.

unity/stdio/SprintfTest.c
```
TEST(sprintf, NoFormatOperations)
{
    char output[5] = "";
    TEST_ASSERT_EQUAL(3, sprintf(output, "hey"));
    TEST_ASSERT_EQUAL_STRING("hey", output);
}
```

The next TEST challenges sprintf() to format a string with %s.

unity/stdio/SprintfTest.c
```
TEST(sprintf, InsertString)
{
    char output[20] = "";

    TEST_ASSERT_EQUAL(12, sprintf(output, "Hello %s\n", "World"));
    TEST_ASSERT_EQUAL_STRING("Hello World\n", output);
}
```

A weakness in both the preceding tests is that they do not guard against sprintf() writing past the string terminator. The following tests watch for output buffer overruns by filling the output with a known value and checking that the character after the terminating null is not changed.

unity/stdio/SprintfTest.c
```
TEST(sprintf, NoFormatOperations)
{
    char output[5];
    memset(output, 0xaa, sizeof output);

    TEST_ASSERT_EQUAL(3, sprintf(output, "hey"));
    TEST_ASSERT_EQUAL_STRING("hey", output);
    TEST_ASSERT_BYTES_EQUAL(0xaa, output[4]);
}

TEST(sprintf, InsertString)
{
    char output[20];
    memset(output, 0xaa, sizeof output);

    TEST_ASSERT_EQUAL(12, sprintf(output, "Hello %s\n", "World"));
    TEST_ASSERT_EQUAL_STRING("Hello World\n", output);
    TEST_ASSERT_BYTES_EQUAL(0xaa, output[13]);
}
```

If we were worried about sprintf() corrupting memory in front of output, we could always make output a character bigger and pass &output[1] to sprintf(). Checking that output[0] is still 0xaa would be a good sign that sprintf() is behaving itself.

In C it is hard to make tests totally fool-proof. Errant or malicious code can go way beyond the end or way in front of the beginning of output. It's a judgment call on how far to take the tests. You will see when we get into TDD how to decide which tests to write.

With those tests, you can see some subtle duplication creeping into the tests. There are duplicate output declarations, duplicate initializations, and duplicate overrun checks. With just two tests, this is no big deal, but if you happen to be sprintf()'s maintainer, there will be many more tests. With every test added, the duplication will crowd out and obscure the code that is essential to understand the test case. Let's see how a *test fixture* can help avoid duplication in TEST() cases.

Test Fixtures in Unity

Duplication reduction is the motivation for a test fixture. A test fixture helps organize the common facilities needed by all the tests in one place. Notice how TEST_SETUP() and TEST_TEAR_DOWN() keep duplication out of the sprintf() tests.

unity/stdio/SprintfTest.c
```c
TEST_GROUP(sprintf);

static char output[100];
static const char * expected;

TEST_SETUP(sprintf)
{
    memset(output, 0xaa, sizeof output);
    expected = "";
}

TEST_TEAR_DOWN(sprintf)
{
}

static void expect(const char * s)
{
    expected = s;
}

static void given(int charsWritten)
{
    TEST_ASSERT_EQUAL(strlen(expected), charsWritten);
    TEST_ASSERT_EQUAL_STRING(expected, output);
    TEST_ASSERT_BYTES_EQUAL(0xaa, output[strlen(expected) + 1]);
}
```

The shared data items defined after the TEST_GROUP() are initialized by TEST_SETUP() before the opening curly brace of each TEST(). The data items are file scope, accessible by each TEST() and all the helper functions. For this TEST_GROUP(), there is no cleanup work for TEST_TEAR_DOWN().

The file scope helper functions, expect() and given(), help keep the sprintf() tests clean and low on duplication.

In the end, it's just plain C, so you can do what you want as far as shared data and helper functions. I'm showing the typical way to structure a group of tests with common data and condition checks.

Now these tests are focused, lean, mean, and to the point.

`unity/stdio/SprintfTest.c`
```
TEST(sprintf, NoFormatOperations)
{
    expect("hey");
    given(sprintf(output, "hey"));
}

TEST(sprintf, InsertString)
{
    expect("Hello World\n");
    given(sprintf(output, "Hello %s\n", "World"));
}
```

Notice that once you understand a specific TEST_GROUP() and have seen a couple examples, writing the next test case is much less work. When there is a common pattern within a TEST_GROUP(), each test case is easier to read, understand, and evolve, as change becomes necessary.

Installing Unity Tests

It's not evident from the example how test cases get run with the necessary pre- and postprocessing. It's done with another macro, the TEST_GROUP_RUNNER(). The TEST_GROUP_RUNNER() can go in the file with the tests or a separate file. To avoid scrolling through the file, I use a separate file. For the two sprintf() tests written, the TEST_GROUP_RUNNER() looks like this:

`unity/stdio/SprintfTestRunner.c`
```
#include "unity_fixture.h"

TEST_GROUP_RUNNER(sprintf)
{
    RUN_TEST_CASE(sprintf, NoFormatOperations);
    RUN_TEST_CASE(sprintf, InsertString);
}
```

Each test case is called through the RUN_TEST_CASE() macro. Essentially, this TEST_GROUP_RUNNER() calls the function bodies associated with each of these macros:

```
TEST_SETUP(sprintf);
TEST(sprintf, NoFormatOperations);
TEST_TEAR_DOWN(sprintf);

TEST_SETUP(sprintf);
TEST(sprintf, InsertString);
TEST_TEAR_DOWN(sprintf);
```

Invoking TEST_SETUP() before each TEST() means that each test starts out fresh, with no accumulated state. TEST_TEAR_DOWN() is called to clean up after each test.

Now that the tests are wired into a TEST_GROUP_RUNNER(), let's see how the TEST_GROUP_RUNNERs are called. For this last step we have to look at main(). You will have a main() for your production code and one, or more, for your test code. The Unity test main() looks like this:

unity/AllTests.c
```
#include "unity_fixture.h"

static void RunAllTests(void)
{
    RUN_TEST_GROUP(sprintf);
}

int main(int argc, char * argv[])
{
    return UnityMain(argc, argv, RunAllTests);
}
```

RUN_TEST_GROUP(GroupName) calls the function defined by TEST_GROUP_RUNNER(). So, each TEST_GROUP_RUNNER() you want to run as part of your test main() has to be mentioned in a RUN_TEST_GROUP. Notice that RunAllTests() is passed to UnityMain().

One unfortunate side effect of using a C-only test harness is that you have to remember to install each TEST() into a TEST_GROUP_RUNNER(), and the runner is invoked by calling UnityMain(). If you forget, tests will compile but not run, potentially giving a false positive.

Because of this opportunity for error, the designers of Unity created a system of code generators that read your test files and produce the needed test runner code. To keep the dependencies low for getting started with Unity, I've opted to not use the code-generating scripts and manually wire all the test code.

When we look at CppUTest in the next section, you will see another solution to that problem. But before we do that, let's look at Unity's output.

Unity Output

The tests should be run as part of the automated test build. A single command builds and runs your test executable. You will see that I build often, with each small change. This is TDD. I set up my development environment to automatically make all whenever a file is saved.

Test output looks like this:

```
❰ make
 compiling SprintfTest.c
 Linking BookCode_Unity_tests
 Running BookCode_Unity_tests
 ..
 -----------------------
 2 Tests 0 Failures 0 Ignored
 OK
```

Notice that when all tests are passing, the output is minimal. At quick glance, a single line of text says "OK," meaning "All tests passing." In the Unix style, the test harness follows the "no news is good news" principle. (When a test case fails, as you will see shortly, it reports a specific error message.) It's pretty self-explanatory, but let's decipher the test output and summary line.

Notice also that a dot (.) is printed before each test case runs. For a long test run, this lets you know something is happening. The line of hyphens (- - -) is just a separator line for the test summary.

- *Tests*—the total number of TEST() cases.
- *Failures*—the total number of TEST() cases that failed.
- *Ignored*—a count of the number of tests in *ignore* state. Ignored tests are compiled but are not run.

Let's add a failing test to see what happens. Look at the test output, and the intentional error in this test case will be evident:

unity/stdio/SprintfTest.c
```
TEST(sprintf, NoFormatOperations)
{
    char output[5];

    TEST_ASSERT_EQUAL(4, sprintf(output, "hey"));
    TEST_ASSERT_EQUAL_STRING("hey", output);
}
```

The failure looks like this:

```
❰ make
 compiling SprintfTest.c
 Linking BookCode_Unity_tests
 Running BookCode_Unity_tests
 ..
 TEST(sprintf, NoFormatOperations)
     stdio/SprintfTest.c:75: FAIL
     Expected 4 Was 3
 -----------------------
 2 Tests 1 Failures 0 Ignored
 FAIL
```

The failure reports the filename and line of the failing test case, the name of the test case, and the reason for failure. If you are coding along with me, your line numbers will probably differ from mine throughout the examples. Also notice the summary line now shows one test *failure*.

You can find more on Unity in Appendix 2, *Unity Quick Reference*, on page 297.

2.3 CppUTest: A C++ Unit Test Harness

Now that you've seen Unity, I'll quickly describe CppUTest, my preferred unit test harness for C and C++. In full disclosure, I'm partial to CppUTest, not only because it is a capable test harness but also because I'm one of its authors. The first examples in this book use Unity. Later examples, starting in Chapter 8, *Spying on the Production Code*, on page 117, use CppUTest.

CppUTest was developed to support multiple OS platforms with a specific goal of being usable for embedded development. The CppUTest macros make it so that test cases can be written without knowledge of C++. This makes it easy for C programmers to use the test harness.

CppUTest uses a primitive subset of C++; it's a good choice for embedded development where not all compilers support the full C++ language. You'll see that the test cases are nearly identical between Unity and CppUtest. You, of course, can use whichever test harness you prefer for your development.

sprintf Test Cases in CppUTest

This CppUTest test case is equivalent to the second Unity test case found in *sprintf Test Cases in Unity*, on page 15.

```
tests/stdio/SprintfTest.cpp
TEST(sprintf, NoFormatOperations)
{
    char output[5] = "";

    LONGS_EQUAL(3, sprintf(output, "hey"));
    STRCMP_EQUAL("hey", output);
}
```

Besides the macro names, the test cases are the same.

sprintf Test Fixture in CppUTest

Let's look at this CppUTest test fixture that is equivalent to the example Unity test fixture found in *Test Fixtures in Unity*, on page 17.

tests/stdio/SprintfTest.cpp
```cpp
TEST_GROUP(sprintf)
{
    char output[100];
    const char * expected;
    void setup()
    {
        memset(output, 0xaa, sizeof output);
        expected = "";
    }
    void teardown()
    {
    }
    void expect(const char * s)
    {
        expected = s;
    }
    void given(int charsWritten)
    {
        LONGS_EQUAL(strlen(expected), charsWritten);
        STRCMP_EQUAL(expected, output);
        BYTES_EQUAL(0xaa, output[strlen(expected) + 1]);
    }
};
```

Again, it is very similar, with all the same concepts represented. One formatting difference is that the CppUTest TEST_GROUP is followed by a set of curly braces enclosing shared data declarations and functions. Everything between the curly braces is part of the TEST_GROUP and accessible to each TEST() in the group. The shared data items (output and expected) are initialized by a special helper function called setup(). As you might guess, setup() is called before each TEST(). Another special function, teardown(), is called after each TEST(). In this example, it is not used. expect() and given() are free-form helper functions that are accessible to all TEST() cases in the TEST_GROUP.

These refactored test cases are identical to the unity test cases:

tests/stdio/SprintfTest.cpp
```cpp
TEST(sprintf, NoFormatOperations)
{
    expect("hey");
    given(sprintf(output, "hey"));
}

TEST(sprintf, InsertString)
{
    expect("Hello World\n");
    given(sprintf(output, "Hello %s\n", "World"));
}
```

One advantage to CppUTest is that tests self-install. There is no need for an external script to generate a test runner or manually write and maintain test wiring code like RUN_TEST_CASE(), TEST_GROUP_RUNNER(), and RUN_TEST_GROUP(). On the minor difference list are the assertion macros; each test harness supports different macros, though there is functional overlap.

You may notice that Unity and CppUTest are suspiciously close in their macros and test structure. Well, there is no real mystery there; they do follow a well-established pattern that I first saw with JUnit, a Java test framework. The more specific similarities are because I contributed the test fixture–related macros to the Unity project.

CppUTest Output

As already explained for Unity, tests run as part of an automated build using make. Test output looks like this:

```
make all
compiling SprintfTest.cpp
Linking BookCode_tests
Running BookCode_tests
..
OK (2 tests, 2 ran, 0 checks, 0 ignored, 0 filtered out)
```

Just like with Unity, when all tests are passing, the output is minimal. Here is how to interpret the summary line of the test run:

- *tests*—the total number of TEST() cases.

- *ran*—the number of TEST() cases that ran (in this case, they passed too).

- *checks*—a count of the number of condition checks made. (Condition checks are calls such as LONGS_EQUAL().)

- *ignores*—a count of the number of tests in *ignore* state. Ignored tests are compiled but are not run.

- *filtered out*—a count of the number of tests that were filtered out of this test run. Command-line options select specific tests to run.

Let's insert an error into the test to see what the output looks like:

tests/stdio/SprintfTest.cpp
```
TEST(sprintf, NoFormatOperations)
{
    char output[5];
    LONGS_EQUAL(4, sprintf(output, "hey"));
    STRCMP_EQUAL("hey", output);
}
```

The failure looks like this:

```
❮ make
compiling SprintfTest.cpp
Linking BookCode_Unity_tests
Running BookCode_Unity_tests
...
stdio/SprintfTest.cpp:75: TEST(sprintf, NoFormatOperations)
    expected <4 0x2>
    but was  <3 0x1>

Errors (1 failures, 2 tests, 2 ran, 1 checks, 0 ignored, 0 filtered out, 0 ms)
```

The failure reports the line of the failing condition check, the name of the test case, and the reason for failure. Also notice the summary line includes a count of test *failures*. The first failure terminates the test case, resulting in a *checks* count of one.

If you ever insert an error on purpose into a test case, make sure you remove it, or you risk baking a bug into your code.

2.4 Unit Tests Can Crash

One other possible outcome during a test run is a crash. Generally speaking, C is not a safe language. The code can go off into the weeds, never to return. sprintf() is a dangerous function. If you pass it an output buffer that is too small, it will corrupt memory. This error might crash the system now. It might crash later. The behavior is undefined. Consequently, a test run may silently exit with an OK, silently exit early showing no errors, or crash with a bang.

When you have a silent failing or crashing test, let the test harness help you confirm what is wrong. Sometimes a production code change will cause a previously passing test to fail, or even crash. So, before chasing the crash, make sure you know which test is failing.

Because the test harness is normally quiet except for test failures, when a test crashes, you probably won't get any useful output. Both Unity and CppUTest have a command-line option for running the test in verbose mode (-v). With -v, each TEST() announces itself before running. Conveniently, the last TEST() mentioned is the one that crashed.

You can also filter tests by test group (-g testgroup) and test case (-n testname). This lets you get very precise about which test cases are running. These are very helpful for chasing down crashes.

2.5 The Four-Phase Test Pattern

In Gerard Meszaros' book, *xUnit Testing Patterns* [Mes07], he describes the Four-Phase Test, which I'll be using throughout this book. The goal of the pattern is to create concise, readable, and well-structured tests. If you follow this pattern, the test reader can quickly determine what is being tested. Paraphrasing Gerard, here are the four phases:

- Setup: Establish the preconditions to the test.
- Exercise: Do something to the system.
- Verify: Check the expected outcome.
- Cleanup: Return the system under test to its initial state after the test.

To keep your tests clear, make the pattern visible in your tests. When this pattern is broken, the documentation value of the test is diminished; the reader has to work harder to understand the requirements expressed by the test.

2.6 Where Are We?

At this point, you should have a good overview of the Unity and CppUTest, and understand how test fixtures and test cases allow a set of tests to be defined.

What you have not seen so far is Test-Driven Development. The tests written for sprintf() are not TDD tests; sprintf() is existing code. I invite you to put your new knowledge to work by doing the following exercises. Then we'll test-drive some new code in the next couple chapters.

2.7 Put the Knowledge to Work

1. Set up a host development system test environment. You can get some help from Appendix 1, *Development System Test Environment*, on page 291. Download the book code, and run the makefile. You can find the book's code by visiting the book's home page at http://www.pragprog.com/titles/jgade. Look at code/README.txt for more information. Run the makefile. All its unit tests pass.

2. Run make -f MakefileUnity.mk in the code directory. The Unity sprintf() tests are built by this makefile.

3. Then run make -f MakefileCppUTest.mk in the code directory. The CppUTest sprintf() tests are built by this makefile.

4. Write more sprintf() tests like the examples shown in this chapter. For Unity, use code/unity/stdio/SprintfTest.c. For CppUTest tests, use code/tests/stdio/SprintfTest.cpp.

5. Modify TEST_GROUP(Sprintf) so that it handles any size sprintf() output.

Those who want really reliable software will discover that they must find means of avoiding the majority of bugs to start with, and as a result, the programming process will become cheaper. If you want more effective programmers, you will discover that they should not waste their time debugging, they should not introduce the bugs to start with.

➢ *Edsger Dijkstra*, The Humble Programmer

CHAPTER 3

Starting a C Module

In this chapter, I'll lead you through some of the first steps you'll take when test-driving a new module in C. In the next chapter, we'll be in full stride as we complete the module. Starting in this chapter and continued throughout this book, we will see whether we can realize Dijkstra's vision of not introducing bugs.[1] The tool we will use is TDD.

3.1 Elements of a Testable C Module

The examples in the book will use the idea of a module. For our purposes, a module is a self-contained part of a system that has a well-defined interface. This does not say how big a module can get. In this book, we'll use small modules; the module examples will coincide with compilation units, although in the wild, not all modules consist of a single compilation unit. You will see that modularity is needed to make testable code. You will also see that modular design is a natural outcome of TDD.

Testability impacts design significantly and positively. In creating modular C, we will draw upon the idea of an *abstract data type*. Barbara Liskov defines ADTs in her *Programming with Abstract Data Types [Lis74]* as follows: "An abstract data type is defined indirectly, only by the operations that may be performed on it and by mathematical constraints on the effects (and possibly cost) of those operations."

In an ADT, a module's data is treated as private; it is encapsulated. There are a couple modularity options we can employ for encapsulating a module's data. The first choice is to hide data using static file scope variables in the .c file, giving access to the functions in the compilation unit. The data is then

---

1. The Edsger Dijkstra quote is from *The Humble Programmer [Dij72]*.

accessible only indirectly through the module's public interface, which is defined in the .h file as a set of function prototypes. This approach works for a module that has a single set of data to manage, something I call a *single-instance module*.

When a module has to manage different sets of data for different clients, we can use the *multiple-instance module*. With a multiple-instance module, structures must be initialized and passed back to a client holding their context. Here is where ADTs come into play. You can declare a typedef of a forward declared struct in a header file like this:

typedef struct CircularBufferStruct * CircularBuffer;

The compiler is happy to allow pointers to incomplete types to be passed around as long as no code dereferences the pointer. Inside the .c file for CircularBuffer, the struct members can be defined, effectively hiding the data so that only the module whose responsibility is the integrity of that structure can manipulate it. If you are familiar with the POSIX pthread library, it uses this technique. FILE, from Unix, is another example of an ADT.

When doing TDD to create modular C, we will use these files and conventions:

- The *header file* defines the module's interface. For single-instance modules, the header file is made up of function prototypes. For abstract data types, in addition to function prototypes, a typedef is created for a pointer to a forward declared struct. Again, hiding the struct hides the data details of the module.

- The *source file* contains the implementation of the interface. It also includes any needed private helper functions and hidden data. The module implementation manages the integrity of the module's data. For ADTs, the forward declared struct members are defined in the source file.

- The *test file* holds the test cases, keeping test code and production code separate. Each module has at least one test file usually containing only one, but sometimes a few, test groups. Test groups are organized around data common to all the tests in the group. When the setup needs of some test cases are significantly different from others, we'll use multiple test groups and maybe multiple test files.

- *Module initialization and cleanup functions*. Every module that manages hidden data should have initialization and cleanup functions. ADTs certainly need them with their totally hidden internals. C++ builds this idea into the language with constructors and destructors. By convention, I'll make Create and Destroy functions for each module. Modules made up of stand-alone functions, like strlen() and sprintf(), that keep no internal state won't need initialization and cleanup.

Following these practices and conventions makes code easier to test and easier to read and evolve. It's not impossible to test code that follows the data structure/function call free-for-all approach—it's just harder. In the first example, I'll use the single-instance module while test-driving an LED driver. We'll use abstract data types later.

3.2 What Does an LED Driver Do?

Let's say that our system uses LEDs to communicate status to the users or developers of the system. We are going to need a driver for the LEDs. Here's what we know about the LED driver requirements:

- The LED driver controls 16 two-state LEDs.
- The driver can turn on or off individual LED without affecting others.
- The driver can turn all LEDs on or off with a single interface call.
- The user of the driver can query the state of any LED.
- At power-on, the hardware default is for LEDs to be latched on. They must be turned off by the software.
- The LEDs are memory-mapped to a 16-bit word (at an address to be determined).
- A 1 in a bit position lights the corresponding LED; 0 turns it off.
- The least significant bit corresponds to LED 1; the most significant bit corresponds to LED 16.

The first four goals are focused on what the LED driver is supposed to do. Goals 5 to 8 describe how the driver will interact with the hardware. In addition to these requirements, there's a design goal: make the driver testable off the target hardware. There is just one bank of LEDs in the target system, so we'll use the single-instance design model.

Before we start, let's figure out what tests we need.

3.3 Write a Test List

It's helpful to create a test list before developing new functionality. The test list is derived from the requirements. The test list defines your best vision of what it means to be *done*. The list does not need to be perfect. It's a temporary document, probably on a note card or notepad. You can also type the list right into the test file as a comment. As you add each test, the corresponding comment line is deleted.

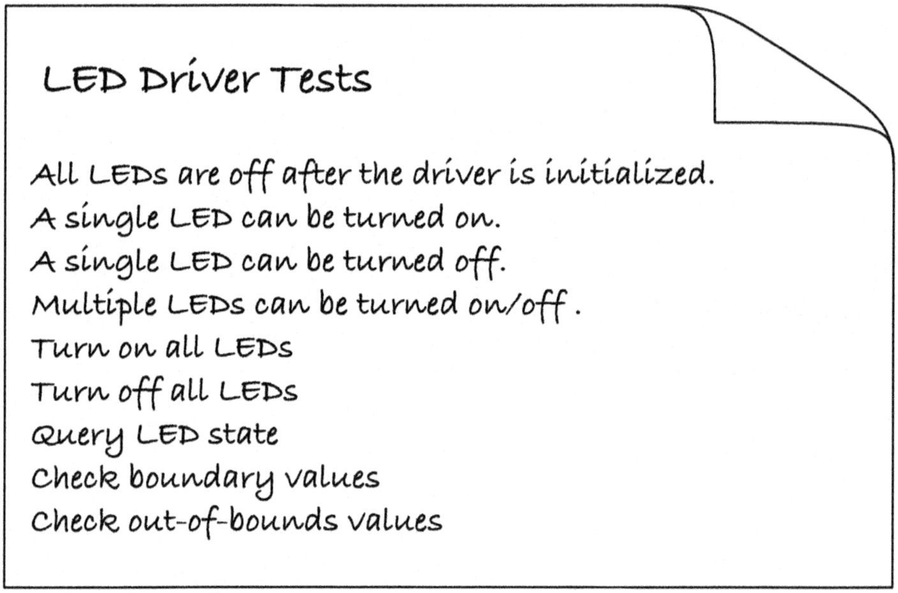

> **LED Driver Tests**
>
> All LEDs are off after the driver is initialized.
> A single LED can be turned on.
> A single LED can be turned off.
> Multiple LEDs can be turned on/off.
> Turn on all LEDs
> Turn off all LEDs
> Query LED state
> Check boundary values
> Check out-of-bounds values

Figure 3— LED driver test list

Don't spend a lot of time composing the list; for the LedDriver, it should take only a couple minutes. My initial test list is shown in Figure 3, *LED driver test list*, on page 30.

Beware of diminishing returns when making a test list. Once you get a few tests down, tests come pretty quickly. When progress slows, you've hit diminishing returns, and that's probably a good time to stop working the test list and start test-driving the design. You will think of other tests as you drive the design. Some of the tests will later be split. Some might be combined. The purpose of the list is to help make sure you don't forget anything. It acts as a map to reorient yourself after a deep dive that is needed to get a test to pass. It's your to-do list.

Some of the tests identified might not have clear outcomes. For example, how do you think the driver should react to out-of-bounds parameters? The answer is not clear. But that's OK. You will probably know your options better when the code comes together. Sometimes more experience clarifies, but sometimes it triggers new questions, ones that cannot be resolved immediately.

In the next section, you will start the TDD test-drive. Before that, I have a question for you. Have you ever been told to tackle the hardest part of the problem first, letting the little things take care of themselves? I have, and it always seemed to be good advice. I am going to turn that advice on its head.

The test-driven developer starts with something small, or easy, that moves the work toward the goal. Each step along the way is verifiable. Capability is added to the production code one test at a time, working toward a robust and well-tested solution. The result is a foundation that can support the more complex behaviors when we get to them. Anticipating the tests to write, and choosing an order to write them in, is a skill you develop over time.

3.4 Writing the First Test

The test list is done, so let's get started. A natural first test is to test that initialization is correct. LEDs are supposed to be off after initialization.

First we'll create the LedDriver test file. By convention, I call it LedDriverTest.c. I usually place test code in a different directory from the production code. I'll put this code in the unity/LedDriver directory and adjust my makefile so it compiles and links with the new test file. Choosing a suitable test name for what we are trying to accomplish, the file should look like this:

unity/LedDriver/LedDriverTest.c
```c
#include "unity_fixture.h"
TEST_GROUP(LedDriver);

TEST_SETUP(LedDriver)
{
}

TEST_TEAR_DOWN(LedDriver)
{
}

TEST(LedDriver, LedsOffAfterCreate)
{
    TEST_FAIL_MESSAGE("Start here");
}
```

If you build and run this test, you'll get this output:

```
❮ make
  compiling LedDriverTest.c
  Linking BookCode_Unity_tests
  Running BookCode_Unity_tests
  Unity test run 1 of 1

  -----------------------
  0 Tests 0 Failures 0 Ignored
```

An initial failing test would indicate that everything is in place, but we did not get a failing test. Add the LedDriverTestGroupRunner.c file to the tests/LedDriver, and add this test case to it like this:

unity/LedDriver/LedDriverTestRunner.c
```
TEST_GROUP_RUNNER(LedDriver)
{
    RUN_TEST_CASE(LedDriver, LedsOffAfterCreate);
}
```

Running make again gives the same results:

```
❰ make
compiling LedDriverTestRunner.c
Linking BookCode_Unity_tests
Running BookCode_Unity_tests
Unity test run 1 of 1

-----------------------
0 Tests 0 Failures 0 Ignored
```

One final bit of wiring is needed. Have main() call the test group runner:

unity/AllTests.c
```
#include "unity_fixture.h"

static void RunAllTests(void)
{
    RUN_TEST_GROUP(LedDriver);
}

int main(int argc, char * argv[])
{
    return UnityMain(argc, argv, RunAllTests);
}
```

With everything wired together properly, we get this failure message:

```
❰ make
compiling AllTests.c
Linking BookCode_Unity_tests
Running BookCode_Unity_tests
Unity test run 1 of 1
.
TEST(LedDriver, LedsOffAfterCreate)
    LedDriver/LedDriverTest.c:15: FAIL
    Start here
-----------------------
1 Tests 1 Failures 0 Ignored
FAIL
```

Now delete the TEST_FAIL_MESSAGE() and see this output:

```
❮ make
compiling LedDriverTest.c
Linking BookCode_Unity_tests
Running BookCode_Unity_tests
Unity test run 1 of 1
.
-----------------------
1 Tests 0 Failures 0 Ignored
OK
```

Now let's make the test check something meaningful. Looking at the test list, the driver has the responsibility to turn off all the LEDs as part of initialization.

How can that be checked? An automatic test can't look at an LED, can it? A retina is needed or a photo cell. Or is it? During hardware software integration we'll have to look at the LEDs, but during unit testing we can *virtually* look at them.

In the target hardware there is a specific address, a memory-mapped I/O address, that is literally wired into the circuitry. The bits written to that address turn on and off specific LEDs. The driver must write a 16-bit zero value to the LED's I/O address during LedDriver_Create() to turn off all the LEDs.

This book is about TDD, so another design goal is that the LedDriver must be testable independent of the hardware (that is, on the development system). If during the test the driver writes to the physical address required by the target hardware, there will be a problem: memory corruption or a memory access fault. Let's *address* how to get this code testable in the development system.

Fake Out the Driver

If the address is passed to the driver, the test case can fake out the driver by passing the address of a bank of *virtual* LEDs instead of the real physical address. The *virtual* LEDs are nothing more than a variable with the same number of bits as the memory-mapped LEDs. The test case can set, reset, and read the variable representing the *virtual* LEDs. The driver does not know that it is being tricked. It's just as happy turning on a bit in RAM as it is setting a bit in a memory-mapped device.

The virtual LEDs idea will work, but what values should we check for? The spec and test list give direction on what values to check. Setting an individual LED bit to zero turns the LED off, while setting it to one turns it on. The hardware powers up with each LED in the on state. Per the spec, the software is responsible for turning all LEDs off during initialization. So, we better make sure that a zero is written to each bit of the virtual LEDs.

> **Save, Make, Run**
>
> In TDD we make a lot of small changes and additions to the code. We build and run tests really often. I suggest you set up your development environment so that a simple keystroke saves your work and initiates a build. I'm using Eclipse for the code examples. I have it set to run make whenever a file is saved. I use the Save All key sequence reflexively.

To test that LEDs are initialized correctly, we write this test:

unity/LedDriver/LedDriverTest.c
```c
TEST(LedDriver, LedsOffAfterCreate)
{
    uint16_t virtualLeds = 0xffff;
    LedDriver_Create(&virtualLeds);
    TEST_ASSERT_EQUAL_HEX16(0, virtualLeds);
}
```

There is some subtlety here. In TEST(LedDriver, LedsOffAfterCreate), virtualLeds is set to 0xFFFF followed by a call to LedDriver_Create(&virtualLeds). Initializing virtualLeds to 0xFFFF makes sure that the test can tell the difference between virtualLeds coincidentally being zero and it being zero because the initialization did its job.

Also, notice the type of virtualLeds. The LEDs are represented by a 16-bit unsigned integer, matching the width of the LEDs in the memory-mapped I/O space. The tests and the production code need to run on at least two machines: the development systems and the target. Consequently, the width of virtualLeds must be specified. As you know, int sizes can vary from one machine architecture to another. Using a portable int type like uint16_t from stdint.h[2] allows us to force the integer length to 16 bits on any machine.

Compiling results in an error, just as expected:

```
❮ make
compiling LedDriverTest.c
LedDriver/LedDriverTest.c: In function 'TEST_LedDriver_LedsOffAfterCreate_':
LedDriver/LedDriverTest.c:16: warning: implicit declaration
                              of function 'LedDriver_Create'
Linking BookCode_Unity_tests
Undefined symbols:
  "_LedDriver_Create", referenced from:
      TEST_LedDriver_LedsOffAfterCreate_ in LedDriverTest.o
ld: symbol(s) not found
```

---

2. stdint.h is only guaranteed to exist in compilers that are C99 or later.

Create the LedDriver.h file and add the prototype for the function LedDriver_Create().
Add the #include to the test file. Compile and see the link error.

```
❮ make
compiling LedDriverTest.c
Linking BookCode_Unity_tests
Undefined symbols:
  "_LedDriver_Create", referenced from:
      TEST_LedDriver_LedsOffAfterCreate_ in LedDriverTest.o
ld: symbol(s) not found
```

After a clean compile, create LedDriver.c and add a skeletal version of LedDriver_Create(). Don't implement the initialization just yet. It should look like the following:

src/LedDriver/LedDriver.c
```
#include "LedDriver.h"

void LedDriver_Create(uint16_t * address)
{
}

void LedDriver_Destroy(void)
{
}
```

We let the test fail to assure it can do its job. Can it detect a specific failure? It looks like this test case can:

```
❮ make
compiling LedDriver.c
Linking BookCode_Unity_tests
Running BookCode_Unity_tests
Unity test run 1 of 1
.
TEST(LedDriver, LedsOffAfterCreate)
    LedDriver/LedDriverTest.c:17: FAIL
    Expected 0x0000 Was 0xFFFF
----------------------
1 Tests 1 Failures 0 Ignored
FAIL
```

The next code example shows the simplest implementation needed to get it to pass:

src/LedDriver/LedDriver.c
```
void LedDriver_Create(uint16_t * address)
{
    *address = 0;
}
```

Building again, we see that the updated test is passing:

```
❰ make
compiling LedDriver.c
Linking BookCode_Unity_tests
Running BookCode_Unity_tests
Unity test run 1 of 1
.
-----------------------
1 Tests 0 Failures 0 Ignored
OK
```

Dependency Injection

Passing the virtualLeds to the driver is a use of *dependency injection*. Instead of the driver *knowing* and depending upon the LED's address at compile time, we inject it at runtime. Only the target system's initialization function will have a compile-time dependency on the physical LED address.

An interesting side benefit of using dependency injection is that the LedDriver is more reusable. The driver could be put in a library and used in systems that have different LED addresses. This is an example of TDD naturally leading to a more flexible design.

Don't Let the Code Get Ahead of the Tests

If you are envisioning the final code, this incomplete implementation is probably bothering you. The address of the LEDs is not stored anywhere, and of course it will need to be stored. Don't store it yet; no failing test requires it. Write a test that won't pass unless you store the address. The next test will force the driver to use the passed-in LED address.

I know it's hard to resist writing code that you know will be needed, but don't write it yet. Let the code follow the tests. Sticking to this discipline produces comprehensive tests and thoroughly tested production code.

Bob Martin composed *The Three Laws of TDD*, shown in *Bob Martin's Three Laws of TDD*, on page 37, which provides guidance on alternating between writing test code and production code. Storing the address before a test requires it is a violation of Bob's third law of TDD.

3.5 Test-Drive the Interface Before the Internals

A good interface is critical for a well-designed module. The first few tests drive the interface design. The focus on the interface means that we're working from the outside of the code being developed to the inside. The test, as the

> **Bob Martin's Three Laws of TDD**
>
> Bob Martin describes Test-Driven Development using these three simple rules:[a]
>
> - Do not write production code unless it is to make a failing unit test pass.
> - Do not write more of a unit test than is sufficient to fail, and build failures are failures.
> - Do not write more production code than is sufficient to pass the one failing unit test.
>
> Even though this sounds restrictive, it is a very productive and fun way to develop software.
>
> ---
>
> a. Found at http://butunclebob.com/ArticleS.UncleBob.TheThreeRulesOfTdd

first user of the interface, gives the callers (or client code) perspective of how to use the code being developed. Starting from the user's perspective leads to more usable interfaces.

I also usually let the first few tests exercise some boundary condition in the code being developed. Choose a simple case but one that exercises a boundary.

The code behind the interface starts with hard-coded return results, so it feels like nothing is being tested. The point is not testing but driving the interface design and getting the simple boundary tests in place.

The main purpose of the driver is to turn LEDs on and off. From the schematic, we found that the LEDs are numbered 01 through 16. To turn on LED 01, when no other LEDs are on, the driver writes 0x0001 to the LED's memory-mapped address. Turning on LED 01 in the test should result in setting virtualLed to 1, as shown in the following test:

unity/LedDriver/LedDriverTest.c
```c
TEST(LedDriver, TurnOnLedOne)
{
    uint16_t virtualLeds;
    LedDriver_Create(&virtualLeds);
    LedDriver_TurnOn(1);
    TEST_ASSERT_EQUAL_HEX16(1, virtualLeds);
}
```

Notice that in this test virtualLeds is not first initialized to 0xFFFF. That was significant for the LedDriver_Create() function, but not here. The initial state does not really matter because LedDriver_Create() takes care of it. This test produces a compilation error as expected.

```
❮ make
compiling LedDriverTest.c
LedDriver/LedDriverTest.c: In function 'TEST_LedDriver_TurnOnLedOne_':
LedDriver/LedDriverTest.c:23: warning: implicit declaration of function 'LedDriver_TurnOn'
Linking BookCode_Unity_tests
Undefined symbols:
  "LedDriver_TurnOn", referenced from:
      TEST_LedDriver_TurnOnLedOne_ in LedDriverTest.o
ld: symbol(s) not found
```

To get rid of the compilation error, add the interface-function prototype to the module's interface declaration in the header file like this:

include/LedDriver/LedDriver.h
```
void LedDriver_TurnOn(int ledNumber);
```

If you typed everything right, the compilation error is gone. Your reward is a link error.

```
❮ make
compiling LedDriver.c
compiling LedDriverTest.c
Linking BookCode_Unity_tests
Undefined symbols:
  "LedDriver_TurnOn", referenced from:
      TEST_LedDriver_TurnOnLedOne_ in LedDriverTest.o
ld: symbol(s) not found
```

To get rid of the link error, again add a skeletal, but wrong, implementation to the .c file.

src/LedDriver/LedDriver.c
```
void LedDriver_TurnOn(int ledNumber)
{
}
```

Building and running now should result in a failing test. Here's what we get:

```
❮ make
compiling LedDriver.c
Linking BookCode_Unity_tests
Running BookCode_Unity_tests
.
-----------------------
1 Tests 0 Failures 0 Ignored
OK
```

Tests pass, but something is wrong. Notice there is only one test in the run. We better update the TEST_GROUP_RUNNER() so it knows about our new test.

unity/LedDriver/LedDriverTestRunner.c
```
TEST_GROUP_RUNNER(LedDriver)
{
    RUN_TEST_CASE(LedDriver, LedsOffAfterCreate);
    RUN_TEST_CASE(LedDriver, TurnOnLedOne);
}
```

There is no need to add anything to main() this time, because the TEST_GROUP_RUNNER() is already installed. Witness the successful link and the new test failure:

```
❮ make
 compiling LedDriverTestRunner.c
 Linking BookCode_Unity_tests
 Running BookCode_Unity_tests
 ..
 TEST(LedDriver, TurnOnLedOne)
     LedDriver/LedDriverTest.c:19: FAIL
     Expected 0x0001 Was 0x0000
 -----------------------
 2 Tests 1 Failures 0 Ignored
 FAIL
```

Now there's a failure, right on cue. To get this test to pass, TurnOn() will need access to the LED's address that was passed into the LedDriver_Create().

Add a *private* file-scope variable to the .c file, and initialize it like this:

src/LedDriver/LedDriver.c
```
static uint16_t * ledsAddress;
void LedDriver_Create(uint16_t * address)
{
    ledsAddress = address;
    *ledsAddress = 0;
}
```

And finally, do the simplest thing possible to get this test to pass. In this case, write a 1 to the LED's address in memory:

src/LedDriver/LedDriver.c
```
void LedDriver_TurnOn(int ledNumber)
{
    *ledsAddress = 1;
}
```

Build the code, and watch it pass the two tests:

```
❮ make
 compiling LedDriver.c
 Linking BookCode_Unity_tests
 Running BookCode_Unity_tests
```

```
..
----------------------
2 Tests 0 Failures 0 Ignored
OK
```

Writing and passing this test helped accomplish a couple things: it defined the interface for one driver function and confirms our approach for intercepting writes going to the hardware. But I bet there is something bothering you.

The Implementation Is Wrong!

Like most engineers, you are probably a little uncomfortable with hard-coding something that is obviously wrong. The final implementation should only set the lowest order bit. But, if you think about it, it is exactly right for the tests written so far. If we were not practicing TDD, where more tests are to follow, leaving this wrong implementation could result in a bug. But we are doing TDD and will write the tests that reveal this weakness.

I can't imagine getting through our test list and leaving this wrong implementation in place. But if you find yourself hard-coding something that is not covered in the current test list, write the test to reveal the weakness immediately or add another item to the test list.

The Tests Are Right

With the implementation being incomplete, you might think that nothing is being tested. Big deal! The test makes sure that a variable is set to one!

Try to think about it a different way. The tests are right! They are a very valuable by-product of TDD. These simple implementations test our tests. Watching the test case fail shows that the test can detect a wrong result. Hard-coding the right answer shows that the test case can detect the right result. The test is right and valuable, even though the production code is incomplete. Later, as the implementation evolves, these seemingly trivial tests will test important behavior and boundary conditions. In essence, we're closing a vise around the code under test, holding the behavior steady (see *Software Vise*, on page 41).

Don't worry, the production code won't be hard-coded and incomplete for long. As soon as you need to turn on a different LED, the hard-coded value will have to go. The real implementation is not much more difficult, but I ask you to resist the temptation to put in more code than is needed by the current test. We're evolving the design. The problem with adding more code than the current tests require is that you probably won't write all the tests you need to keep future, and present, bugs out of the code.

> ### Software Vise
>
> "When we have tests that detect change, it is like having a vise around our code. The behavior of the code is fixed in place. When we make changes, we can know that we are only changing one piece of behavior at a time. In short, we're in control of our work."
>
> —Michael Feathers, *Working Effectively with Legacy Code [Fea04]*

Adding code before it is needed by the tests adds complexity. Sometimes you will be wrong about the need, resulting in carrying the complexity unnecessarily. Also, there is no end to the thinking "I will need it." Where should you stop? In practicing TDD, we stop when the code is not needed by the current tests. Loose ends are cataloged in the test list.

TDD is structured procrastination. Put off writing the *right* production code until the tests force us to. Implementation completeness, the ultimate objective, is reached only after *all* the correct tests are in place.

Choose the Next Test

What test is next? We could write a new test that would force us to eliminate the simple-minded implementation. But I'd rather evolve the interface to get a better picture of the module being built. Let's turn off the LED just turned on. Turn on and turn off complement each other and will come in handy in the coming tests that verify that LED manipulations do not interfere with each other. One other point, we could actually deploy this code to the target if all we needed to do was turn on LED 1. It's settled—let's write a test to turn off LED 1:

unity/LedDriver/LedDriverTest.c
```
TEST(LedDriver, TurnOffLedOne)
{
    uint16_t virtualLeds;
    LedDriver_Create(&virtualLeds);
    LedDriver_TurnOn(1);
    LedDriver_TurnOff(1);
    TEST_ASSERT_EQUAL_HEX16(0, virtualLeds);
}
```

I'm not going to show all the steps this time. Go ahead and add the LedDriver_TurnOff() prototype to the .h file, add an empty implementation of the function to the .c files, and install the test case into the test group runner just like before. Incrementally we're getting rid of compiler errors and then linker errors. The new test builds but fails because LedDriver_TurnOff() doesn't actually turn anything off.

```
❮ make
compiling LedDriverTest.c
Linking BookCode_Unity_tests
Running BookCode_Unity_tests
...
TEST(LedDriver, TurnOffLedOne)
    LedDriver/LedDriverTest.c:28: FAIL
    Expected 0x0000 Was 0x0001
-----------------------
3 Tests 1 Failures 0 Ignored
FAIL
```

You are probably getting uncomfortable again, because you know I'm going to make you hard-code the LED value again to get this test to pass. Right you are. Make the code pass like this:

src/LedDriver/LedDriver.c
```c
void LedDriver_TurnOff(int ledNumber)
{
    *ledsAddress = 0;
}
```

All the tests pass again.

```
❮ make
compiling LedDriver.c
Linking BookCode_Unity_tests
Running BookCode_Unity_tests
...
-----------------------
3 Tests 0 Failures 0 Ignored
OK
```

At this point, the interface of the LED driver is taking shape. We have three tests and a skeletal implementation of the driver.

We'll return to the code in the next chapter, but first let's discuss these small steps we're taking.

3.6 Incremental Progress

People new to TDD are often bothered by an early version of code like this. We're testing nothing (you might think), just some hard-coded return values; the tests are tiny, and we're bouncing between activities. Let me explain a little more.

Do TSTTCPW: Fake It and Then Make It

Back when I was first learning extreme programming, Kent Beck wrote this catchy acronym on the board: DTSTTCPW.[3] It has a real nice ring to it; I like to think of words that rhyme with it. It stands for Do The Simplest Thing That Could Possibly Work. When you have written only a few simple tests, the simplest thing is usually faking it. The LedDriver faked it by hard-coding the values written to the LED's address. Once you have some more tests, faking won't be simple—it will be simpler to use the real solution or part of the real solution.

In traditional development, having the hard-coded values could be a serious problem. It's easy to forget shortcuts like this when they are buried in the implementation. In TDD it's no big deal because you will go back to them. As you design more tests, the weaknesses are revealed. If you are concerned that you will forget, add a test to the test list.

When I first saw Kent fake the return result, I was bothered. But I tried it and found it worked. As Kent suggested, I made sure I wrote all the needed tests. After quite a bit of TDD experience, I had an important revelation. Even though the implementation is nowhere near correct, the tests are correct!

I've taught many people TDD and shown them "fake it 'til you make it." Often they ask, "When do you stop faking and write the real code?" My simple rule of thumb is that as soon as it is more trouble to fake it than it is to make it, you make it. You will see what I mean soon.

Keep Tests Small, Focused

It's worth taking notice of a couple things. You might wonder why there is a second test case for turning off LED 1. The easiest thing to do to test turning off LED 1 would be to add a little more code to the TEST(LedDriver, TurnOnLedOne). But that would have made the test less focused. There would be two reasons for that test to fail: LedDriver_TurnOn() is broken or LedDriver_TurnOff() is broken.

In the second test, notice that there is no check to see whether LedDriver_TurnOn() worked. TEST(LedDriver, TurnOnLedOne) makes that check, so there is no need to keep checking it in this and the other tests to come.

Programmers new to TDD usually put too much in each test. It hurts readability and focus. There is no limit to the number of lines or assertions in a test case, just like there is no limit to the number of lines in a function. Keep tests readable, small, and focused. The steps of the Four-Phase Test pattern

---

3. See http://www.c2.com/cgi/wiki?DoTheSimplestThingThatCouldPossiblyWork.

(setup, exercise, verify, and cleanup) should be visible in your test cases. When tests get too big or unclear, they lose their documentation value. When tests get unclear, readers are not sure what they are trying to accomplish. Keep your tests small, focused, and well named; they will repay the effort for years to come.

Ideally a single code problem will result in a single test failure. By the way, this ideal will never be met, but it's still good to have the ideal.

Refactor on Green

Another integral part of TDD is *refactoring*. Refactoring is the regular cleaning of the code and design. We'll be refactoring as we continue developing the LedDriver in the next chapter. We'll also go in-depth into refactoring in Chapter 12, *Refactoring*, on page 219.

The only safe time to refactor is when the tests are passing. Said more emphatically, don't refactor when tests are not passing! When tests are failing, you don't have the behavior locked in. Structural changes, while hunting down a failing test, can make it very difficult to get back to all tests passing. Passing tests are the safety net, making the acrobatics of refactoring safe. Tests are passing, so let's see whether there are any problems in our new code.

With a well-developed sense of *smell*, you will detect a whiff of *code smells* before the *design rot* becomes too advanced to easily fix.

The test code has developed a smell, duplication. virtualLeds are being created in each test case, and LedDriver_Create() is called in each test case. TEST(LedDriver, LedsOffAfterCreate) needs to stay as it is because it deals with a special case. The duplication in the other two tests should be moved out of the test cases like this:

unity/LedDriver/LedDriverTest.c
```
TEST_GROUP(LedDriver);
static uint16_t virtualLeds;
TEST_SETUP(LedDriver)
{
    LedDriver_Create(&virtualLeds);
}

TEST_TEAR_DOWN(LedDriver)
{
}

TEST(LedDriver, LedsOffAfterCreate)
{
```

```
        uint16_t virtualLeds = 0xffff;
        LedDriver_Create(&virtualLeds);
        TEST_ASSERT_EQUAL_HEX16(0, virtualLeds);
}
TEST(LedDriver, TurnOnLedOne)
{
        LedDriver_TurnOn(1);
        TEST_ASSERT_EQUAL_HEX16(1, virtualLeds);
}
TEST(LedDriver, TurnOffLedOne)
{
        LedDriver_TurnOn(1);
        LedDriver_TurnOff(1);
        TEST_ASSERT_EQUAL_HEX16(0, virtualLeds);
}
```

Tests are documentation; they should be carefully named. Once the test is passing, make sure the name expresses the test's intention.

3.7 Test-Driven Developer State Machine

You can think of TDD as working through a state machine, like the one shown in Figure 4, *TDD state machine*, on page 46. Each step of the way, you are focused on solving one specific problem. First, you have to decide the next increment of behavior and express the desired outcome in a test. Then you have to make the compiler happy as you design the interface and get the header file and test to agree (sometimes the name you choose is already taken; you find that out during this step).

With the interface and test in agreement, expect a link error, and then add the skeletal implementation that is intentionally wrong. Watching the test fail is a good sign that your test can detect when the code is broken. If you find that the test passes while expecting a failure, it might indicate that the test has a mistake in it. This is pretty common when cutting and pasting the last test to make the next test. Also, when using Unity, or any test harness that requires multiple steps to install a test, the failing test shows that your test is installed into the test runner.

Once the test passes, you know you have the desired behavior, but your work isn't done yet. The code needs to be left clean. While making the test pass, it's OK to make a mess. Just don't leave the mess; refactor it out.

Why do these small steps? They allow you to focus on solving one problem at a time.

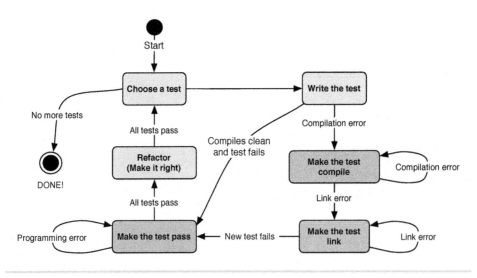

Figure 4— TDD state machine

3.8 Tests Are FIRST

In *Agile in a Flash [OL11]*, Tim Ottinger and Jeff Langr tell us five critical attributes of unit tests. Tests need to be *FIRST* to be most effective.

F   Fast: Tests are fast, so fast that developers run them with every small change without waits that break the flow.

I   Isolated: Tests are isolated. One test does not set up the next test. Tests also isolate failures.

R   Repeatable: Tests are repeatable; repeatable means automated. Tests run in a loop always giving the same result.

S   Self-verifying: Tests verify their outcome, reporting a simple "OK" when they pass while providing concise details when they fail.

T   Timely: Tests are timely. Programmers write them just in time, in lockstep (but just before) the production code, preventing bugs.

It is a challenge to test-drive C. TDD is best applied to self-contained units of functionality. In common C programming practice, the self-contained units of functionality are often missing; module boundaries are not very evident, and the language constructs are limited.

In object-oriented languages, functions are gathered around common data and accessed through the interface defined by the functions. The language supports self-contained units directly. Self-contained units are more testable.

That's why TDD is more natural when applied to OO programming languages. Although C is not an OO language, there is nothing stopping us from applying valuable lessons from the OO world.

When we make tests FIRST, it leads to modular designs, which are designs that can stand the test of time. Let's look at how we'll keep code modular and testable.

3.9 Where Are We?

In this chapter, we got a start on the LedDriver. The LedDriver is not a complicated example, but it's best to start with a simple example to show the mechanics and thought processes of TDD.

We have a test list that will help drive design and meet the needs of the users of the driver. These first few tests have delivered a skeleton of the test fixture and of the driver. We're ready to add more meat to the bone.

Probably some of you are concerned about the loose ends in this code, the partial implementations. Don't fret. You can't work on everything at once anyway. We are methodically and incrementally adding and verifying behavior. We're procrastinating, but here procrastination is not a bad word.

We broke the dependency from the driver to hardware by passing the LED's address to the driver. This design decision gave us the opportunity to fake out the driver, allowing it to intercept bit patterns destined for the hardware.

TDD is kind of like crossing a mountain stream on the rocks that protrude from the rushing water. The path is not perfectly straight, as the Debug-Later Programming approach may appear. But we get across the stream with dry shoes. DLP is like making a flying leap to cross the stream in one bound. If the stream is narrow, this might work. More often we end up in the stream fighting unexpected currents to get to done. Each test moves the code toward the goal of being done, as illustrated in Figure 5, *TDD stepping-stones*, on page 48. TDD's crooked path has less risk because the code is always passing its currently defined tests. There is less risk of bugs impeding our progress. We're partway across the stream. We'll get the rest of the way across in the next chapter.

3.10 Put the Knowledge to Work

1. Write a test list for a first-in first-out CircularBuffer that holds a series of ints.

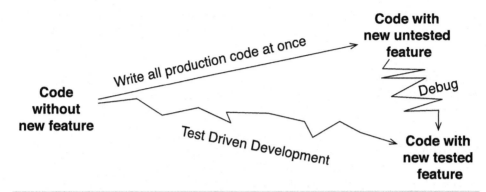

Figure 5— TDD stepping-stones

2. Start your own LedDriver so that you can follow along in the next chapter. You will find starter files in code/SandBox. Build instructions are in code/README.txt.

3. Start test-driving the CircularBuffer. Choose tests that check the initial state and explore its interface. Only choose tests that can pass with hard-coded return results. You will need to modify the makefile so it can find the CircularBuffer files. You will get a chance to finish it after the next chapter.

When you find yourself in a hole, stop digging.
➢ Will Rogers

CHAPTER 4

Testing Your Way to Done

In the previous chapter, we started LedDriver. In this chapter, we'll finish it...if there is anything such as finished in software development. Starting a task is very different from sustaining it or finishing it. In this chapter, you will see the steady state, the basic rhythm, of TDD. We'll grow the driver, one test at a time, until it's *done*.

Before we jump back into it, let's review where we left off in the previous chapter. The skeletal header, source, and test files are in place and part of our automated build. The LedDriver's interface is partially defined, and we have a list of anticipated tests. We also have a test fixture that tests the driver independent of the target hardware. All three of our tests are passing.

If you want to refresh your memory about the current state of the LedDriver, you can find it in Appendix 4, *LedDriver After Getting Started*, on page 309.

4.1 Grow the Solution from Simple Beginnings

The simple-minded implementation in the previous chapter gets more robust incrementally. Each test drives the implementation to a more complete state.

The next test turns on a couple of LEDs. That is enough to force a more general and complete implementation. Notice which LEDs are turned on in the test that follows, and see if you can easily determine whether the expected value in virtualLeds is correct.

```
unity/LedDriver/LedDriverTest.c
TEST(LedDriver, TurnOnMultipleLeds)
{
    LedDriver_TurnOn(9);
    LedDriver_TurnOn(8);
    TEST_ASSERT_EQUAL_HEX16(0x180, virtualLeds);
}
```

Tests are documentation, and a good document should be easy to understand. If you want well-written tests, you must carefully select your test data.

Someone who works with binary and hexadecimal should find it pretty easy to confirm that test data. I chose LEDs 8 and 9 because the arithmetic is fairly simple and the two bits are in separate nibbles, making their combination easy to recognize in hex.

I expect this test to compile; there were no interface changes. Next you want a failing test, but if you build and run right now there is no failing test. The test has not been added into the TEST_GROUP_RUNNER(). Once you do, it fails because we did *the simplest thing that could possibly work* at the end of the previous chapter, and it doesn't work for this test.

```
❮ make
compiling LedDriverTest.c
Linking BookCode_Unity_tests
Running BookCode_Unity_tests
Unity test run 1 of 1
....
TEST(LedDriver, TurnOnMultipleLeds)
        LedDriver/LedDriverTest.c:60: FAIL
        Expected 0x0180 Was 0x0001
-----------------------
4 Tests 1 Failures 0 Ignored
FAIL
```

No surprise here. The test fails as expected, proving the implementation inadequate by this test. What was the DTSTTCPW before this test is no longer DTSTTCPW; it doesn't work.

Instead of just assigning *ledsAddress = 1, we do some bit fiddling like this:

src/LedDriver/LedDriver.c
```
void LedDriver_TurnOn(int ledNumber)
{
    *ledsAddress |= (1 << ledNumber);
}
```

Will the test pass? That's the goal. I'm bullish as I save and build.

```
❮ make
compiling LedDriver.c
Linking BookCode_Unity_tests
Running BookCode_Unity_tests
Unity test run 1 of 1
...
TEST(LedDriver, TurnOnLedOne)
        LedDriver/LedDriverTest.c:43: FAIL
        Expected 0x0001 Was 0x0002
```

```
TEST(LedDriver, TurnOnMultipleLeds)
        LedDriver/LedDriverTest.c:60: FAIL
        Expected 0x0180 Was 0x0300
-----------------------
4 Tests 2 Failures 0 Ignored
FAIL
```

What's with those two failures? This was supposed to pass! The previously passing TEST(LedDriver, TurnOnLedOne) and the new TEST(LedDriver, TurnOnMultipleLeds) are both failing. There must be some small mistake. It can't be big; only one line was changed. Small logic mistakes happen all the time. One of the big benefits of TDD is catching small problems while they are easy to find and fix. A key to this is detecting them right away.

If this mistake had been discovered in the fully integrated system, finding it would take much longer. There would have been multiple changes bundled with it. The fault could have been with the caller asking for the wrong LED rather than the driver controlling the wrong LED. It's this defect prevention aspect of TDD that helps developers keep a rapid steady pace.

Let's find the problem. Look carefully at the TEST(LedDriver, TurnOnLedOne) output, and you can see that 0x0001 was expected but the result was a 0x0002. The bit shifter between your ears might tell you that the bit was shifted one position too many to the left. No print statements or debuggers needed, and we've isolated the problem: ledNumber needs to be converted to a bit offset by subtracting one from it prior to using it as a shift count.

Off-by-one errors and other logic errors are very easy to make, but their consequence can be catastrophic as a hidden bug. In Debug-Later Programming, mature bugs are hunted down. In TDD, we see them in the larvae stage and squash them before they infest the code.

One of the goals of running tests on the development system is to find and fix most errors before running on the hardware, avoiding extra target uploads and lengthy *Debug on Hardware* (DOH!) sessions. Of course, there will still be problems that can be found only on the hardware, but we can avoid DOH! for many of the problems along the way.

The *off-by-one* error is fixed like this:

src/LedDriver/LedDriver.c
```c
void LedDriver_TurnOn(int ledNumber)
{
    *ledsAddress |= 1 << (ledNumber - 1);
}
```

```
< make
compiling LedDriverTest.c
Linking BookCode_Unity_tests
Running BookCode_Unity_tests
Unity test run 1 of 1
....
-----------------------
4 Tests 0 Failures 0 Ignored
OK
```

Ahhh, having a passing test feels much better. It is fixed now, never to be broken again, at least not without us knowing right away.

Now that all tests pass, it's a good time to look for ways to improve the code. That bit manipulation is a little tough on the eyes. Let's refactor the bit manipulation into its own helper function.

src/LedDriver/LedDriver.c
```
static uint16_t convertLedNumberToBit(int ledNumber)
{
    return  1 << (ledNumber - 1);
}
void LedDriver_TurnOn(int ledNumber)
{
    *ledsAddress |= convertLedNumberToBit(ledNumber);
}
```

It's easier to see the ideas in the code when you extract them and wrap them in an intention-revealing name. You might be concerned with the added overhead for extracting the bit manipulation. You can see I chose a static function to avoid adding to the global namespace. If we are really concerned about the memory footprint, we could also make convertLedNumberToBit() an inline[1] function or a preprocessor macro. That may be unnecessary with today's optimizing compilers.

Steady Progress

Each test moves the implementation closer to done. Often, there is a natural sequence to the tests, like the stones in a mountain stream. Sometimes there is more than one path. Let's hop to the next stone, testing that we're on the right path.

unity/LedDriver/LedDriverTest.c
```
TEST(LedDriver, TurnOffAnyLed)
{
    LedDriver_TurnOn(9);
```

---

1. inline is part of the C99 standard.

```
    LedDriver_TurnOn(8);
    LedDriver_TurnOff(8);
    TEST_ASSERT_EQUAL_HEX16(0x100, virtualLeds);
}
```

The test fails (assuming you installed it in the TEST_GROUP_RUNNER).

```
❮ make
compiling LedDriverTest.c
Linking BookCode_Unity_tests
Running BookCode_Unity_tests
Unity test run 1 of 1
.....
TEST(LedDriver, TurnOffAnyLed)
     LedDriver/LedDriverTest.c:68: FAIL
     Expected 0x0100 Was 0x0000
-----------------------
5 Tests 1 Failures 0 Ignored
FAIL
```

Notice that the test turns on LED 9 before turning on and off LED 8. Without turning on some other LED, the current brute-force implementation would have passed. The existing simple implementation used to turn off LED 1 (*ledsAddress = 0;) turns off all LEDs. LedDriver_TurnOff() does not mask the bits that should not be affected. To force the writing of the masking code, we have to make sure some LED will be left in the *on* state.

This test would be better if we had LedDriver_TurnAllOn() to work with. Let's comment out this test, implement the turn all on function, and then come back to this test. We just stepped back one stone and are taking a different path. Here's the test for turning all LEDs on:

unity/LedDriver/LedDriverTest.c
```
TEST(LedDriver, AllOn)
{
    LedDriver_TurnAllOn();
    TEST_ASSERT_EQUAL_HEX16(0xffff, virtualLeds);
}
```

And its implementation:

src/LedDriver/LedDriver.c
```
void LedDriver_TurnAllOn(void)
{
    *ledsAddress = 0xffff;
}
```

Before we move on, let's refactor out the magic numbers for all LEDs on and off here and in LedDriver_Create().

src/LedDriver/LedDriver.c
```c
enum {ALL_LEDS_ON = ~0, ALL_LEDS_OFF = ~ALL_LEDS_ON};

void LedDriver_TurnAllOn(void)
{
    *ledsAddress = ALL_LEDS_ON;
}
```

With the ability to turn on all LEDs, here is the revised test for turning off any LED:

unity/LedDriver/LedDriverTest.c
```c
TEST(LedDriver, TurnOffAnyLed)
{
    LedDriver_TurnAllOn();
    LedDriver_TurnOff(8);
    TEST_ASSERT_EQUAL_HEX16(0xff7f, virtualLeds);
}
```

After installing TEST(LedDriver, TurnOffAnyLed) and then watching it fail, we add the code to LedDriver_TurnOff(). I predict it will work right the first time. What do you think?

src/LedDriver/LedDriver.c
```c
void LedDriver_TurnOff(int ledNumber)
{
    *ledsAddress &= ~(convertLedNumberToBit(ledNumber));
}
```

Tests are passing once again. Notice that LedDriver_TurnOff() took advantage of the recently extracted convertLedNumberToBit().

```
❮ make
compiling LedDriver.c
Linking BookCode_Unity_tests
Running BookCode_Unity_tests
Unity test run 1 of 1
......
-----------------------
6 Tests 0 Failures 0 Ignored
OK
```

I wonder, can the software read the state of the LEDs? The LEDs I/O-mapped address is probably write-only. It's best not to guess. I holler to our hardware engineer to get a quick answer:

> *James:* Hey Gary, can we read the state of the LEDs with software?
>
> *Gary:* That's a stupid question; of course not. Read the schematic!
>
> *James, a little peeved:* Thanks, Gary, love you like a brother.

I think Gary had a bad weekend, but I'm glad I asked. The driver, as currently implemented, won't work in the real hardware because the production code uses the LED memory location for reading and writing. How do we prove the hardware is not read? It's easier than it sounds. Add a test that shows that the driver is not getting the current LED state from the hardware by first setting virtualLeds to 0xFFFF. Remember that during initialization LedDriver_Create turns off all the LEDs.

unity/LedDriver/LedDriverTest.c
```c
TEST(LedDriver, LedMemoryIsNotReadable)
{
    virtualLeds = 0xffff;
    LedDriver_TurnOn(8);
    TEST_ASSERT_EQUAL_HEX16(0x80, virtualLeds);
}
```

In the current implementation, the driver reads from virtualLeds, causing this test to fail and giving this message:

```
❮ make
  compiling LedDriverTest.c
  Linking BookCode_Unity_tests
  Running BookCode_Unity_tests
  Unity test run 1 of 1
  .......
  TEST(LedDriver, LedMemoryIsNotReadable)
  {
          LedDriver/LedDriverTest.c:80: FAIL
          Expected 0x0080 Was 0xFFFF
  -----------------------
  7 Tests 1 Failures 0 Ignored
  FAIL
```

After initially forgetting to install the test case...the newly installed test fails. (I'm going to stop mentioning that the test must be installed into the TEST_GROUP_RUNNER(). If you are following along writing this code, you probably forget a couple times, and the unexpected passing test will warn you.) To make the test pass, record the LED's state in a *private* file-scope variable ledsImage. Initialize it in LedDriver_Create().

src/LedDriver/LedDriver.c
```c
enum {ALL_LEDS_ON = ~0, ALL_LEDS_OFF = ~ALL_LEDS_ON};

static uint16_t * ledsAddress;
static uint16_t ledsImage;

void LedDriver_Create(uint16_t * address)
{
    ledsAddress = address;
```

```
    ledsImage = ALL_LEDS_OFF;
    *ledsAddress = ledsImage;
}
```

As a record of the current LED states, use ledsImage in the functions LedDriver_TurnOn(), LedDriver_TurnOff(), and LedDriver_TurnAllOn().

src/LedDriver/LedDriver.c
```
void LedDriver_TurnOn(int ledNumber)
{
    ledsImage |= convertLedNumberToBit(ledNumber);
    *ledsAddress = ledsImage;
}
void LedDriver_TurnOff(int ledNumber)
{
    ledsImage &= ~(convertLedNumberToBit(ledNumber));
    *ledsAddress = ledsImage;
}
void LedDriver_TurnAllOn(void)
{
    ledsImage = ALL_LEDS_ON;
    *ledsAddress = ledsImage;
}
```

The tests are running green again.

```
❰ make
compiling LedDriver.c
Linking BookCode_Unity_tests
Running BookCode_Unity_tests
Unity test run 1 of 1
.......
-----------------------
7 Tests 0 Failures 0 Ignored
OK
```

Let's remove a bit more duplication and make this code easier for future readers by extracting *ledsAddress = ledsImage; into a helper function.

src/LedDriver/LedDriver.c
```
static void updateHardware(void)
{
    *ledsAddress = ledsImage;
}

void LedDriver_TurnAllOn(void)
{
    ledsImage = ALL_LEDS_ON;
    updateHardware();
}
```

The implementation for LedDriver_TurnOn() and LedDriver_TurnOff() looks pretty complete, with one exception: there are no boundary checks. Let's decide whether bounds checks are needed.

Test Boundary Conditions

In some designs, the responsibility for assuring that no out-of-bounds LEDs are controlled may be somewhere else. In that case, the design would not call for boundary checking. But in this case, the LedDriver will be used by the application-level code, so boundary checks are the driver's responsibility.

This test checks the upper and lower bounds of the legal LED values. The tests act as a detailed requirement. The really cool part about this document is that it executes, making sure the requirement is met.

```
unity/LedDriver/LedDriverTest.c
TEST(LedDriver, UpperAndLowerBounds)
{
    LedDriver_TurnOn(1);
    LedDriver_TurnOn(16);
    TEST_ASSERT_EQUAL_HEX16(0x8001, virtualLeds);
}
```

Unsurprisingly, this test compiles and runs the first time.

```
❮ make
  compiling LedDriverTest.c
  Linking BookCode_Unity_tests
  Running BookCode_Unity_tests
  Unity test run 1 of 1
  ........
  ----------------------
  8 Tests 0 Failures 0 Ignored
  OK
```

What should happen when you manipulate an out-of-bounds LED? Should the driver write over adjacent memory, silently ignore the bad parameters, corrupt the stack, or produce a runtime error?

Of all those, the last one sounds best. If the code detects the wrong LED number, there is certainly a programming error.

Before we get to how to handle the runtime error, let's make sure that the out-of-bounds values do no harm—part of a Hippocratic Oath for LED drivers. This test exercises the driver with some fence-post values and a way out-of-bounds value.

unity/LedDriver/LedDriverTest.c
```
TEST(LedDriver, OutOfBoundsChangesNothing)
{
    LedDriver_TurnOn(-1);
    LedDriver_TurnOn(0);
    LedDriver_TurnOn(17);
    LedDriver_TurnOn(3141);
    TEST_ASSERT_EQUAL_HEX16(0, virtualLeds);
}
```

Running the tests...

```
< make
compiling LedDriverTest.c
Linking BookCode_Unity_tests
Running BookCode_Unity_tests
Unity test run 1 of 1
.......
TEST(LedDriver, OutOfBoundsChangesNothing)
       LedDriver/LedDriverTest.c:100: FAIL
       Expected 0x0000 Was 0x0010
-----------------------
9 Tests 1 Failures 0 Ignored
FAIL
```

I thought this would pass, just by accident, but it didn't. When you shift a bit totally out of the variable, shouldn't the variable be zero? If inquiring minds really need to know, insert TEST_ASSERT_EQUAL_HEX16(0, virtualLeds) after each LedDriver_TurnOn() call, and read *Inquiring Minds and LedDriver_TurnOn(3141)*, on page 59 to understand the test output.

Sometimes testing unhandled out-of-bounds conditions will crash the test run. For instance, an out-of-bounds for an array on the stack can corrupt the stack. Out-of-bounds in this case won't do any damage; it just gives an odd result.

To make the test pass, add guard clauses to LedDriver_TurnOn() and LedDriver_TurnOff() like this:

src/LedDriver/LedDriver.c
```
void LedDriver_TurnOn(int ledNumber)
{
    if (ledNumber <= 0 || ledNumber > 16)
        return;

    ledsImage |= convertLedNumberToBit(ledNumber);
    updateHardware();
}
```

> ### Inquiring Minds and LedDriver_TurnOn(3141)
>
> I just had to know. So, I did the experiment, sprinkling in the TEST_ASSERT_EQUAL_HEX16(0, virtualLeds) assertions. On my machine, turning on LED 3141 actually sets the bit associated with LED 5. This is undefined behavior and we should not count on it to be portable or even to survive the next compiler release. Maybe preventing this type of misuse is the job of static analysis.
>
> To confirm my hunch, I turned on LED 33, like this:
>
> ```
> unity/LedDriver/LedDriverTest.c
> TEST(LedDriver, OutOfBoundsChangesNothing)
> {
>     LedDriver_TurnOn(-1);
>     TEST_ASSERT_EQUAL_HEX16(0, virtualLeds);
>     LedDriver_TurnOn(0);
>     TEST_ASSERT_EQUAL_HEX16(0, virtualLeds);
>     LedDriver_TurnOn(17);
>     TEST_ASSERT_EQUAL_HEX16(0, virtualLeds);
>     LedDriver_TurnOn(33);
>     TEST_ASSERT_EQUAL_HEX16(0, virtualLeds);
>     LedDriver_TurnOn(3141);
>     TEST_ASSERT_EQUAL_HEX16(0, virtualLeds);
> }
> ```
>
> If my 32-bit rotation hypothesis is correct, I would expect the low-order bit to be set. Here are the results confirming my hunch:
>
> ```
> ❬ make
> compiling LedDriverTest.c
> Linking BookCode_Unity_tests
> Running BookCode_Unity_tests
> Unity test run 1 of 1
> .........
> TEST(LedDriver, OutOfBoundsChangesNothing)
>         LedDriver/LedDriverTest.c:99: FAIL
>         Expected 0x0000 Was 0x0001
> -----------------------
> 9 Tests 1 Failures 0 Ignored
> FAIL
> ```
>
> The tests are a good way to design experiments around your code. When the experiment is done, don't leave those crufty interspersed assertions in the tests.

```c
void LedDriver_TurnOff(int ledNumber)
{
    if (ledNumber <= 0 || ledNumber > 16)
        return;

    ledsImage &= ~(convertLedNumberToBit(ledNumber));
    updateHardware();
}
```

Run the makefile, and see the tests pass:

```
❮ make
  compiling LedDriverTest.c
  Linking BookCode_Unity_tests
  Running BookCode_Unity_tests
  Unity test run 1 of 1
  .........
  -----------------------
  9 Tests 0 Failures 0 Ignored
  OK
```

Wait a second. The code just got ahead of the tests.(See *Do You Have a Test for That?*, on page 61 for some advice on preventing the production code from getting ahead of the tests.) The guard clause in LedDriver_TurnOff() is not tested. The copied code from LedDriver_TurnOn() was tested in TEST(LedDriver, OutOfBoundsChangesNothing), but it is not tested in its new home.

Sure, you feel perfectly safe copying tested code, but beware—the two copies are likely to diverge in the future. Tests are not just for getting the code right in the first place but keeping it right over the long run. So, delete or comment out the pasted code and add an out-of-bounds test for LedDriver_TurnOff(). You want to see it fail first.

Let's rename TEST(LedDriver, OutOfBoundsChangesNothing) to TEST(LedDriver, OutOfBoundsTurnOnDoesNoHarm)—the name now focusses on the out-of-bounds behavior of LedDriver_TurnOn(). A quick copy/paste/edit gives the LedDriver_TurnOff() variant: of the test.

unity/LedDriver/LedDriverTest.c
```c
TEST(LedDriver, OutOfBoundsTurnOffDoesNoHarm)
{
    LedDriver_TurnOff(-1);
    LedDriver_TurnOff(0);
    LedDriver_TurnOff(17);
    LedDriver_TurnOff(3141);
    TEST_ASSERT_EQUAL_HEX16(0, virtualLeds);
}
```

The test should have failed, but it passed!

```
❮ make
  compiling LedDriverTest.c
  Linking BookCode_Unity_tests
  Running BookCode_Unity_tests
  Unity test run 1 of 1
  ..........
  -----------------------
  10 Tests 0 Failures 0 Ignored
  OK
```

> ### Do You Have a Test for That?
>
> Test-Driven Development has its roots in Extreme Programming. Pair programming, another XP practice, involves two developers working side by side doing TDD. It's a fun and productive way to work. Pair programming is a helpful technique to staying on track, keeping the quality high, and learning from each other. Essentially, it is a real-time code review and problem-solving session.
>
> Letting the production code get ahead of the tests is such a common mistake, especially when you are learning TDD, that Kent Beck taught a technique for dealing with it. If your partner writes production code before the test, ask, "Do you have a test for that?" Whenever you hear that, don't make excuses; write a new test. Or push the keyboard to your partner to write the missing test.
>
> If you are programming solo, make sure to ask yourself that from time to time too!

Copy/paste almost got us in trouble...again; the LEDs are all off to start with! The LEDs must be on to be able to tell whether LedDriver_TurnOff() does its job. This should help.

unity/LedDriver/LedDriverTest.c
```c
TEST(LedDriver, OutOfBoundsTurnOffDoesNoHarm)
{
    LedDriver_TurnAllOn();
    LedDriver_TurnOff(-1);
    LedDriver_TurnOff(0);
    LedDriver_TurnOff(17);
    LedDriver_TurnOff(3141);
    TEST_ASSERT_EQUAL_HEX16(0xffff, virtualLeds);
}
```

Now we get the failure and can copy and paste in the LED guard clause.

Now back to the runtime error. Rather than silently having a runtime error, the driver should let someone know about the error. Let's invoke the RUNTIME_ERROR() macro. RUNTIME_ERROR() logs an error recording the message provided as well as the file and line number. Here is its declaration:

include/util/RuntimeError.h
```c
void RuntimeError(const char * message, int parameter,
                  const char * file, int line);

#define RUNTIME_ERROR(description, parameter)\
    RuntimeError(description, parameter, __FILE__, __LINE__)
```

In production, RuntimeError() puts an entry into an event log. During test, stub out RuntimeError() so the last error can be captured and checked. The stub header looks like the following:

```
mocks/RuntimeErrorStub.h
void RuntimeErrorStub_Reset(void);
const char * RuntimeErrorStub_GetLastError(void);
int RuntimeErrorStub_GetLastParameter(void);
```

Here's the stub implementation:

```
mocks/RuntimeErrorStub.c
#include "RuntimeErrorStub.h"
static const char * message = "No Error";
static int parameter = -1;
static const char * file = 0;
static int line = -1;

void RuntimeErrorStub_Reset(void)
{
    message = "No Error";
    parameter = -1;
}
const char * RuntimeErrorStub_GetLastError(void)
{
    return message;
}
void RuntimeError(const char * m, int p, const char * f, int l)
{
    message = m;
    parameter = p;
    file = f;
    line = l;
}
int RuntimeErrorStub_GetLastParameter(void)
{
    return parameter;
}
```

As you can see, the stub version of RuntimeError() just captures the error description. The other two functions give a way to reset the stub and access to the captured message.

The stub version of RuntimeError() is linked in during test. It lets the test check that out-of-bounds produces a RuntimeError(). This is shown in the following code.

```
unity/LedDriver/LedDriverTest.c
TEST(LedDriver, OutOfBoundsProducesRuntimeError)
{
    LedDriver_TurnOn(-1);
    TEST_ASSERT_EQUAL_STRING("LED Driver: out-of-bounds LED",
            RuntimeErrorStub_GetLastError());
    TEST_ASSERT_EQUAL(-1, RuntimeErrorStub_GetLastParameter());
}
```

Watch the test fail.

```
❮ make
compiling LedDriverTest.c
Linking BookCode_Unity_tests
Running BookCode_Unity_tests
Unity test run 1 of 1
..........
TEST(LedDriver, OutOfBoundsProducesRuntimeError)
    unity/LedDriver/LedDriverTest.c:138: FAIL
    Expected 'LED Driver: out-of-bounds LED' Was 'No Error'
-----------------------
11 Tests 1 Failures 0 Ignored
FAIL
```

Now add the call to RUNTIME_ERROR(); the test passes.

```
❮ make
compiling LedDriver.c
Linking BookCode_Unity_tests
Running BookCode_Unity_tests
Unity test run 1 of 1
...........
-----------------------
12 Tests 0 Failures 0 Ignored
OK
```

Executable Reminders

We decided that the out-of-bounds LED number should issue a runtime error. What if we could not decide? We could add an item to the test list and come back to it later. We could also add an *executable reminder*.

Most unit tests harnesses have some provision for ignoring a test. In Unity and CppUTest, change TEST() to IGNORE_TEST(). The ignored test must still compile, but it does not run.

You can use ignored tests as an executable reminder. A good thing about an executable reminder is that it will be hard to lose. You see evidence of it with every test run.

unity/LedDriver/LedDriverTest.c
```
IGNORE_TEST(LedDriver, OutOfBoundsToDo)
{
    /* TODO: what should we do during runtime? */
}
```

Notice the ! in the sequence of dots. Also the *ignored* count is now 1. The reminder is subtle, but it is there.

```
< make
  compiling LedDriverTest.c
  Linking BookCode_Unity_tests
  Running BookCode_Unity_tests
  Unity test run 1 of 1
  ..........!
  -----------------------
  12 Tests 0 Failures 1 Ignored
  OK
```

To see what test is ignored, run the test with the verbose flag set. When verbose is switched on, all tests are announced before they are run, including any ignored tests.

```
< $ ./BookCode_Unity_tests -v
  TEST(LedDriver, LedsOffAfterCreate) PASS
  TEST(LedDriver, TurnOnLedOne) PASS
  TEST(LedDriver, TurnOffLedOne) PASS
  TEST(LedDriver, TurnOnMultipleLeds) PASS
  TEST(LedDriver, TurnOffAnyLed) PASS
  TEST(LedDriver, AllOn) PASS
  TEST(LedDriver, LedMemoryIsNotReadable) PASS
  TEST(LedDriver, UpperAndLowerBounds) PASS
  TEST(LedDriver, OutOfBoundsTurnOnDoesNoHarm) PASS
  TEST(LedDriver, OutOfBoundsTurnOffDoesNoHarm) PASS
  TEST(LedDriver, OutOfBoundsProducesRuntimeError) PASS
  IGNORE_TEST(LedDriver, OutOfBoundsToDo)
  12 Tests 0 Failures 1 Ignored
  OK
```

4.2 Keep the Code Clean—Refactor as You Go

On several occasions, we've refactored some small problems out of the code. When there is something to refactor, refactor it. Code problems, detected early, never get a chance to grow up into the big bad code problems some of you are wrestling with in your legacy code bases. But first, a reminder. Only refactor code when the tests are passing! Otherwise, you're asking for trouble.

LedDriver_TurnOn() and LedDriver_TurnOff() have some duplicate code and magic numbers. Cutting and pasting and hard-coded constants are helpful to get the code to have the right behavior but is a long-term liability to leave the duplication and magic numbers. In Chapter 12, *Refactoring*, on page 219, we will go deeper into this topic, but for now let's just look at eliminating these two smells by extracting the duplicate code into a helper and defining constants for the magic numbers.

Copy, Don't Cut

When you extract a new function, copy—don't cut—the duplicate code. Define the function and paste the code into the new function body. Add parameters and the return value as needed, and then compile. In an easy-to-undo operation, switch to the new code and see it pass its tests. If you happen to comment out the old code, delete it now.

With tests passing, replace the other uses of duplicate code with the new helper.

The reason we get the extracted function compiling before cutting to it is to make it easy to get back to working code if we make a mistake. We don't want to burn our old bridge, the currently working code, before the new bridge is in place.

After the new helper function is integrated and passes its tests, replace the magic numbers with symbolic constants. Here are the constants and the extracted function:

src/LedDriver/LedDriver.c
```c
enum {FIRST_LED = 1, LAST_LED = 16};
static BOOL IsLedOutOfBounds(int ledNumber)
{
    return (ledNumber < FIRST_LED) || (ledNumber > LAST_LED);
}
```

IsLedOutOfBounds() is not needed by users of the driver. So, do not mention it in the .h file. Also, declare it as static, keeping it out of the global namespace.

Here's the refactored LedDriver_TurnOn() and LedDriver_TurnOff():

src/LedDriver/LedDriver.c
```c
void LedDriver_TurnOn(int ledNumber)
{
    if (IsLedOutOfBounds(ledNumber))
        return;

    ledsImage |= convertLedNumberToBit(ledNumber);
    updateHardware();
}
void LedDriver_TurnOff(int ledNumber)
{
    if (IsLedOutOfBounds(ledNumber))
        return;

    ledsImage &= ~(convertLedNumberToBit(ledNumber));
    updateHardware();
}
```

The bit manipulation code doesn't fit the level of abstraction of the refactored functions. Let's make it consistent by extracting a couple of helper functions—one at a time, of course. Here's the refactored code:

src/LedDriver/LedDriver.c
```c
static void setLedImageBit(int ledNumber)
{
    ledsImage |= convertLedNumberToBit(ledNumber);
}
void LedDriver_TurnOn(int ledNumber)
{
    if (IsLedOutOfBounds(ledNumber))
        return;

    setLedImageBit(ledNumber);
    updateHardware();
}

static void clearLedImageBit(int ledNumber)
{
    ledsImage &= ~convertLedNumberToBit(ledNumber);
}
void LedDriver_TurnOff(int ledNumber)
{
    if (IsLedOutOfBounds(ledNumber))
        return;

    clearLedImageBit(ledNumber);
    updateHardware();
}
```

We've eliminated a little more duplication. Why am I making such a big deal about it? Duplicate code is a big problem in software. Read *DRY: Don't Repeat Yourself*, on page 69 to see what a couple software development gurus have to say about duplicate code.

Solve One Problem at a Time

The small steps help keep you focused on solving one problem at a time. Humans do much better when solving one problem at a time.

For example, by compiling the replacement code before calling it, we're solving the design problem of "What should the extract function look like?" Getting syntax right and a decent API is a different problem from getting the behavior right.

Also, changing one caller to IsLedOutOfBounds() at a time, you find subtle mistakes more quickly. Less code was changed, so any problem is easier to see.

Let me stress that when a refactoring breaks a previously working test, don't debug. Undo and inspect your work. If the problem is really obvious, then give a fix a try, but be conscious of how many undos it will take to get back to green. If the first or second change does not pass the tests, you're digging a hole. Stop digging.

4.3 Repeat Until Done

The core of the driver is in place. The turn on and turn off functionality works top to bottom. Now you continue adding tests and production code until all the meat is on the skeleton. Let's look at the updated test list in Figure 6, *LedDriver test list—evolved*, on page 68.

I've crossed off the completed tests and also added tests that were not originally anticipated, at least not to the level of detail that TDD drove us to. Test lists evolve; it's expected, and there is nothing wrong with it. As we dig in, we learn more, and the ideas for new tests come as a consequence of our evolving understanding.

Let's add LED query next. Recall that the hardware is not designed to support reading the state of an LED. That functionality is encapsulated in the driver.

unity/LedDriver/LedDriverTest.c
```
TEST(LedDriver, IsOn)
{
    TEST_ASSERT_FALSE(LedDriver_IsOn(11));
    LedDriver_TurnOn(11);
    TEST_ASSERT_TRUE(LedDriver_IsOn(11));
}
```

In the previous test, the LEDs are initially off; then we turn one on and check that it is now on. Compiling, you get an error. Fix the compilation error by adding this prototype to the header:

include/LedDriver/LedDriver.h
```
BOOL LedDriver_IsOn(int ledNumber);
```

Fix the link error by adding this hard-coded implementation. It will cause the test to fail:

src/LedDriver/LedDriver.c
```
BOOL LedDriver_IsOn(int ledNumber)
{
    return FALSE;
}
```

Now code the winning return result:

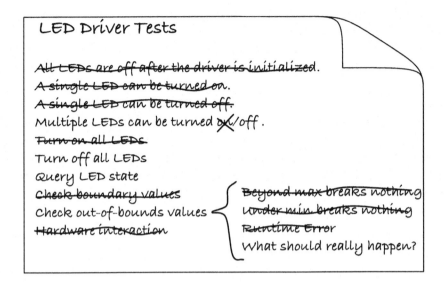

Figure 6— **LedDriver** test list—evolved

```
src/LedDriver/LedDriver.c
BOOL LedDriver_IsOn(int ledNumber)
{
    return ledsImage & (convertLedNumberToBit(ledNumber));
}
```

```
❮ make
compiling LedDriver.c
Linking BookCode_Unity_tests
Running BookCode_Unity_tests
Unity test run 1 of 1
...........!.
-----------------------
13 Tests 0 Failures 1 Ignored
OK
```

You might wonder why the TEST(LedDriver, IsOn) is not testing more LEDs. What to put into the test is a judgment call. If you can think of a test that would fail, add it. If more tests won't fail, then you're done.

There is a black-box aspect to the tests: you are testing through the external interface. There is also a white-box aspect to the tests: you know the implementation. TDD unit tests often are more like gray-box tests. So, there is a gray area here on how exhaustive the test must be. Knowing the implementation, I think these tests are pretty good.

> ### DRY: Don't Repeat Yourself
>
> Duplicate bounds checks are a violation of the DRY principle. The DRY principle, found in Dave Thomas and Andy Hunt's *The Pragmatic Programmer [HT00]*, is described like this:
>
> "Every piece of knowledge must have a single, unambiguous, authoritative representation within a system. " —From *The Pragmatic Programmer [HT00]*
>
> With duplicate code, the same idea is expressed in more than one place. What's the big deal? Here are a few considerations.
>
> First, there is a maintenance liability to having the same idea coded in more than one place. In our example, you can anticipate that the bounds check will be expressed in four places once we implement the LED query functions. Maybe there will be other places as well. This form of duplication will likely cause maintenance problems. A change in requirements, or implementation, would mean visiting each place and changing it. If one is forgotten, you have a new bug! Maybe it won't bite you in this case, but it is best to be vigilant and remove all duplication, thus preventing the possibility of inconsistent behavior.
>
> Second, leaving the duplication makes the code more detailed and less abstract, putting an extra burden on the programmer. Without extracting the duplication into a well-named function, the reader must interpret and analyze the code, not just in one place but in all places the duplicate code appears.
>
> Third, with the duplication removed, the overall code memory usage could decrease. Your mileage will vary.
>
> On the downside, extracting code into functions could make the code execute more slowly. Not that this will never matter, but don't let the performance factor outweigh improved design and readability unless there is proof the code is contributing to a specific performance problem. We can talk more about this issue in Section 12.5, *But What About Performance and Size?*, on page 249.

LedDriver_IsOn() should guard against invalid LED numbers, just as the LED control functions did. There is a decision to make: should an invalid LED be considered on or off? Or should they be neither on nor off? Something about that last option bothers me; I'm not quite sure that clients of the driver want that uncertainty. OK, it's settled, at least for now. LEDs outside this universe are off. Here's the test:

unity/LedDriver/LedDriverTest.c
```c
TEST(LedDriver, OutOfBoundsLedsAreAlwaysOff)
{
    TEST_ASSERT_FALSE(LedDriver_IsOn(0));
    TEST_ASSERT_FALSE(LedDriver_IsOn(17));
}
```

```
< make
compiling LedDriver.c
Linking BookCode_Unity_tests
Running BookCode_Unity_tests
Unity test run 1 of 1
...........!..
-----------------------
14 Tests 0 Failures 1 Ignored
OK
```

Interestingly enough, this test passes when there is no guard clause, and it's not because the test is not installed in the test runner. I suspect this is machine dependent. To make sure the test case can really detect the wrong behavior, hard-code return TRUE;.

src/LedDriver/LedDriver.c
```
BOOL LedDriver_IsOn(int ledNumber)
{
    return TRUE;
    /* return 0 != (ledsImage & convertLedNumberToBit(ledNumber)); */
}
```

You should see these results when you run make:

```
< make
compiling LedDriver.c
Linking BookCode_Unity_tests
Running BookCode_Unity_tests
Unity test run 1 of 1
...........!.
TEST(LedDriver, IsOn)
    LedDriver/LedDriverTest.c:193:  FAIL
    Expected FALSE Was TRUE
 .
TEST(LedDriver, OutOfBoundsLedsAreAlwaysOff)
    LedDriver/LedDriverTest.c:211:  FAIL
    Expected FALSE Was TRUE
-----------------------
14 Tests 2 Failures 1 Ignored
OK
```

Now that the test is failing, add the needed production code:

src/LedDriver/LedDriver.c
```
BOOL LedDriver_IsOn(int ledNumber)
{
    if (IsLedOutOfBounds(ledNumber))
        return FALSE;

    return ledsImage & (convertLedNumberToBit(ledNumber));
}
```

Building the code, all the tests run.

Finish off the query duo; implement LedDriver_IsOff(). I won't bother showing the .h file. To keep duplication at a minimum, implement LedDriver_IsOff() by inverting the result of LedDriver_IsOn().

src/LedDriver/LedDriver.c
```
BOOL LedDriver_IsOff(int ledNumber)
{
    return !LedDriver_IsOn(ledNumber);
}
```

What did you say? "Do you have a test for that?" You learn fast. In all the excitement of cut-and-paste reuse, I forgot the boundary tests for LedDriver_IsOff().

Better write the test, checking the out-of-bounds markers. Good catch! No harm done, this time.

unity/LedDriver/LedDriverTest.c
```
TEST(LedDriver, IsOff)
{
    TEST_ASSERT_TRUE(LedDriver_IsOff(12));
    LedDriver_TurnOn(12);
    TEST_ASSERT_FALSE(LedDriver_IsOff(12));
}
```

Before running the test, insert an error into LedDriver_IsOff().

src/LedDriver/LedDriver.c
```
BOOL LedDriver_IsOff(int ledNumber)
{
    return FALSE; /* !LedDriver_IsOn(ledNumber); */
}
```

The error fails the new test.

```
❮ make
  compiling LedDriver.c
  compiling LedDriverTest.c
  Linking BookCode_Unity_tests
  Running BookCode_Unity_tests
  Unity test run 1 of 1
  ...........!...
  TEST(LedDriver, IsOff)
     LedDriver/LedDriverTest.c:202:  FAIL
      Expected TRUE Was FALSE
  -----------------------
  15 Tests 1 Failures 1 Ignored
  FAIL
```

To wrap up LedDriver_IsOff(), we have to make sure that out-of-bounds LEDs are always off.

unity/LedDriver/LedDriverTest.c
```
TEST(LedDriver, OutOfBoundsLedsAreAlwaysOff)
{
    TEST_ASSERT_TRUE(LedDriver_IsOff(0));
    TEST_ASSERT_TRUE(LedDriver_IsOff(17));
    TEST_ASSERT_FALSE(LedDriver_IsOn(0));
    TEST_ASSERT_FALSE(LedDriver_IsOn(17));
}
```

And not surprisingly, it works.

A case can be made for not adding the previous test; no code was needed for it to pass. I tend to add them for completeness and as documentation.

```
❮ make
compiling LedDriver.c
compiling LedDriverTest.c
Linking BookCode_Unity_tests
Running BookCode_Unity_tests
Unity test run 1 of 1
............!....
----------------------
16 Tests 0 Failures 1 Ignored
OK
```

We have two items left on the test list—turn off multiple LEDs and turn all off. Here's turn off multiple:

unity/LedDriver/LedDriverTest.c
```
TEST(LedDriver, TurnOffMultipleLeds)
{
    LedDriver_TurnAllOn();
    LedDriver_TurnOff(9);
    LedDriver_TurnOff(8);
    TEST_ASSERT_EQUAL_HEX16((~0x180)&0xffff, virtualLeds);
}
```

We expect this test to pass, because LedDriver_TurnOff() is already generalized. But inject an error anyway to make sure the test is wired in.

If you look at the test file, you will see that I added the TurnOffMultipleLeds test after TurnOnMultipleLeds, keeping similar tests together. Usually I keep the tests in the order they are developed in, unless there is some affinity as in this case. I also structured them similarly to make interpreting them a little easier.

Here is the final test from the test list:

`unity/LedDriver/LedDriverTest.c`
```
TEST(LedDriver, AllOff)
{
    LedDriver_TurnAllOn();
    LedDriver_TurnAllOff();
    TEST_ASSERT_EQUAL_HEX16(0, virtualLeds);
}
```

Again follow the same drill. Watch the new test fail. Then, finish the implementation.

`src/LedDriver/LedDriver.c`
```
void LedDriver_TurnAllOff(void)
{
    ledsImage = ALL_LEDS_OFF;
    updateHardware();
}
```

```
❮ make
compiling LedDriver.c
Linking BookCode_Unity_tests
Running BookCode_Unity_tests
Unity test run 1 of 1
............!....
----------------------
18 Tests 0 Failures 1 Ignored
OK
```

Are we done? When you think you are done, it's time to take a step back.

4.4 Take a Step Back Before Claiming *Done*

Before you claim to be *done*, take a look at your work and see whether there is any cleanup needed. After a quick review, the production code looks clean; functions are short and focused, names are readable, and we got rid of magic numbers as we proceeded.

There are magic numbers in the LedDriverTest.c file for the boundary values. They could be removed, but I'll leave them for now. I think it makes the tests a little bit easier to read. Once again, it's a judgment call.

As the design evolved, our test strategy evolved too. Maybe that should be revisited. The early tests relied on the value of virtualLeds. Later tests depended upon the query functions. You could refactor the tests so that more of the tests depend on the query functions added to the driver. Of course, you'd want some test cases that verify that the right bit patterns are sent to the hardware.

How far to take the refactoring is a judgment call. The judgment should be based on detecting code smell and envisioning a better form for the code. We'll spend a chapter on that in Chapter 12, *Refactoring*, on page 219.

4.5 Where Are We?

Our first TDD session is done. We have seen TDD at the detailed level. We should have a fair idea of what TDD is and what it is not.

If we had marked up the test list to include the added tests (I probably would not; I'd just add ones that I plan to do later), it would look like Figure 7, *LedDriver test list—final*, on page 75. You can see that the anticipated tests evolved quite a bit. This is natural and what would be expected as you get into the details. We moved from writing the test list to implementing tests when we noticed the diminishing returns for the effort needed for additional tests in the test list.

You can find a complete listing of the LedDriver and its tests online in the code download. You will find both the CppUTest and the Unity versions of the test code as well there. Take a few minutes to look at the differences between Unity and CppUTest test cases and test fixtures. They are very similar.

I'll use CppUTest for the rest of the code examples. In Section 6.9, *Why a C++ Test Harness for Testing C?*, on page 101, I'll summarize why I and others doing TDD for embedded C prefer a C++ test harness. Of course, it is up to you to choose the right test harness for your work.

I expect you have a few questions about TDD and how TDD can be effectively used for embedded development. The next couple chapters answer some of the common questions that come up after a TDD introduction. Others you will have to answer through your own experiences. After we get through the questions, we'll get back into more TDD and code.

At first TDD is foreign and requires discipline to keep the tests before the code. As you become more experienced, the feedback from TDD becomes its own reward. You will find yourself addicted to tests and the rapid feedback they provide. You might become Pavlov's Programmer anticipating the test results. You won't be comfortable without them.

4.6 Put the Knowledge to Work

1. Do the LED driver example from start to finish on your own. The exercises in the previous chapter show you where to start.

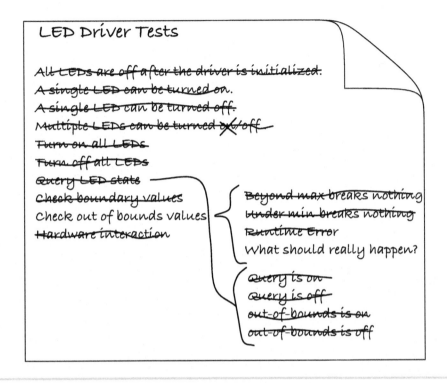

Figure 7— **LedDriver** test list—final

2. Finish the CircularBuffer that you started at the end of the previous chapter.

3. Our hardware engineer informed us she could save $0.12/board if the LEDs used inverted logic. Modify the LedDriver and its tests to use inverted logic.

   How could our tests or design be improved so that most of the tests don't care about inverted logic?

4. Our company just completed the version of the board with inverted LED logic. We find out that some of the previous version are still in the field. How should the LedDriver and its tests be modified to support both versions of the hardware? Conditional compilation is not part of a correct answer. We want one binary.

5. The production board's silkscreen is wrong! LED 1 is labeled 16, Led 2 is 15, and so on. How do you modify the tests and code to work with the real hardware?

Idealism increases in direct proportion to one's distance from the problem.
➢ *John Galsworthy*

CHAPTER 5

Embedded TDD Strategy

The previous chapter shows how an LED driver, a hardware-dependent piece of code, is developed using TDD and tested off the target on the host development system. You may wonder, are these tests valid when they are not run on target hardware? They are valuable, but along with the benefits, there are risks that must be considered and contained.

Testing off the target hardware also allows difficult-to-cause errors to be easily injected. Without this ability, a lot of code may go untested until that fateful day when the hardware error we anticipated occurs but the corrective action is wrong.

In this chapter, we'll look at specific progress blockers and time wasters common for embedded software and how to adapt TDD to help eliminate the target hardware bottleneck.[1]

5.1 The Target Hardware Bottleneck

Concurrent hardware and software development is a reality for many embedded projects. If software can be run only on the target, you will likely suffer unnecessarily from one or more of these time wasters:

- Target hardware is not ready until late in the project, delaying software testing.

- Target hardware is expensive and scarce. This makes developers wait and build up mounds of unverified work.

---

1. This chapter is based upon work previously published through the *Agile Times [Gre04]*, *Embedded Systems Conference [Gre07]*, and *IEEE [Gre07a]*.

- When target hardware is finally available, it may have bugs of its own. The mound of untested software has bugs too. Putting them together makes for difficult debugging, long days, and plenty of finger pointing.
- Long target build times waste valuable time during the edit, compile, load, and test cycle.
- Long target upload times waste valuable time during the edit, compile, load, and test cycle.
- Long target upload times lead to batching numerous changes in one build, which means that more can go wrong, leading to more debugging.
- Compilers for the target hardware are typically considerably more expensive than native compilers. The development team may have a limited number of licenses available, adding expense and possible delays.

Not all development efforts suffer from all those problems. But it is likely that every embedded development effort suffers from at least some of them, and these problems will block software development progress. Bob Martin's prime directive says, "We will not be blocked!"[2] Don't allow our progress to be blocked by lack of the target hardware. Don't wait for a long tool chain to do its job. Don't wait for a long upload. Don't wait in line to test your code.

Embedded developers have traditionally turned to the evaluation board for relief from one of the causes of the target hardware bottleneck.[3] An eval board provides an execution environment prior to target availability or when target hardware is too expensive for each developer to have their own. It's a very useful weapon in the embedded developer's arsenal, defending you from late and defect-laden projects, but it's really not enough. Eval boards suffer from long build and upload times but do provide a platform that works and is relatively inexpensive. Developers could have one for themselves early in the development cycle.

Here is where your development system and *dual-targeting* come into play as an effective way to cope with the target-hardware bottleneck.

5.2 Benefits of Dual-Targeting

Dual-targeting means that from day one, your code is designed to run on at least two platforms: the final target hardware and your development system.

---

2. http://butunclebob.com/ArticleS.UncleBob.ThePrimeDirectiveOfAgileDevelopment
3. An eval board is a circuit board used in development with the same processor configuration as the target system and ideally some of the same I/O.

In the LED driver example, the code is ultimately intended to run on an embedded target, but first it is written and tested on the development system. The goal is not some esoteric or academic pursuit; it is a pragmatic technique to keep development going at a steady pace. We avoid the waste and risk that comes with creating an inventory of unverified work. Nancy and Ron, in the following story, describe how they put dual-targeting to work on their project.

> **Excerpt from:** *Taming the Embedded Tiger [SM04]*
> *by: Nancy Van Schooenderwoert and Ron Morsicato*
>
> When you try to run newly written software on your embedded platform, you are tackling many unknowns simultaneously. A problem on the board, the CPU circuitry, the connectors, or the cabling can masquerade as a software bug, sending you off on a huge and frustrating waste of time. Hardware that worked perfectly one minute can be buggy the next—intermittent hardware bugs are horrendous to deal with. We needed a practical way to completely isolate the software under test to avoid debugging hardware and software simultaneously!
>
> Our application ran on a desktop PC as well as on the target CPU. We maintained this capability throughout development, even after we had good hardware. With so many hardware components at early stages in their own development, we simply could not risk having to troubleshoot with multiple unknowns. Very little of the application had to interact directly with hardware.
>
> This test technique required all the team members to have a clear understanding of the boundary between "pure" code and hardware-specific code. That, in itself, was good for software design and modularity. Finally, by continuing with the dual-targeting strategy, we were able to maintain an environment that was amenable to automation.

Dual-targeting solves several problems. It allows you to test code before the hardware is ready, and you can avoid the hardware bottleneck throughout the development cycle. You also avoid the finger pointing that goes with simultaneous hardware software debugging. It is a practice that keeps you moving fast.

Dual-targeting, like TDD, has another benefit: it influences your design. Paying attention to the boundaries between software and hardware produces more modular designs, in other words, designs with hardware independence. Unless you are building a one-of-a-kind product, hardware independence will remove some of the burden in future platform migrations. Hardware will change, that's a given. When it does, you'll be better prepared, having automated unit tests and code that already runs on multiple target platforms.

5.3 Risks of Dual-Target Testing

Testing code in the development system builds confidence in your code before committing it to the target, but there are risks inherent in the dual-target

> **Dual-Target Bonus Benefits**
>
> A side benefit of dual-targeting for test purposes is that the code will be easier to port in the future to different hardware platforms. How many of you are working with ten- or fifteen-year-old code that has been ported to several platforms? It's a significant issue for embedded. Hardware changes, often out of our control, will happen. Starting with dual-targeted code might just make it easier to move your code to the next unforeseen target hardware platform.
>
> In addition, when the time comes to port your code to yet another platform, you have the tests to support the porting effort, helping to lock in the desired behavior.

approach. Most of these risks are because of differences between the development and target environments. These include:

- Compilers may support different language features.
- The target compiler may have one set of bugs, while the development system native compiler has another set of bugs.[4]
- The runtime libraries may be different.
- The include filenames and features may be different.
- Primitive data types might have different sizes.
- Byte ordering and data structure alignments may be different.

Because of these risks, you may find that code that runs failure free in one environment experiences test failures in other environments.

The fact that there are potential differences in execution environments should not discourage you from dual-targeting. On the contrary, these are all workable obstacles on the path to getting more done. But it's best to take this path with eyes open and knowledge of some of the spear-filled pits that await further down the path.

With the benefits and risks enumerated, let's see how the embedded TDD cycle overcomes the challenges, without compromising the benefits.

5.4 The Embedded TDD Cycle

The embedded TDD cycle is an extension of the core TDD microcycle, described in Section 1.4, *The TDD Microcycle*, on page 6. It is designed to overcome the target-hardware bottleneck.

---

4. The day this paragraph was written, a popular open source compiler had 3,427 open bug reports. Seventy-four new bugs arrived the previous week, while fifty-four bugs were closed. The bugs were winning by twenty.

TDD is most effective when the build and test cycle takes only a handful of seconds. A longer build and test time usually results in taking bigger steps; with the bigger steps come more things that can be broken, leading to more debugging when the test finally is run. The need for a fast feedback loop leads us to move the TDD microcycle off the target to run natively on the development system. The TDD microcycle is the first stage of the embedded TDD cycle, as depicted in Figure 8, *The embedded Test-Driven Development cycle*, on page 82.

Stages 2–4 are designed to mitigate the risk of using the development platform to run unit tests. Stage 5 makes sure that the fully integrated system delivers working features. Without the TDD approach, stage 5 is where many embedded testing efforts begin.

Let's look at each stage in a little more detail.

Stage 1—TDD Microcycle

The first stage is run most frequently, usually every few minutes. During this stage, you write the bulk of the code and compile it to run on your host development system. Testing it on the development system gives fast feedback, not encumbered by the constraints of hardware reliability or availability. There are no target compiles or lengthy uploads delaying feedback. The development system is a proven and stable execution environment; it often has a richer debugging environment (which you won't use much[5]) than the target. You will also be able to run your code through tools like `valgrind`, `profil`, and `gcov`. Also, each developer has a development system or can get one tomorrow.

During this stage, you write code that is platform independent. You look for opportunities to disconnect software from hardware, as much as is practical. The boundary between hardware and software becomes evident and is recorded in your test cases.

As mentioned earlier, there is a risk to running code on the development system when it is eventually going to run in a foreign execution environment. It's best to confront that risk regularly because sometimes there are problems...enter stage 2.

Stage 2—Compiler Compatibility Check

Periodically, compile for the target, using the cross-compiler you expect to use for production compilations. This stage is an early warning system

---

5. You won't use your debugger as much because TDD reveals mistakes as you make them. The cause is usually obvious, not requiring a debugger.

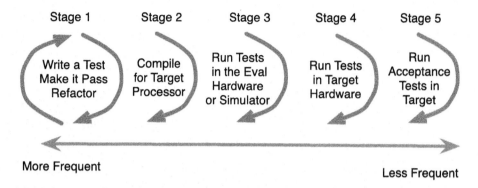

Figure 8— The embedded Test-Driven Development cycle

for compiler incompatibilities. It warns of porting problems such as unavailable header files, incompatible language support, and missing language features. This leads to code that uses only those facilities available in both development environments.

Early in an embedded development project, the tool chain may not yet be decided, and you may think this stage cannot be executed. Take your best guess about the tool chain, and compile against that compiler. You could use your suite of tests as part of your compiler evaluation criteria. As the compiler market changes, you also could use your suite of tests to evaluate new compiler vendors or versions.

You don't need to run stage 2 with every code change. You should do a target cross-compile whenever you use some new language feature, include a new header file, or make a new library call.

That said, it's best to make this happen automatically as part of a nightly build or your *continuous integration* build, where builds run on every check-in. See *Continuous Integration*, on page 84.

Stage 3—Run Unit Tests in an Eval Board

There is a risk that the compiled code will run differently in the host development system and the target processor. To mitigate this risk, run the unit tests on an eval board. Using an eval board shows when the code's behavior differs between the development system and the target processor. You will see, in a true story coming up in *Runtime Libraries Have Bugs*, on page 84, that this risk is real.

In an ideal world, we'd have the target hardware, and we would not need to use eval hardware. If it's late in the development cycle, we may have reliable target hardware making this stage appear unnecessary. So if every developer has ready access to the target hardware and we have high confidence in the hardware, this stage could be eliminated. But don't make this decision lightly.

Having the ability to run in an eval board may come in handy even after the target is ready. If there is some suspicious target behavior, you could quickly rule in or out target hardware problems by running tests in the eval platform.

These test runs should be built into the continuous integration build and run at least daily.

Stage 4—Run Unit Tests in the Target Hardware
The objectives here are the same as stage 3 while exercising the real hardware. One additional aspect to this stage is that you could also run target hardware-specific tests. These tests allow you to characterize or learn how the target hardware behaves.

An additional challenge in this stage is limited memory in the target. You might find that all the tests do not fit into the target. In that case, you can organize the tests into separate test suites where each suite fits in memory. This does result in more complicated build automation.

Stage 5—Run Acceptance Tests in the Target
Finally, we make sure the product features work by running automated and manual acceptance tests in the target. Here you have to make sure that any of the hardware-dependent code that can't be fully tested automatically is tested manually. You already know what that is.

At different points in the project life cycle, some of the stages might be either impossible or not so critical. For example, when there is no hardware early in the project, stages 4 and 5 are not possible to complete. Similarly, if the target is available and appears reliable, the eval board tests could be suspended until there is some question of target reliability. Off-target TDD, stage 1, is still where the bulk of the code is written and tested regardless of target availability.

5.5 Dual-Target Incompatibilities

The world is real, not ideal. Consequently, there will be differences in and out of the target. To test production code in both environments, you need code that works the same in both environments. Let's look at some of the portability problems you might encounter.

> ### Continuous Integration
>
> Continuous integration is a companion practice of Test-Driven Development. In continuous integration, team members integrate and check in changes to their version control system main branch regularly, usually many times a day. As a precondition to check in, all tests must pass.
>
> An automated build is needed for successful CI. It has to be easy to build the system. If the build is a tedious manual process with numerous mouse clicks and file copies, you won't build as often as you should. The goal is a single command build.
>
> In the dual-target approach suggested in this chapter, the test build must be automated. But that's not the end of it. The production build should also be automated. In the mouse-heavy IDEs of today, this may take some doing.
>
> With a single command build, you can automate the running of the build. The current state of the art is the *continuous integration server*. The CI server watches for check-ins to the code repository and initiates a complete build and test sequence once the check-in is complete. If a build breaks or any test failures occur, the team is notified usually by email. Fixing the build becomes the number-one responsibility of the team.
>
> An embedded build would be done in two stages, first for the development system tests. If successful, the target build would run next. If your product deploys to more execution platforms, you would want a build for each.
>
> CI is a risk reduction strategy and a time-saver. When developers go for long periods of time without integrating, the difficulty and risk of the integration grows. Like TDD, if testing is hard, do it all the time—it gets easier. With CI the mind-set is similar. If integration is hard, do it all the time. You avoid those long and error-prone code merges. Merges are smaller, and they are assisted by automated tests created via TDD.
>
> There are good open source tools, such as CruiseControl and Hudson, to help automate CI builds and error notifications.

Runtime Libraries Have Bugs

Shocking but true, runtime libraries have bugs. A few years back, I was working with a client adopting TDD. We were porting the test harness to a new target processor. We ran into a little snag. The target version of strstr() did not behave like all other versions of strstr() before it.

CppUTest compiled with no problem. The unit test harness had its own suite of unit tests, so the first order of business was to run those tests in the target. We waited through the upload, we ran the tests, and then we got some odd failures. Hmmm, the tests ran fine on the development system but failed on the target. What could that be?

We fired up the in-target debugger and started stepping through the code. After some digging, we discovered that strstr(), from the standard library, was not handling empty strings properly. Instead of working like strstr() does in the rest of the free world, where an empty string is contained in every string, this implementation reported that the empty string was not part of any string. We found a bug in the target compiler's implementation of the standard library function strstr()!

Once we understood the incompatibility, we modified the code so that it would pass on both systems, covering up the strstr() bug. We introduced a new platform-specific function called PlatformSpecificStrStr(). The GCC implementation looks like this:

```
int PlatformSpecificStrStr(const char * s, const char * other)
{
    return strstr(s, other) != NULL;
}
```

The target compiler's implementation covers up the bug so that all platforms work the same. It looks like this:

```
int PlatformSpecificStrStr(const char * s, const char * other)
{
//strstr on the XXXX processor library does not handle "" correctly
//"" should be found in any string.
//The conditional logic works around that problem
if (strlen(other) == 0)
    return TRUE;
else if (strlen(s) == 0)
    return FALSE;
else
    return strstr(s, other) != NULL;
}
```

We added the comment because the reason for the check was not obvious. To someone who knows the standard C library, that code looks unneeded. The comment explains why the seemingly unnecessary conditional logic is there.

Interestingly enough, the existing production code was peppered with the same kludge to overcome the bug in the target library implementation. Someone should have fixed that long ago.

Incompatible Header Files

Header file compatibility can present a significant portability problem. There can be different signatures, function names, defines, and include paths for essentially the same functionality. An example of this kind of incompatibility is the safer versions of sprintf(). In the Unix world, there is snprintf(), and in the Windows world there is _snprintf(), two functions that do almost the same thing.

Many C programmers use conditional compilation to handle platform-specific code. I suggest you avoid conditional compilation because it makes a mess of the code. It also makes it hard to see what code is really compiled under various situations.

Rather than conditional compilation, you could use a platform-specific header file that can map names like this:

```
#define snprintf _snprintf
```

This kludge works, but it is ugly. There is a better way.

In the development of CppUTest, we decided to isolate platform-specific code in one place. Each platform has a directory to hold the platform-specific code. We created a header file that defines function prototypes for operations that have to be implemented in a platform-specific way. Then we created an implementation for each platform, isolating it in a directory for that target. We used the compiler and linker, instead of the preprocessor.

We also created platform-independent test cases that describe how these functions must behave. For example, this is one of many test cases that define how snprintf() should behave:

```
TEST(PlatformSpecificSprintf, OutputFitsInBuffer)
{
    char buf[10];

    int count = PlatformSpecificSprintf(buf, sizeof buf, "%s", "12345");
    STRCMP_EQUAL("12345", buf);
    LONGS_EQUAL(5, count);
}
```

Here's the prototype that was added to the header file, right next to the other platform-specific prototypes:

```
int PlatformSpecificSprintf(char *str, size_t size, const char *format, ...);
```

Starting with the Visual C++ implementation and its variable-length argument list support, the implementation looks like this:

```
int PlatformSpecificSprintf(char *str, size_t size, const char *format, ...)
{
    int result;
    va_list args;
    va_start(args, format);
```

```
    memset(str, 0, size);
    result = _vsnprintf( str, size-1, format, args);
    va_end(args);
    return result;
}
```

The gcc code is the same, with the exception of a missing underscore.

Both builds passed their tests. Before cutting over to the new code, we added another test to make sure both implementations behaved the same when the buffer is not big enough to hold the whole string. We did not want CppUTest to have a buffer overrun. Reading the Unix-defined behavior for vsnprintf(), it says that if the output is truncated, the return value is the number of characters (excluding the trailing \0), which would have been written if space had been available. That led to this test, which passed just fine...with gcc.

```
TEST(SimpleString, PlatformSpecificSprintf_doesNotFit)
{
    char buf[10];

    int count = PlatformSpecificSprintf(buf, sizeof buf, "%s", "12345678901");
    STRCMP_EQUAL("123456789", buf);
    LONGS_EQUAL(11, count);
}
```

However, the test failed for Visual C++. Visual C++ and GNU do not agree. Insufficient buffer space in Visual C++ results in a -1 return value.

Initially, we had no interest in the precision of the Unix-style return value, and neither did any of the rest of the CppUTest code. So, we dumbed down the gcc version to mimic the Visual C++ version like this:

```
int PlatformSpecificSprintf(char *str, size_t size, const char *format, ...)
{
   va_list args;
   va_start(args, format);
   size_t count = vsnprintf( str, size, format, args);
   if (size < count)
       return -1;
   else
       return count;
}
```

Later, CppUTest needed the Unix-style return value for a new feature, and PlatformSpecificSprintf() had to evolve to meet the new need.

This incompatibility problem was solved by making a common interface that was independent of either platform's native function and then implementing the function for each platform.

In the prior two examples, the solution to an incompatibility was to implement a form of an adapter in C. An adapter converts the interface needed by the client to the interface provided by the server. This is a common pattern for solving platform dependency problems. It is described in the book *Design Patterns [GHJV95]*. The adapter pattern is very helpful for managing dependencies between code you control and code you don't control.

5.6 Testing with Hardware

Where practical, tests with hardware should be automated. Let's look at three kinds of tests we can create that interact with the hardware:

- Automated hardware tests
- Partially automated hardware tests
- Automated hardware tests with external instrumentation

Automated Hardware Tests

Your embedded hardware will probably have areas that are well-suited for automated testing. Other areas of the hardware will probably need special instruments to test hardware functionality. Where possible, you should write tests that help you learn what the hardware does and give you confidence that the hardware is working. As the inevitable hardware changes happen, your tests can help you see when a new hardware design has problems. You might find that some of these tests are valuable during production and may want some included in a built-in test sequence that ships with the product.

Let's say your design uses a Common Flash-Memory Interface (CFI)–compliant device. There are operations we can use to interrogate the flash memory device to see whether it is responding properly. For example, when a 0x98 is written to flash offset 0x55, a CFI-compliant flash memory device will respond with Q, R, and Y when offsets 0x10, 0x11, and 0x12 are read, respectively. The device must be reset after the query by writing a 0xff. This simple test, run on the target, will pass if the device is responding properly. It's not a thorough test, but it is a quick sanity test.

```
TEST(Flash, CheckCfiCommand)
{
    FlashWrite(0x55, 0x98);
    CHECK( FlashRead(0x10) == 'Q' );
    CHECK( FlashRead(0x11) == 'R' );
    CHECK( FlashRead(0x12) == 'Y' );
    FlashWrite(0, 0xff);
}
```

In the following story, the tests that software developers put together to test-drive their code became an invaluable tool for their hardware developer colleagues.

No Fear of Change
by: Randy Coulman, embedded software development engineer

We started a new project involving several custom hardware devices, all with an embedded processor and FPGA. We resolved to avoid problems we had in the past with buggy FPGA designs and fixes breaking other features. As with most projects with concurrent hardware/software development, we needed to start developing the software well before the hardware was available. We had a mostly complete spec for the hardware.

We decided that the best approach was to write tests for the hardware. We started with the most foundational feature of the hardware and wrote tests for it. We called these *hardware acceptance tests*. Since we didn't have hardware yet, we also wrote a simple simulation that would pass the test. We continued on this way, writing tests for features of the hardware and simulations that passed them. We used TDD to write unit tests for our software as we went along as well.

When the hardware became available, the integration effort was much shorter and simpler than it had been in the past. We encountered three types of problems:

- Places where certain language constructs worked differently on the embedded processor than they did on our development platform
- Places where the compiler was generating memory access code that the FPGA didn't support
- Places where we misinterpreted the hardware spec

Initially, the hardware acceptance tests were for the software team's benefit. Over time, the EEs came to trust our tests more and more. We had implemented a set of automated builds that would compile the software on the desktop platform and run all the tests against our hardware simulation and then install the latest software and FPGA binary on our target hardware, run the hardware acceptance tests (and some others as well), and report the results. At the request of the EEs, we added a "sandbox build" where they could drop in a new FPGA binary and have the automated tests run against it. Once it was passing all of the tests, they would then deliver the binary for us to integrate into the system. This allowed them to verify their work even if they were working in the middle of the night while the software engineers were home in bed.

These hardware acceptance tests have caught several regressions in the FPGA, allowing our EEs to upgrade their toolset, recompile their designs, and be confident that they didn't break anything. Overall, the integration effort was much less than in the past, and we've been able to continue to add new features over time with great confidence.

Partially Automated Hardware Tests

The LedDriver example, completed in the previous chapter, shows how a hardware-dependent piece of code can be tested outside the target. But, how do you know it really turns on the right LEDs? The LedDriver *thinks* it is controlling LEDs, but any number of mistakes could lead to software that thinks it is doing the right thing but actually does nothing or possibly something harmful.

So, you have to make sure the *last inch* of code, right next to the hardware, is right.

What kind of problems could we have with the LedDriver? It can be initialized with the wrong base address. It is possible that you misread the spec and the bits are inverted. It is possible that the schematic and the silk screen don't match. Maybe some of the connections on the board are not right. You're not just testing software; you're testing an embedded system. So, to be sure that the LedDriver really turns on the right LED at the right time, you have to look at it!

This is a good application for a partially automated test. A partially automated test displays a cue prompting the operator to manually interact with the system or view some system output. In this case, we would verify that a specific LED is either on or off. This would be repeated for each LED. This could also be part of built-in test capability shipped with the product or used to support manufacturing.

Manual tests are more expensive to run than automated tests, but they can't be completely avoided. If we are effective at minimizing the code that depends on the hardware, it is likely that the hardware-dependent code will not be changed very often. Consequently, the manual acceptance test will likely not need to be rerun as often. You will have to decide when these are run. A new hardware revision or changes to the hardware-dependent code would trigger a manual retest. You might also consider short and long versions of the partially automated tests, running the short one regularly and the longer one less frequently or when necessitated by change.

Tests with External Instrumentation

Special-purpose external test equipment can help automate hardware-dependent tests. This story was ahead of its time.

In the late 1980s, we developed a digital telecommunication monitoring system that monitored 1.544 Mbps (T1) signals. A major part of the behavior depended on a custom application-specific integrated circuit (ASIC). The ASIC monitored the T1 signals in real time; our embedded software interrogated the ASIC and reported performance information on demand and alarm conditions as they occurred. Testing this system required specialized test equipment to generate T1 signals and inject errors found in the real world.

After tiring of the manual tests that involved poking buttons on the T1 signal generator, our test engineer, Dee, dug into the instrument's capabilities and discovered it could be controlled through a serial port. Dee started writing test scripts. Her scripts instructed the external signal generator to corrupt the digital transmission with a specific bit error rate, then interrogate the system under test to see whether it reported the correct diagnosis. Incrementally, she automated her manual procedure, growing the automated test suite each day. The regression test grew to have wide functional coverage. This practice allowed Dee to report defects to the group within one day of their introduction.

Dee was not popular at first, walking from the lab smiling with a fresh list of bugs. After a while, the development team met the challenge and grew to rely on the morning bug report. A healthy competition developed; developers worked diligently to produce bug-free code. They used the test scripts before releasing to check their work. The quality improved.

We had zero defects reported from our installed base of thousands of units. Many other products developed at about the same time, by teams using manual test practices, had long bug lists and expensive field retrofits. This test investment had a great return.

5.7 Slow Down to Go Fast

Using Test-Driven Development for embedded software has its challenges. Some of those challenges will be unique to your development efforts. In spite of the challenges, putting TDD to work in the embedded environment is worth the effort.

As hardware and requirements evolve, existing functionality usually needs to be preserved. The next product's specification usually starts with "The product does everything the current product does plus...." The automated tests produced through TDD are a safety net, detecting unwanted changes to production code behavior during product evolution.

TDD helps you go faster. It may feel like TDD slows you down as you change from the developer's juggling act that many of us have found ourselves performing to the careful and thoughtful process encompassed by TDD. Slowing down is exactly what is needed to go fast! The careful, thoughtful, and verified work leads to higher quality.

5.8 Where Are We?

In this chapter, we looked at the problem of cross-platform development and the all too common scarcity of hardware. We discussed the need to isolate hardware dependencies. The more successful we are at that, the longer the useful life you can expect from your code and your tests. If you let hardware dependencies permeate the code, hardware evolution (and obsolescence) will accelerate the aging of your code and shorten its useful life. It may also shorten your life through the stress of keeping an aging code base alive.

We looked at the embedded TDD cycle and how to keep the pace of development unencumbered by cross development issues. We also looked at the advantages of dual-targeting and how to contain the risk of testing off the target.

Often, the foremost question on the embedded developer's mind is how to apply TDD effectively in a cross development environment. But there are other issues, too. In the next chapter, we'll look at some of the other common concerns of embedded developers as they think of how to apply TDD to their development efforts.

5.9 Put the Knowledge to Work

1. Test some of your production code off the target. Choose something simple that has few external dependencies.

2. Compile CppUTest or Unity for your target. Run the unit tests.

3. Write a script that uploads your test executable, runs it, and reports pass or fail.

CHAPTER 6

Yeah, but...

The initial discussion of TDD always raises quite a few questions that reflect real concerns. In the following sections, I'll try to address some of the questions and concerns that might be on your mind. I don't expect I'll totally convince you, though I hope to show you what is possible. To really convince yourself, you will need your own TDD experiences.

6.1 We Don't Have Time

We all need more time. Where will we find time to write all this test code? There is barely enough time to write the production code we need. There are more lines of test code than production code for the LedDriver. But does that really matter?

If people programmed error-free and at a constant rate, then there is some reason for concern. But people do neither. The time-consuming parts of programming are thinking, problem solving, and confirming solutions. Confirming solutions can be done many ways, Debug Later Programming (DLP) or TDD to name two. The important question is, did writing the test impede or speed your progress?

Many proficient practitioners proclaim that TDD makes them go faster. They report a productive and sustainable pace. The speedup comes from reducing current and future debug times, and from having a cleaner code base with tests as executable documentation.

What if TDD takes a little more time? There are other costs besides development time: customer dissatisfaction, lost sales, field service, warranty repair, defect management...the list goes on. Maybe it is worth it to you and your customers to spend more time and deliver fewer problems to the field. Also, you may become one of those people who goes faster with TDD.

If you look only at the time it takes to get the production code written, you are not looking at the whole job. You still have to get the bugs out. How much time do you currently spend testing and debugging code? The most popular answer I have heard, from polling conference attendees, is 50 percent. That is a lot of time. The first place to look for the time to do TDD is in your current practice. You should be able to trade some reactive debug time for the proactive TDD approach. In the next few sections, we'll look at some common unit test approaches that could be at least partially replaced by TDD.

Manual Test

If you are manually unit testing, use some of that time. If you are in a legacy code environment, you won't leave manual testing completely behind, but you could start to develop new code using TDD or write tests for some of the untested legacy code.

The initial investment in manual test may be lower than automating tests, but it is not sustainable; it has a nearly zero future return. A change to manually tested code nullifies the prior manual tests. You have to run the tests again. Because they are manual, we tend to rationalize running only a subset of the tests. When you don't rerun the right tests, you get the joy and cost of a future bug.

Custom Test Harness

From time to time, we have all written a test main() and a few test stubs that exercises newly written code. The test main() exercises the code under test, and stubs provide indirect inputs and log their parameters so we can inspect the behavior. You have created a custom test harness.

These tests are very helpful; they improve the quality of the code so that we are integrating better working code into the product. But too often, after integration, the tests fall into disrepair, as all testing moves to the integrated system. The tests fall out of sync with the production code, and the return on investment is diminished. Your custom test harness was helpful for a while.

Often custom test harnesses have a poor return on investment. They often become incompatible and are discarded after very few uses. The custom-crafted test main() also takes more effort than writing tests that plug into a test harness like CppUTest or Unity.

Unit Test by Single-Step

Another manual unit test approach is to single-step through the code under test with a debugger. This is a slow and inherently nonrepeatable process. When change comes, as it always does, the single-step unit test has to be repeated. Because it's a long and tedious process, it is likely to be a less thorough job the second, third, and Nth times through. We're only human; we make mistakes and miss subtle interactions within the code.

The shelf life of these tests is even worse than the shelf life of the test main() approach. Any single change invalidates prior tests. You have to start over and do it again. So, the manual test effort will tend to grow over time. But you can't afford that time, so you don't rerun all the needed single-step tests, and what happens? A bug creeps in, costing future effort too.

Documented and Reviewed Unit Test Process

I consulted at a company that had a very well-defined process. Well-defined and big are usually synonymous when it comes to processes. Their process manual was big. Their process police force was big, and they had a big stick.

They were assessed at CMM level three. They had good conformance and enforcement. One area covered by their process was unit testing. The process consisted of first documenting the unit test procedure and then getting the procedure reviewed and approved. Then they had to record evidence of executing the process. I asked the engineer, Dave, how they used this procedure. Here is how that conversation went:

> *James:* *How do you do unit testing?*
>
> *Dave:* *We have a unit testing standard. We write a unit test plan for each function.*
>
> *James:* *Does the unit test plan get reviewed?*
>
> *Dave:* *Yeah, we do a formal technical review on the plan.*
>
> *James:* *When do you perform the unit test plan?*
>
> *Dave:* *We run it before the code has been through its formal technical review.*
>
> *James:* *So if there are holes in the test plan, the reviewer can make suggestions and improvements to fill those holes.*
>
> *Dave:* *Yes, that's how it goes.*
>
> *James:* *What does the unit test plan look like?*
>
> *Dave:* *We follow the standard template and add the plan as comments before every function in the source code. The plan becomes part of the code. It includes a*

series of operations performed on the code, checking various conditions. We make sure we check each branch.

James: *What is it like to run the tests?*

Dave: *We use the debugger or the emulator and single-step through each statement and verify it does the right thing. We're really thorough.*

James: *It sounds like it. It takes a lot of time I bet.*

Dave: *Sure does.*

James: *What happens the next time you change that function?*

Confidently Dave says: *We do part of the tests over, based on what we changed.*

James, knowing the answer to the question: *Does code like this need to change very often?*

Dave says accusingly: *Yes, the systems engineers never can make up their mind.*

James: *What happens as there are more changes?*

Dave: *We rerun those parts of the unit test affected by the change.*

James: *How do you know what part of the plan needs to be rerun?*

Dave: *It's a judgment call.*

This big process took a lot of effort. It made everybody feel good because of all the investment in the software quality. Unfortunately, this kind of effort too often returns little on the investment. When the manual unit test process is repeated, the process gets boring, shortcuts naturally follow, and bugs find their way into the code.

I suggest test automation over test documentation. Test automation is the gift that keeps on giving. If you're using a process that is similar to Dave's, it's time to stop! Spend your unit test dollars somewhere else. By the way, the tests are documentation too. Dave's company had product safety requirements; we settled on reviewing the test cases to help assure the cases were thorough.

Where Do Your Unit Test Dollars Go?

When you look at how to pay for the unit tests that are written as part of TDD, take an honest look at your current process. Maybe your process is ad hoc or you write a test main or you document a unit test procedure or single-step through the code. Those activities cost a lot to implement but have a very limited payback.

You are already paying for unit tests either directly as mentioned or indirectly through long debug cycles. Consider spending some of your unit test effort on TDD rather than your current process. With TDD the tests are run with every change, the tests evolve along with the code, and the investment is returned many times over.

6.2 Why Not Write Tests After the Code?

It's hard to shift from DLP to TDD, and this is a common reaction: "Let's just write the tests after." This practice has a name, Test-After Development. You will get benefit from writing tests after, but not as much benefit as letting tests drive your production code. Test-After Development is about testing, where TDD is about much more. Here are a few examples of benefits you won't get from writing tests after development:

- TDD influences design. When you test after you do not get as much positive design impact, TDD leads to better APIs and more cohesive modules that are loosely coupled.
- TDD prevents defects. As you make small mistakes, TDD finds them immediately. When you test after, you might find many of your mistakes, but some will escape detection where TDD would have found them. These mistakes eventually populate your bug database.
- When you write tests after, you also will have to spend valuable time hunting down the root cause of the test failures, while in TDD the root cause is usually obvious.
- TDD is more rigorous and provides better test coverage—the right test coverage. Test coverage is not the goal of TDD, but test coverage will suffer when tests are written after code.

6.3 We'll Have to Maintain the Tests

Yes, you will have to maintain the tests. When you don't have tests, you don't have to maintain them, but you do have to do those tedious manual retests. You get value from having the tests that makes the maintenance effort worth the investment.

Tests have to be kept clean and expressive and free from duplication. It takes time to learn these skills. After you gain skill at TDD and designing test cases, you will find that tests do not have to be difficult to maintain.

6.4 Unit Tests Don't Find All the Bugs

It is true, TDD will not prevent all bugs, but that does not make a case for not doing TDD. I like to think of TDD as helping make really solid building blocks by making sure each line of code does what we expect. Having each block behave as intended makes it possible for the system to behave as needed.

You will still need integration tests, acceptance tests, exploratory tests, and load tests. TDD will eliminate many of the problems so that the higher-level tests are finding appropriate problems. Integration tests should find integration problems, acceptance tests should show that the code meets its requirements, and load tests should help determine whether the system meets its design limits. When changes occur, there will be implications at the unit test level, and the TDD tests will help assure that changes have only the intended consequences.

A single wrong bit can spell disaster for software-controlled systems. Software is amazingly complex, and mistakes are amazingly easy to make. Years ago one of my colleagues, Joe, designed a multiprocessor communication infrastructure that was part of our product platform. From time to time we would report some hard-to-reproduce bugs in the platform. Joe would disappear for weeks while he tracked down these hard-to-find bugs. Eventually he would emerge from his cube and claim, "It wasn't a bug, just a typo!"

I did not know TDD then, but this is definitely a case of the code at a low level not doing what the programmer expected. Joe's mistake may have been minor, but the resulting bugs were in no way minor. Small mistakes don't mean small bugs. Mistakes small and large cause a lot of wasted effort. TDD may not prevent all bugs, but it does a very effective job of preventing many mistakes from becoming bugs.

6.5 We Have a Long Build Time

It's common for the build time in big embedded projects to take hours—a cell phone manufacturer I worked with had a six-hour build. But, the edit/build/unit test cycle time must be measured in seconds, not minutes or hours. To get into a TDD rhythm, you need a fast incremental build—you don't need to build the whole system for TDD. You can build parts of the system independently when dependencies are managed.

If your build time is too long, you will probably need multiple unit test builds to keep the incremental build time down. Multiple unit tests builds should not be too difficult to set up, because your product likely already has some structure based around libraries, components, and subsystems. The exact mechanics of setting up each build depend on your development environment and the unit test harness being used. In essence, you set up different make files or different make targets to generate the different test executables.

The real challenge with testing modules, or groups of modules together, is that you need modular code! The all too prevalent data structure and function call free-for-all antipattern makes breaking the system apart for testing more difficult. Starting in the next chapter, we will look at techniques for breaking dependencies that can help in creating smaller, more focused test builds.

6.6 We Have Existing Code

Most of you reading this book have an existing product code base you work with day in and day out. Most likely you have few or no automated unit tests. Does that mean you cannot do TDD? Of course not. Do you need to write tests for all your existing code before you begin? Come on, be serious. It would be great to have the unit tests, but it is not practical to write them all after the fact, stopping product development.

The recommended prescription for legacy code (code without tests) is to incrementally add tests while delivering new product functionality. We'll look at this topic in detail in Chapter 13, *Adding Tests to Legacy Code*, on page 253. As a brief preview, here are the techniques for adding tests and getting TDD going for your product:

- Use TDD for new functions and modules.
- Add tests when changing existing code.
- Add tests when fixing bugs.
- Invest in some strategic tests proactively.

6.7 We Have Constrained Memory

Constrained memory is the reality for many embedded developers. Running tests in the development system won't reveal the same memory constraints found in the target. Here are a few things to help TDD in constrained memory situations:

- Use dual-targeting so the bulk of your code is tested off-target.
- Make a lab version of your target system with plenty of memory to hold all production code and test cases.

- Find a small test harness. Unity is a good choice.

- As described in Section 6.5, *We Have a Long Build Time*, on page 98, create multiple test runners, each with a subset of tests that fit into the limited memory.

- Track memory usage for your target build.

Let's talk a little about tracking memory usage. Let's say that your target system has 1MB of flash memory. You could graph your usage each iteration, as shown in Figure 9, *Flash usage graph*, on page 101.

Your continuous integration system would build the target flash memory binary image and also create a map file. A simple shell script could read the map file and calculate the code area usage. Each iteration, the team pulls that number from the build and puts it on their Big Visible Chart (BVC). When the consumption of this limited resource has an unexpected spike, as in iteration 7, the team can see there is a problem. The build records would reveal when and what was changed to cause the bump in usage. The chart illustrates a drop in flash usage—they must have found some flash hog and put it on a diet.

The team could also establish budgets for flash or RAM usage for each iteration or feature, and set that number in the CI build. The build could fail if the budgeted usage is exceeded—bringing it to the attention of the team immediately during the iteration. The BVC is a very handy tool and could be used for tracking any critical resource such as CPU idle time or I/O data rate. You can see that a BVC for resource consumption could give early warning.

6.8 We Have to Interact with Hardware

Tests that interact with hardware can be written and tested off the target. This is an important topic, and we spend a lot of time on it. Recall the LedDriver, first shown in Chapter 3, *Starting a C Module*, on page 27. This did not prove that the code will work in the hardware, but the tests do show that the code meets our understanding of what the hardware is supposed to do. When the LedDriver is integrated with the hardware, any misunderstandings can be fixed in the production code and the tests.

LedDriver is a simple driver; many drivers will have more complex interactions with the hardware. Several chapters in the book (starting in Chapter 7, *Introducing Test Doubles*, on page 107) are dedicated to exploring the use of test stubs in test-driving interactions between modules as well as interactions from the software to the hardware.

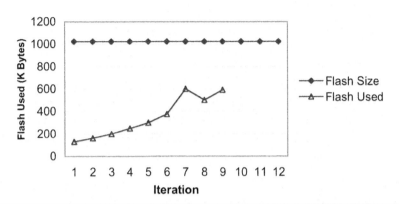

Figure 9— Flash usage graph

We'll take control of the clock, one of the often critical hardware interactions. You will see that time is just a function call. We'll control time so that testing of time-dependent code is thorough and practical.

We'll also get right next to the silicon in Chapter 10, *The Mock Object*, on page 163 where we will simulate the complex interactions between a device driver and the hardware. No, don't let "simulate" give you the wrong impression. Simulate often means creating software, and maybe hardware, that can be as complex as the thing being built or simulated. Test doubles and mocks are not simulators; they simulate specific interaction scenarios. Simulating a sequence of interactions is much less complex than a simulation of the whole and is very effective.

6.9 Why a C++ Test Harness for Testing C?

Much of CppUtest could be written in straight C, but straight C cannot directly handle the self-installation of test cases. Unity and other C-only test harnesses require a two-step (and sometimes three-step) process to install test cases. This makes it easy to make mistakes. For example, if you write a test case and then forget to install it, it will appear to pass when actually it has not even run.

Having multiple entries for each test makes refactoring tests more difficult. If you rename or split a test, you have duplicate work. It's more likely you'll just leave the bad name when renaming is hard, so it's best if we use a test harness that makes it easy to do the right thing.

As you've seen, the designers of Unity[1] addressed the test installation problem with a Ruby script that reads test cases and generates a test caller.

CppUTest's designers[2] chose a different approach. We used some of the C++ capabilities to install each test into a list of all tests. If you are not very familiar with C++, the explanation might be a little foreign. One of the important features of C++ provides built-in language support for initializing objects. The declaration of a file scope object will be initialized before main() runs, using the object's constructor. A constructor is like an init function for a struct. Basically, the TEST() macro creates a file scope C++ object whose constructor installs the TEST() into the list of all tests.

I would not dismiss CppUTest, even if your target has only a C compiler. Sometimes when you compile with a different compiler, you can find problems you wouldn't have found before. Testing in the host development system can help identify portability problems. Self-installed tests help eliminate *lost* test cases. Some users of CppUTest report that their reluctance to use C++ was lessened as a side effect of using a C++ test harness. It allowed them to experiment with C++ in the test cases, and they now use it in their production code too.

If your target does not have a C++ compiler or you're still concerned about using CppUTest, have a look at the Ruby script that comes with CppUTest that converts CppUTest tests to Unity tests. This lets you work first in the development compiler environment and automatically convert test cases to Unity for target execution.

6.10 Where Are We?

You probably still have questions about how to fit TDD into your development effort. The LedDriver example was simple in that the driver had only a single dependency. It helped you get the feel of TDD. You will have *easy* code like this to write in your work. Don't feel you must solve the biggest testing challenges first. The simpler testing challenges help you develop the testing and incremental development skills needed for going after the bigger challenges.

Don't worry, TDD is not just for testing the easy stuff. The complexities of systems come from dependencies on other parts of the system. In the next part of this book, we will look at applying TDD to modules that have dependencies that make writing automated tests a challenge.

---

1. Greg Williams, Mark Karlesky, and Mark Vander Voord
2. Michael Feathers, Bas Vodde, and your humble author

6.11 Put the Knowledge to Work

1. Think of 100 reasons why TDD could never work for you. Then go review your bug list.

2. List bug root causes, and consider which of them might get prevented by TDD.

3. Pretend that TDD might work for you and try it.

Part II

Testing Modules with Collaborators

You can fool some of the people all of the time and all of the people some of the time, but you cannot fool all of the people all of the time.

➢ Abraham Lincoln

CHAPTER 7

Introducing Test Doubles

So far, we have developed and written tests for self-contained code, which is code without dependencies. These are, and have always been, the easier parts of any system development, the easily sharable parts, and the reusable parts. A more formidable challenge for TDD is testing code in the middle, which consists of the modules that must work through other modules, functions, and data stores to get their job done. This part of the book is dedicated to demonstrating techniques to effectively test the code in the middle.

7.1 Collaborators

A collaborator is some function, data, module, or device outside the code under test (CUT) that the CUT depends upon. We've already seen a very simple collaborator in LedDriver. At first glance, it looks like a stand-alone module with no collaborators. First glances can be deceptive—it does have a collaborator, as you can see in Figure 10, *Testing the LedDriver*, on page 108. In production, ledsAddress points to the memory-mapped I/O address required by the hardware. During testing, the LedDriver is given the address of virtualLeds, which is a word of memory standing in for the actual hardware. The test case indirectly monitors the driver's behavior by inspecting virtualLeds after each operation.

virtualLeds is a simple *test double*.[1] A test double impersonates some function, data, module, or library during a test. The CUT does not know it is using a double; it interacts with the double the same way it interacts with the real collaborator.

---

1. Test doubles are described in Gerard Meszaros' book *xUnit Testing Patterns* [Mes07].

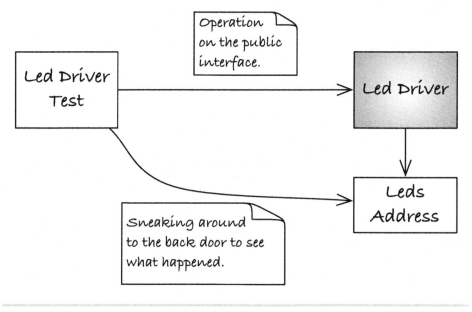

Figure 10— Testing the **LedDriver**

You have probably used test doubles before. In the simplest form, the test double is a stub taking the place of the actual production code. You've written them, but you probably considered the stub a short-term solution to not having the real code. Once you had the real code, you stopped using the stubs. In TDD, the test doubles are used and maintained throughout the life of the production code, facilitating automated unit testing.

7.2 Breaking Dependencies

Real code has dependencies. One module interacts with several others to get its job done. Code resists automated tests when it interacts with the operating system, hardware devices, or sometimes other modules. The bad news is that these problem dependencies make test automation difficult or maybe prohibitively expensive. The good news is that we can design code to be testable; we can break problem dependencies.

The key to breaking dependencies is a more rigorous use of interfaces, encapsulation, and data hiding and less reliance on unprotected global data. To design more modular and testable C, we employ a header file to publish the interface of a module. A testable module is one that interacts with other modules through the module's interface.

When the interactions between modules are through interfaces, collaborators can be designed to be swapped out, and test versions of the collaborators can be inserted. We use the substitute collaborators only when needed; if you can test with the real production code collaborator, then do it. If the collaborator gets in the way of your automated tests, then it is time to use a test double.

Collaborators can get in the way when is it hard to control their behavior. For example, to test the proper reaction to a network failure, we need to be able to cause the failure at the right instant for the test case. Networks might not fail when we want them to, and they also tend to fail when we don't want them to. To test code that interacts with a network, we need to be able to insert a test version of the network communication API.

Test doubles solve the problem of testing a precisely timed network failure. Let's say there is a message sequence involving four messages. When there is a communications failure, the recovery varies based on which message was the last sent. To be confident that the code meets its requirements, you need to test the various failure modes. Does the code recover properly when the network fails after the third message? "Pull the plug now, Harry!" might work, but it is hardly repeatable. Testing this scenario requires taking control of the collaborator and causing the error at exactly the right moment.

Refer to the left of the following graphic and you'll see a dependency graph of a handful of modules.

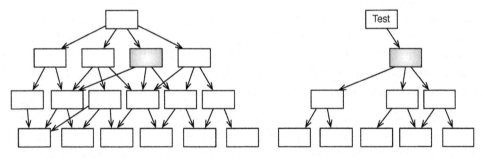

The module in the middle...   ...has baggage.

Your mission, should you choose to accept it, is to test the gray module in the middle. As you investigate the dependencies, it's clear that the gray box has a lot of baggage. The dependency graph on the right shows the module to test and the web of dependencies that might hinder getting the code into a test harness. There are hidden runtime dependencies and initializations that will be hard to anticipate and discover. Where does it end? We can confidently accept the mission because the problem dependency chains can be broken using one or more test doubles.

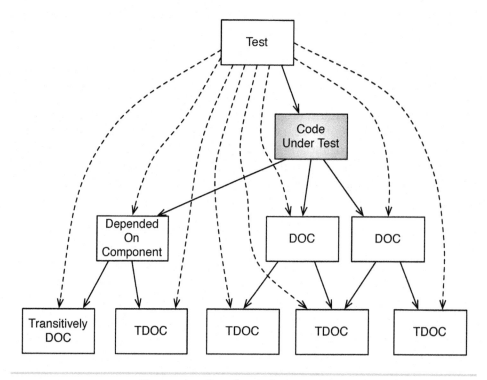

Figure 11— Test dependency octopus

Without test doubles, we have the dependency mess shown in Figure 11, *Test dependency octopus*, on page 110. At the top is the test case, acting as the client to the CUT. The test case's dependencies make it look like an octopus. The dashed lines are the tentacles reaching to the CUT's collaborating modules or data structures. Gerard calls these *Depended on Components* (DOC).

As discussed in Section 2.5, *The Four-Phase Test Pattern*, on page 25, tests are responsible for the four phases of each test: setup, exercise, verify, and cleanup. The test's dependency mess comes from fulfilling its responsibility in the Four-Phase Test pattern. The test case must set up and clean up the DOCs. There can be *transitively depended on components* to initialize too.[2] If you do not give up, you might find your whole system being initialized in the test case. After the test cases exercise the CUT, you may need to consult the DOCs and transitively depended on components to check proper CUT behavior. It can be a mess.

---

2. The transitive property of dependencies says if A depends on B and B depends on C, then A depends on C.

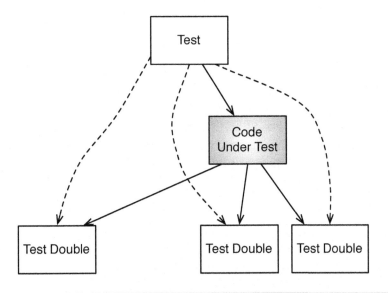

Figure 12— Managing test dependencies with test doubles

Aside from making the test complex, the test's knowledge of the direct and transitive dependencies makes the test fragile. Future changes to the design are likely to result in test breakage as dependencies evolve. Unmanaged dependencies in test code are dangerous, just as they are in production code.

Figure 12, *Managing test dependencies with test doubles*, on page 111 shows how we can use test doubles to simplify testing and reduce knowledge of transitively depended on components. The test double stands in for the real collaborator; the CUT cannot tell the difference. The double is the collaborator from the CUT's point of view.

The test doubles are not full simulations of the thing being replaced, just as a stunt double is not the same as the leading man. The stunt double knows his part; he can fall off a building really well. A different double might be needed to fall off a horse. Doubles take the place of the leading man in very specific situations. This helps test doubles stay simple, much simpler than the thing being replaced.

Test doubles provide indirect inputs (return values) to the CUT or to capture and possibly check indirect outputs (parameters) sent by the CUT to the test double.

There are a number of variants of the test double concept. Read *Test Doubles Variations*, on page 114 to see a few of the variations.

7.3 When to Use a Test Double

Not all interactions will use test doubles. My rule of thumb is to use the real code when you can and use a test double when you must. You will need to use judgment to decide when to fake and when not to fake.

For example, if the CUT uses a linked list as one of its collaborators, there is no need to use a fake linked list. Use the real one. The test case consults the linked list during the verify stage of the Four-Phase Test pattern to see whether the right additions, deletions, and modifications were made to the linked list.

Here are some common reasons to use a test double:

Hardware independence
Having test doubles for hardware interactions will allow testing independently from the hardware. It also provides the ability to feed a wide variety of inputs into the core of the system that may be very difficult or time-consuming to do in the lab or field.

Inject difficult to produce input(s)
Some computed or hardware-generated event scenarios may be difficult to produce. By adjusting the return result of a test double, the CUT might have all it needs to trigger some unlikely execution path.

Speed up a slow collaborator
If tests don't run fast, you will likely stop running them as often as you should. A slow collaborator, such as a database, a network service, or some number crunching, can be faked out by returning a result controlled by the test case, speeding up the test.

Dependency on something volatile
The classic example of a volatile collaborator is the clock. You have some event that is supposed to happen at 8:42 a.m.—either you get one chance a day or you have to reset the clock. But with a double standing in for the clock, it can be 8:42 a.m.—or the last day of leap year—whenever you want.

Dependency on something under development
Design often encompasses unknown areas, especially when hardware and software are concurrently developed. As you approach an area of the unknown, develop a test double with the interface that best meets the CUT's needs. Progress on the CUT can continue, while at the same time exploring the CUT's needs of the currently unimplemented service.

Dependency on something that is difficult to configure
If a DOC is difficult to set up and get into one or more desired states, it may be best to substitute the DOC with a test double. A database is a good example of a DOC that you could test with but is difficult to set up.

Choosing to use test doubles for the CUT is not an all-or-nothing proposition. Most often you will have a variety of real and fake collaborators, as shown in Figure 13, *Using test doubles and real collaborators*, on page 115. Also, for some tests you will want to use the production code collaborator, and for others you will want the test double.

7.4 Faking It in C, What's Next

We've talked conceptually about the problems that test doubles are designed to address. We have defined some of the variations on test doubles that fit differing testing needs. We have listed some of the situations where test doubles are almost always used. What we have not done is show you the mechanics of substituting the test double for the production code.

C has only these primitive mechanisms: linker substitution, function pointer substitution, and preprocessor substitution. So, when do you use, or not use, each substitution technique?

Link-time substitution
Use link-time substitution when you want to replace the DOC for the whole unit test executable. Also, you will need to use linker substitution to substitute a module where you do not control the interface. Using this technique is especially helpful for off-target testing and eliminating dependencies on third-party libraries, hardware-dependent modules, or the operating system. You'll see an example of this in the next chapter.

If you also have to test the DOC, then you need a separate test executable that contains the DOC and does not contain the test double. We'll use link-time test doubles in the next chapter.

Function pointer substitution
Use function pointer substitution when you want to replace the DOC for only some of the test cases. You could use function pointers substitution everywhere that you control the interface, but it is more complicated, uses some RAM, and compromises function declaration readability, at least until you get used to it. Function pointers allow great control over which functions get overridden and which do not. Function pointer substitution is detailed in Chapter 9, *Runtime-Bound Test Doubles*, on page 147.

> ### Test Doubles Variations
>
> In Gerard's book, he identifies different types of doubles. We'll use spies, stubs, mocks, and exploding fakes in this book. It is good to know there are other kinds of doubles.
>
> | Name | Variation |
> |---|---|
> | Test dummy | Keeps the linker from rejecting your build. A dummy is a simple stub that is never called. It is provided to satisfy the complier, linker, or runtime dependency. |
> | Test stub | Returns some value, as directed by the current test case. |
> | Test spy | Captures the parameters passed from the CUT so the test can verify that the correct parameters have been passed to the DOC. The spy can also feed return values to the CUT just like a test stub. |
> | Mock object | Verifies the functions called, the call order, and the parameters passed from the CUT to the DOC. It also is programmed to return specific values to the CUT. The mock object is usually dealing with a situation where multiple calls are made to it, and each call and response are potentially different. |
> | Fake object | Provides a partial implementation for the replaced component. The fake usually has a simplified implementation when compared to the replaced implementation. |
> | Exploding fake | Causes the test to fail if it is called. |
>
> These terms are helpful when talking about the different kinds of behavior and capability needed by the test double. Often a distinction is not needed, though, so I suggest you don't get too hung up on the terms in practice. You will find that people generally use the terms *fake*, *mock*, and *stub* interchangeably.

Preprocessor substitution

Use preprocessor substitution when linker and function pointer substitutions can't do the job. You can break a chain of unwanted includes with the preprocessor. You can also use it selectively or temporarily to override names. CppUTest uses preprocessor substitution to override the standard library's free(), malloc(), calloc(), and realloc() functions, allowing it to monitor heap usage. It uses the GCC command-line switch -include to force an include at the beginning of every file. Here is an example of a forced include file that allows CppUTest to monitor the heap:

```
#include <stdlib.h>

void* cpputest_malloc(size_t size, const char *, int);
void* cpputest_calloc(size_t count, size_t size, const char *, int);
void* cpputest_realloc(void *, size_t, const char *, int);
void cpputest_free(void* mem, const char *, int);
```

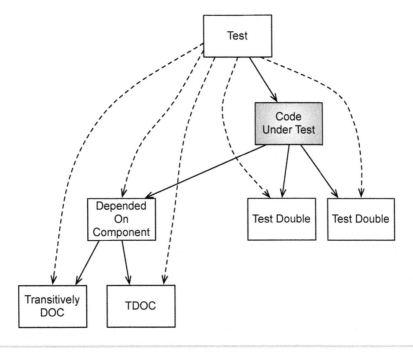

Figure 13— Using test doubles and real collaborators

```
#define malloc(a) cpputest_malloc(a, __FILE__, __LINE__)
#define calloc(a, b) cpputest_calloc(a, b, __FILE__, __LINE__)
#define realloc(a, b) cpputest_realloc(a, b, __FILE__, __LINE__)
#define free(a) cpputest_free(a, __FILE__, __LINE__)
```

Preprocessor substitution is the substitution of last choice. The problem is that the compiled code in the CUT is actually different. It permeates changes to the code far and wide. When tempted to use preprocessor substitution, consider an alternative: wrapping the code and providing a new interface that you do control that gives substitutability through the linker or function pointers.

Combined link-time and function pointer substitution

We can combine link-time and function pointer substitution to work together. A link-time stub can be created that contains a function pointer. Initially the function pointer is initialized to NULL. In this case, the stub has default do-nothing behavior. A test case can override the NULL pointer and provide exactly the stub function needed for the test. This is helpful when you want the flexibility of the function pointer but do not want to change the interface to the DOC.

7.5 Where Are We?

In this chapter, we looked conceptually at the problem of dependencies. We looked at a few ideas of how to separate the code under test from its collaborator by using test doubles. There are a variety of different kinds of test doubles and substitution techniques that are available to you in C.

In the next few chapters, we'll put the various test doubles and substitution techniques to work as we do TDD for some modules in the middle or close to the hardware. Always choose the simplest approach that works and keeps the design clean.

Your existing legacy code may have dependency problems much worse than this. TDD helps avoid that mess by making dependency problems visible. We'll look at how to start taming legacy code in Chapter 13, *Adding Tests to Legacy Code*, on page 253.

7.6 Put the Knowledge to Work

Create a block diagram of your system. Identify collaborators and collaborations that you expect to make automated tests difficult.

CHAPTER 8

Spying on the Production Code

In the previous chapter, we looked at some of the challenges of testing modules that interact with other parts of the system. I described some of the techniques needed in C to overcome these challenges. In this chapter, we'll look at an example module that has problem hardware and OS dependencies. We'll use interfaces, test doubles, and link-time substitution to manage the problem dependencies.

To manage dependencies on the Code Under Test execution environment, all access to the execution environment must go through defined interfaces. Interface calls can be intercepted and inspected by replacing a problem Depended on Component with a test double. The test case can control the test double's return results, driving the CUT indirectly. The essential idea is that the test case and the test doubles together form a software test fixture that surrounds the CUT, driving its inputs and monitoring and checking its outputs.

The test case takes the role of the client, driving the direct inputs on the CUT, while the test doubles play the role of the DOC. The test doubles can monitor data intended for the DOC and provide indirect input as return results that drive the CUT as needed by the test case.

In this chapter, we will create core system functionality that needs to interact with the hardware and operating system. We won't let this code directly access the hardware or OS. We'll make it go through a thin layer that can be replaced with a test double, a spy that will help verify the behavior of the code under test.

As embedded software developers, you have probably heard the terms *OS abstraction layer* and *hardware abstraction layer*. These layers give us portability between execution environments. We're using the same idea to make the core logic of the system testable. Now you have another good reason to introduce these layers in your code.

In the closing of the previous chapter, you saw three techniques for sneaking test doubles into the test runner, one of which was link-time substitution. We'll use link-time substitution in this situation, because we want to completely eliminate the OS and hardware dependencies in the test executable.

We will also use the CppUTest test harness for the rest of the book. CppUTest tests look very similar to Unity tests. You may want to look again at Section 2.3, *CppUTest: A C++ Unit Test Harness*, on page 21 or Appendix 3, *CppUTest Quick Reference*, on page 303, for a refresher.

8.1 Light Scheduler Test List

We're developing light-scheduling features of a home automation system. The first cut of the test list is in Figure 14, *Light Scheduler test list*, on page 119.

The test list is roughly in the order we expect to implement the tests. Don't worry too much about getting the test order exactly right; you will change the order as you go. You will discover forgotten tests or find that an item in the test list is really multiple tests. Don't spend too much time on the test list. If you try to get it perfect, you are definitely spending too much time on it.

8.2 Dependencies on Hardware and OS

Let's see how we can design and test the light-scheduling portion of a home automation system. The component that handles light scheduling is called the LightScheduler, shown in context in Figure 15, *Initial light scheduler design*, on page 120. The LightScheduler has transitive dependencies on the hardware and the operating system (OS). If left unbroken, these dependencies mean that the light scheduler will be testable only in the target hardware.

The design works like this. The client of the LightScheduler is in the AdminConsole subsystem. The AdminConsole instructs the LightScheduler to turn on and off the lights at specific times during the week. Every minute, the LightScheduler is pinged through an OS callback from TimeService. The ping triggers the LightScheduler to check its internally maintained schedule of light control actions. At the appropriate time, the LightScheduler tells the LightController to turn on or off a light by its id.

Each design element has focused responsibilities. The scheduler owns the overall application logic, while LightController and TimeService interact with the

> **Light Scheduler Tests**
>
> Lights are not changed at initialization
> Time is wrong, day is wrong, no lights are changed
> Day is right, time is wrong, no lights are changed
> Day is wrong, time is right, no lights are changed
> Day is right, time is right, the right light is turned on
> Day is right, time is right, the right light is turned off
> Schedule every day
> Schedule a specific day
> Schedule all weekdays
> Schedule weekend days
> Remove scheduled event
> Remove non-existent event
> Multiple scheduled events at the same time
> Multiple scheduled events for the same light
> Remove non scheduled light schedule
> Schedule the maximum supported number of events (128)
> Schedule too many events

Figure 14— Light Scheduler test list

hardware and OS. LightController and TimeService are parts of larger hardware and operating system abstraction layers.[1]

By following the dependency arrows, you can see that the LightScheduler transitively depends on the hardware and OS. The dependencies could mean that LightScheduler can be tested only in the target. But with our separation of responsibilities, it's easy to disconnect the problem dependencies during test. Let's look at how we can use the linker to break the transitive dependency on the hardware and OS.

8.3 Link-Time Substitution

To break the dependencies on the production code, think of the collaborators only in terms of their interfaces. In Figure 16, *The light scheduler instructs collaborators through their interfaces*, on page 121, we can see the separation

---

1. Note that not all interface functions are shown in the UML diagrams, just a few representative functions. This is common for informal usage of UML.

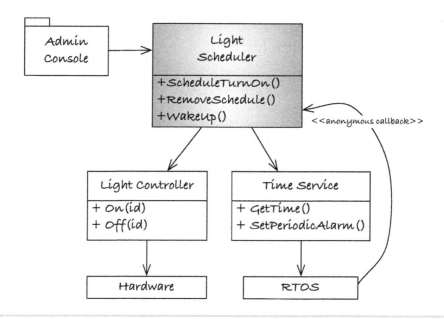

Figure 15— Initial light scheduler design

of the interface from the implementation. The interface is represented by the header file, and the implementation is represented by the source file, as we have discussed. LightScheduler is bound to the production code implementation at link time. Michael Feathers, author of *Working Effectively with Legacy Code* [Fea04], calls this a link seam. And at a seam we have flexibility.

The unit tests take advantage of the link seam by providing alternative implementations for LightController and TimeService, as shown in Figure 17, *Light scheduler unit test structure*, on page 122.

Though there are other ways to accomplish this, a good way to structure the test build is to compile all production code into a library. Test doubles are left as object (.o) files. When building for test, the makefile explicitly links the test double object files before linking to the production code library. This allows the test doubles to override production code with same names. This is described in more detail in Appendix 1, *Development System Test Environment*, on page 291.

8.4 Spying on the Code Under Test

The spy is on a covert operation. It intercepts the inputs destined for the production code, later providing it to the test case. As part of its covert mission,

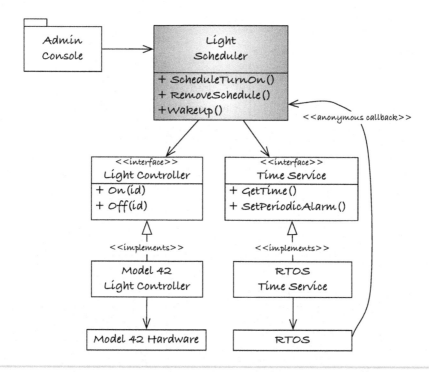

Figure 16— The light scheduler instructs collaborators through their interfaces.

it may also feed return results to the client code, getting the CUT to do the test's bidding. Very sneaky indeed.

After setting up the initial LightScheduler files (I use the shell scripts provided with CppUTest to create the initial files), write a test case that helps you envision the roles of the LightControllerSpy and FakeTimeService in the testing of LightScheduler. This tests helps you decide what facilities are needed in the test fixture.

tests/HomeAutomation/LightSchedulerTest.cpp
```
TEST(LightScheduler, ScheduleOnEverydayNotTimeYet)
{
    LightScheduler_ScheduleTurnOn(3, EVERYDAY, 1200);
    FakeTimeService_SetDay(MONDAY);
    FakeTimeService_SetMinute(1199);
    LightScheduler_WakeUp();

    LONGS_EQUAL(LIGHT_ID_UNKNOWN, LightControllerSpy_GetLastId());
    LONGS_EQUAL(LIGHT_STATE_UNKNOWN, LightControllerSpy_GetLastState());
}
```

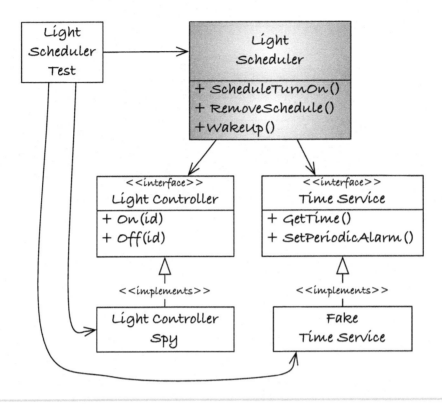

Figure 17— **Light scheduler unit test structure**

Dissecting this test case one line at a time, we see the test schedules the light with id equal to 3 to turn on every day at the 1,200th minute of the day (8 p.m.). The test takes control of the clock, telling the FakeTimeService that it should report that it is Monday at 7:59 p.m. Then the test simulates a callback to LightScheduler_WakeUp(), like the production TimeService will do every minute. Finally, the test checks the expected outcome. The literal constants for EVERYDAY and MONDAY, along with similar constants, will be part of the LightScheduler interface.

There are no scheduled events due, so LightController functions should not be called. The spy is debriefed after the covert mission by checking its secret test-only interface made up of LightControllerSpy_GetLastId() and LightControllerSpy_GetLastState(). LightControllerSpy_GetLastId() returns the id of the light that was controlled or LIGHT_ID_UNKNOWN when there has been no light control. LightControllerSpy_GetLastState() returns LIGHT_OFF, LIGHT_ON, or LIGHT_STATE_UNKNOWN. LIGHT_STATE_UNKNOWN means that the light has not been changed since initialization. If the mission is successful, the debrief should show that no light instructions were given.

TEST(LightScheduler, ScheduleOnEverydayNotTimeYet) looks like a decent test, but it's too big for a first test. There are two test doubles and skeletons of the production code to write. In addition, all the pieces must be wired together. Still, it is good to have this goal articulated. Comment out this test, and save it for later.

A natural first test is one that specifies what should happen during initialization, like this:

tests/HomeAutomation/LightSchedulerTest.cpp
```
TEST(LightScheduler, NoChangeToLightsDuringInitialization)
{
    LONGS_EQUAL(LIGHT_ID_UNKNOWN, LightControllerSpy_GetLastId());
    LONGS_EQUAL(LIGHT_STATE_UNKNOWN, LightControllerSpy_GetLastState());
}
```

This test can be put together more quickly and keep the feedback coming rapidly. Nothing is needed for LightScheduler, letting us focus on the test double.

What if we have not yet chosen our OS, or the light-controlling hardware is still on the drawing board? Does that have to paralyze us while we make those decisions? No, it does not. We can treat those two areas as DOCs and define interfaces that perfectly meet the needs of the code under test. Interfaces let us break dependencies on unknowns. We develop right up to the unknown, defining what we want from it. The tests are helping to drive the design.

There is a subtle positive side benefit to programming when you don't know all the details—it can lead to a more abstract interface, one that does not get polluted with low-level implementation details. Since it does not reveal the implementation, it allows different potential implementations for different targets.

Write a few tests to drive the new fake, not so much to make sure the fake works—usually there is little that can go wrong—but to document the fake's behavior. You could drive the fake fully from the production code, but by writing tests for it, you also document the fake's behavior.

You non-C++ programmers are going to have to put up with a little bit of C++. When CppUTest is used to test C code, you have to enclose C function declarations in an extern "C" block. You will see this in the following example. extern "C" tells the compiler to generate calls to the enclosed functions using C calling conventions. If you don't, you will get linker errors reporting that the linker cannot find functions you know are there. The names will look the same to you, but not to the linker.

tests/HomeAutomation/LightControllerSpyTest.cpp
```cpp
#include "CppUTest/TestHarness.h"

extern "C"
{
#include "LightControllerSpy.h"
}

TEST_GROUP(LightControllerSpy)
{
    void setup()
    {
      LightController_Create();
    }

    void teardown()
    {
       LightController_Destroy();
    }
};

TEST(LightControllerSpy, Create)
{
    LONGS_EQUAL(LIGHT_ID_UNKNOWN, LightControllerSpy_GetLastId());
    LONGS_EQUAL(LIGHT_STATE_UNKNOWN, LightControllerSpy_GetLastState());
}

TEST(LightControllerSpy, RememberTheLastLightIdControlled)
{
    LightController_On(10);
    LONGS_EQUAL(10, LightControllerSpy_GetLastId());
    LONGS_EQUAL(LIGHT_ON, LightControllerSpy_GetLastState());
}
```

The spy's header includes the header file of the interface it is replacing. The spy is an implementation of the LightController interface. Including that header is a way to stress that point.

tests/HomeAutomation/LightControllerSpy.h
```c
#include "LightController.h"

enum
{
    LIGHT_ID_UNKNOWN = -1, LIGHT_STATE_UNKNOWN = -1,
    LIGHT_OFF = 0, LIGHT_ON = 1
};

int LightControllerSpy_GetLastId(void);
int LightControllerSpy_GetLastState(void);
```

You might wonder why the spy's header file defines the literal values for the light states instead of the production code header. Those values are used for interrogating the spy during test. They would pollute the production code.

The spy's implementation defines a *dead drop*,[2] made from file scope data, where the spy stores intelligence during its important covert operation.

tests/HomeAutomation/LightControllerSpy.c
```c
#include "LightControllerSpy.h"

static int lastId;
static int lastState;
```

The create function initializes the spy's dead drop.

tests/HomeAutomation/LightControllerSpy.c
```c
void LightController_Create(void)
{
    lastId = LIGHT_ID_UNKNOWN;
    lastState = LIGHT_STATE_UNKNOWN;
}
```

During the spy's mission, critical information is intercepted through the interface of the replaced collaborator.

tests/HomeAutomation/LightControllerSpy.c
```c
void LightController_On(int id)
{
    lastId = id;
    lastState = LIGHT_ON;
}
void LightController_Off(int id)
{
    lastId = id;
    lastState = LIGHT_OFF;
}
```

The one being spied on suspects nothing. The intelligence is retrieved from the dead drop through secret accessor functions after the CUT is exercised.

tests/HomeAutomation/LightControllerSpy.c
```c
int LightControllerSpy_GetLastId(void)
{
    return lastId;
}
int LightControllerSpy_GetLastState(void)
{
    return lastState;
}
```

---

2. A secret location where a spy leaves material to be picked up

As you can see, this spy is quite simple to write. Let's do something similar to take control of the clock in the next section.

8.5 Controlling the Clock

Time is usually a big deal in embedded systems. Time, a volatile input, makes testing a challenge. Waiting for timed events in tests makes the tests take too long, longer than they have to be. The bottom line is that the tests have to take over the clock.

Abstracting the clock is important too. Real-time operating systems often define nonstandard time functions, and this can lead to portability problems. If you want code that runs on more than one platform, abstract the clock. The abstraction provides a perfect place to insert your fake clock. In production, use a thin adapter to convert the embedded application's time API to the underlying OS calls. You get a shot of testability with a portability chaser.

The test stub needed for the TimeService is kind of the opposite of the LightControllerSpy. The test is not interested in what the CUT passes to the TimeService. But it is interested in controlling what the TimeService returns to the CUT. This is known as an indirect input. Take a look at its tests to reveal its behavior:

tests/HomeAutomation/FakeTimeServiceTest.cpp
```
TEST(FakeTimeService, Create)
{
    Time time;
    TimeService_GetTime(&time);
    LONGS_EQUAL(TIME_UNKNOWN, time.minuteOfDay);
    LONGS_EQUAL(TIME_UNKNOWN, time.dayOfWeek);
}

TEST(FakeTimeService, Set)
{
    Time time;
    FakeTimeService_SetMinute(42);
    FakeTimeService_SetDay(SATURDAY);
    TimeService_GetTime(&time);
    LONGS_EQUAL(42, time.minuteOfDay);
    LONGS_EQUAL(SATURDAY, time.dayOfWeek);
}
```

Now that the test doubles are assembled, let's look again at the test list in Figure 14, *Light Scheduler test list*, on page 119. Like I mentioned earlier, the list is roughly in the order we think we'll implement them. We'll start with the easiest tests first.

8.6 Make It Work for None, Then One

The fully implemented LightScheduler will have to manage a collection of scheduled items. Starting with a test case that involves many scheduled events makes for too much code. A good way to attack and conquer this problem is to start with the cases of *no* scheduled items and then *one* scheduled item, saving the *many* case for later. This is a common approach for engineering collection behavior using TDD.

The *do nothing* tests provides the shortest path to a passing test. All that is needed is the interface definitions for the production code calls. Don't worry that it seems that nothing is being tested. The objective here is to get these boundary tests right. Later when the full implementation is in place, these tests will continue to assure correct behavior of these boundary cases. You will be tempted to put in more code than an empty function body; don't do it. It is a path to untested code.

It looks like there are two areas of scheduler tests. Many of the scheduler tests will be concerned with the time and day matching, while other tests are concerned with the managing of multiple scheduled events. You really don't have to decide the whole test path up front, but I find it helpful to use the *0-1-N pattern* when there is collection behavior. First we handle the *zero* cases where there is nothing scheduled, or no events trigger. Then we handle the *one* event variation that drives the support for all the day and time variations. After the day and time variations are passing their tests, we will shift our focus to add support for the *N* cases where multiple scheduled events are test-driven.

Here's what the *no* scheduled items test looks like:

```
tests/HomeAutomation/LightSchedulerTest.cpp
TEST(LightScheduler, NoScheduleNothingHappens)
{
    FakeTimeService_SetDay(MONDAY);
    FakeTimeService_SetMinute(100);
    LightScheduler_WakeUp();
    LONGS_EQUAL(LIGHT_ID_UNKNOWN, LightControllerSpy_GetLastId());
    LONGS_EQUAL(LIGHT_STATE_UNKNOWN, LightControllerSpy_GetLastState());
}
```

It may seem that there's no need to set the day and minute on the FakeTimeService; there are no scheduled events, so any time will do. We'll still set the day and minute so they are at least valid values. Only a skeleton of LightScheduler_WakeUp() is needed to satisfy this test.

Here is the initial TEST_GROUP():

tests/HomeAutomation/LightSchedulerTest.cpp
```cpp
TEST_GROUP(LightScheduler)
{
    void setup()
    {
      LightController_Create();
      LightScheduler_Create();
    }

    void teardown()
    {
       LightScheduler_Destroy();
       LightController_Destroy();
    }
};
```

Now we're ready for that test we used to envision the test fixture capabilities.

tests/HomeAutomation/LightSchedulerTest.cpp
```cpp
TEST(LightScheduler, ScheduleOnEverydayNotTimeYet)
{
    LightScheduler_ScheduleTurnOn(3, EVERYDAY, 1200);
    FakeTimeService_SetDay(MONDAY);
    FakeTimeService_SetMinute(1199);
    LightScheduler_WakeUp();

    LONGS_EQUAL(LIGHT_ID_UNKNOWN, LightControllerSpy_GetLastId());
    LONGS_EQUAL(LIGHT_STATE_UNKNOWN, LightControllerSpy_GetLastState());
}
```

Because no lights are actually controlled during the previous test, only empty implementations are needed for the production code. The test drives the fixture development and the API for scheduling a light. Also, LightScheduler_ScheduleTurnOn() would just be a skeletal implementation like this:

src/HomeAutomation/LightScheduler.c
```c
void LightScheduler_ScheduleTurnOn(int id, Day day, int minuteOfDay)
{
}

void LightScheduler_WakeUp(void)
{
}
```

Now for the moment we've been waiting for; let's turn on a light. I chose the EVERYDAY test case because that requires less production code to pass the test in this early stage.

```
tests/HomeAutomation/LightSchedulerTest.cpp
```
```c
TEST(LightScheduler, ScheduleOnEverydayItsTime)
{
    LightScheduler_ScheduleTurnOn(3, EVERYDAY, 1200);
    FakeTimeService_SetDay(MONDAY);
    FakeTimeService_SetMinute(1200);

    LightScheduler_WakeUp();

    LONGS_EQUAL(3, LightControllerSpy_GetLastId());
    LONGS_EQUAL(LIGHT_ON, LightControllerSpy_GetLastState());
}
```

Let's think a little about how we'll implement the LightScheduler. We'll need a struct to hold the information about each schedule light control. With that struct we'll create an array to hold the 128 separate scheduled events (128 is the design limit from the requirements). LightScheduler_ScheduleTurnOn(), and similar operations, will use the next unused slot in the array. LightScheduler_WakeUp() will go through the array and see whether any scheduled lights need to be controlled.

Given that we have an idea of how to proceed, let's turn on a light, scheduled for every day at the right time. We need this struct and initialization:

```
src/HomeAutomation/LightScheduler.c
```
```c
typedef struct
{
    int id;
    int minuteOfDay;
} ScheduledLightEvent;

static ScheduledLightEvent scheduledEvent;

void LightScheduler_Create(void)
{
    scheduledEvent.id = UNUSED;
}
```

You are probably wondering why ScheduledLightEvent only has fields for id and minuteOfDay. Also, where is the array to hold the different scheduled events? Before we get into the whys, take a look at the implementation and see that nothing else is yet needed.

```
src/HomeAutomation/LightScheduler.c
```
```c
void LightScheduler_ScheduleTurnOn(int id, Day day, int minuteOfDay)
{
    scheduledEvent.id = id;
    scheduledEvent.minuteOfDay = minuteOfDay;
}
```

```c
void LightScheduler_WakeUp(void)
{
    Time time;
    TimeService_GetTime(&time);

    if (scheduledEvent.id == UNUSED)
        return;
    if (time.minuteOfDay != scheduledEvent.minuteOfDay)
        return;

    LightController_On(scheduledEvent.id);
}
```

It is tempting to add more fields to ScheduledLightEvent and make scheduledEvent an array. But we don't need it yet. In Debug-Later Programming, we add all the stuff we think we'll need right away. There is virtually no end to "I'm going to need it soon" thinking. So in TDD, we generally only add what is needed by the current tests.

By that reasoning, you might question the need to introduce the Scheduled-LightEvent data structure. I chose to introduce it now because it is not much extra syntactical weight to carry, and it will make converting to an array easier. I think ahead, but I act only on some things.

Why not add the array? I'd like to focus on the collection aspect of the scheduler separately and rather not carry around the array index syntax. These are judgment calls.

Now back to the code. Notice that the structure definition is in the .c file and not the .h file. We're purposely hiding those details so that the LightScheduler can manage them.

You can see what the test list would look like if I added some of the details of the specific tests written and scratched out the completed tests in Figure 18, *LightSchedulerTestList-revised1*, on page 131.

This test drives us to add the API for scheduling a light to turn off.

tests/HomeAutomation/LightSchedulerTest.cpp
```cpp
TEST(LightScheduler, ScheduleOffEverydayItsTime)
{
    LightScheduler_ScheduleTurnOff(3, EVERYDAY, 1200);
    FakeTimeService_SetDay(MONDAY);
    FakeTimeService_SetMinute(1200);
    LightScheduler_WakeUp();

    LONGS_EQUAL(3, LightControllerSpy_GetLastId());
    LONGS_EQUAL(LIGHT_OFF, LightControllerSpy_GetLastState());
}
```

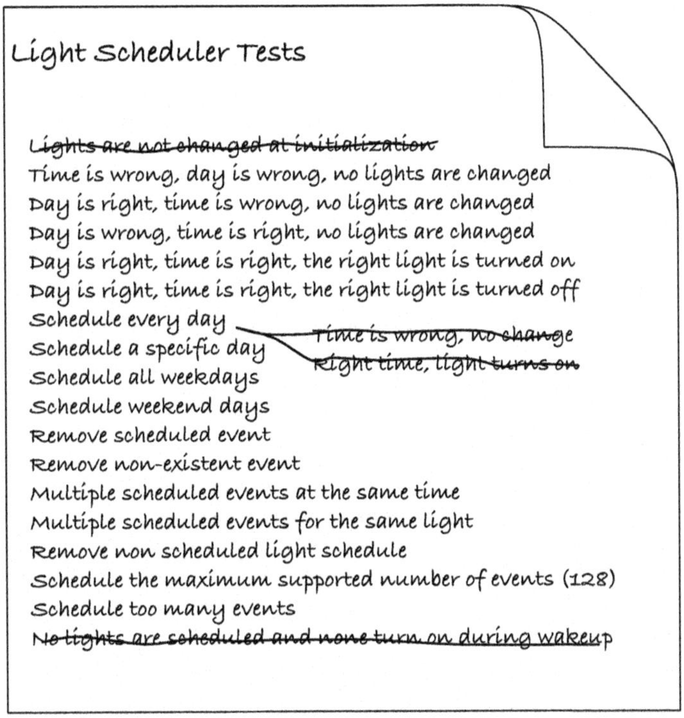

Light Scheduler Tests

~~Lights are not changed at initialization~~
Time is wrong, day is wrong, no lights are changed
Day is right, time is wrong, no lights are changed
Day is wrong, time is right, no lights are changed
Day is right, time is right, the right light is turned on
Day is right, time is right, the right light is turned off
Schedule every day — Time is wrong, ~~no change~~
Schedule a specific day — Right time, light ~~turns on~~
Schedule all weekdays
Schedule weekend days
Remove scheduled event
Remove non-existent event
Multiple scheduled events at the same time
Multiple scheduled events for the same light
Remove non scheduled light schedule
Schedule the maximum supported number of events (128)
Schedule too many events
~~No lights are scheduled and none turn on during wakeup~~

Figure 18— LightSchedulerTestList-revised1

Given our current tests, LightScheduler_WakeUp() can turn on or off a light that is scheduled for EVERYDAY. We are all set to continue adding scheduling scenarios and driving the implementation.

Here is the current state of LightScheduler_WakeUp():

```c
src/HomeAutomation/LightScheduler.c
void LightScheduler_WakeUp(void)
{
    Time time;
    TimeService_GetTime(&time);
    if (scheduledEvent.id == UNUSED)
        return;
    if (time.minuteOfDay != scheduledEvent.minuteOfDay)
        return;
    if (scheduledEvent.event == TURN_ON)
        LightController_On(scheduledEvent.id);

    else if (scheduledEvent.event == TURN_OFF)
        LightController_Off(scheduledEvent.id);
}
```

The corresponding LightScheduler_ScheduleTurnOn() looks like the following, with LightScheduler_ScheduleTurnOff() being almost identical.

src/HomeAutomation/LightScheduler.c
```c
void LightScheduler_ScheduleTurnOn(int id, Day day, int minuteOfDay)
{
    scheduledEvent.minuteOfDay = minuteOfDay;
    scheduledEvent.event = TURN_ON;
    scheduledEvent.id = id;
}

void LightScheduler_ScheduleTurnOff(int id, Day day, int minuteOfDay)
{
    scheduledEvent.minuteOfDay = minuteOfDay;
    scheduledEvent.event = TURN_OFF;
    scheduledEvent.id = id;
}
```

The LightScheduler's interface has evolved to this point:

include/HomeAutomation/LightScheduler.h
```c
#ifndef D_LightScheduler_H
#define D_LightScheduler_H
enum Day {
    NONE=-1, EVERYDAY=10, WEEKDAY, WEEKEND,
    SUNDAY=1, MONDAY, TUESDAY, WEDNESDAY, THURSDAY, FRIDAY, SATURDAY
};

typedef enum Day Day;

void LightScheduler_Create(void);
void LightScheduler_ScheduleTurnOn(int id, Day day, int minuteOfDay);
void LightScheduler_ScheduleTurnOff(int id, Day day, int minuteOfDay);
void LightScheduler_WakeUp(void);
#endif   /* D_LightScheduler_H */
```

Refactor to Remove Duplications

With tests passing, we can refactor out the small bits of duplication in LightScheduler_ScheduleTurnOn/Off(). Then we'll spend a little time cleaning up LightScheduler_WakeUp() a little.

First we extract the duplicate code into its own static function:

src/HomeAutomation/LightScheduler.c
```c
static void scheduleEvent(int id, Day day, int minuteOfDay, int event)
{
    scheduledEvent.minuteOfDay = minuteOfDay;
    scheduledEvent.event = event;
    scheduledEvent.id = id;
}
```

Once that compiles, convert LightScheduler_ScheduleTurnOn() to use scheduleEvent(). Then do the same with LightScheduler_ScheduleTurnOff():

src/HomeAutomation/LightScheduler.c
```c
void LightScheduler_ScheduleTurnOn(int id, Day day, int minuteOfDay)
{
    scheduleEvent(id, day, minuteOfDay, TURN_ON);
}

void LightScheduler_ScheduleTurnOff(int id, Day day, int minuteOfDay)
{
    scheduleEvent(id, day, minuteOfDay, TURN_OFF);
}
```

Why not just expose scheduleEvent() and eliminate the new LightScheduler_ScheduleTurnOn/Off() functions? My reasoning is that the parameter list was already long enough; adding another parameter makes it longer and further burdens the client code. I prefer to enumerate a list of functions than to pass an enumerated type. It's safer and more descriptive.

Refactor for Responsibility

In this code, you'll see that LightScheduler_WakeUp() was refactored to separate responsibilities. We did two function extractions to get the code to speak to us better.

src/HomeAutomation/LightScheduler.c
```c
void LightScheduler_WakeUp(void)
{
    Time time;
    TimeService_GetTime(&time);

    processEventDueNow(&time, &scheduledEvent);
}
```

LightScheduler_WakeUp() is the function we will provide to the TimeService as a periodic callback function. Right now it processes a single event but later will process each event in the collection of scheduled events.

src/HomeAutomation/LightScheduler.c
```c
static void processEventDueNow(Time * time, ScheduledLightEvent * lightEvent)
{
    if (lightEvent->id == UNUSED)
        return;

    if (lightEvent->minuteOfDay != time->minuteOfDay)
        return;

    operateLight(lightEvent);
}
```

processEventDueNow() is responsible for conditionally triggering a single event. This function is all set to be called from a loop when we add support for multiple events.

src/HomeAutomation/LightScheduler.c
```
static void operateLight(ScheduledLightEvent * lightEvent)
{
    if (lightEvent->event == TURN_ON)
        LightController_On(lightEvent->id);
    else if (lightEvent->event == TURN_OFF)
        LightController_Off(lightEvent->id);
}
```

operateLight() captures the idea behind the if/else chain.

Refactor the Tests

Notice the duplication in the tests. The test cases are not really long, but they are hard to read with all the details to interpret. The repeated operations and checks can be extracted into helper functions, leaving the tests easier to read.

tests/HomeAutomation/LightSchedulerTest.cpp
```
TEST(LightScheduler, ScheduleOnEverydayNotTimeYet)
{
    LightScheduler_ScheduleTurnOn(id, EVERYDAY, 1200);
    setTimeTo(SUNDAY, 1199);
    LightScheduler_WakeUp();
    checkLightState(LIGHT_ID_UNKNOWN, LIGHT_STATE_UNKNOWN);
}
```

The helpers are part of the TEST_GROUP(LightScheduler), working to isolate the details. The code is as follows:

tests/HomeAutomation/LightSchedulerTest.cpp
```
void setTimeTo(int day, int minuteOfDay)
{
    FakeTimeService_SetDay(day);
    FakeTimeService_SetMinute(minuteOfDay);
}
void checkLightState(int id, int level)
{
    LONGS_EQUAL(id, LightControllerSpy_GetLastId());
    LONGS_EQUAL(level, LightControllerSpy_GetLastState());
}
```

With the details isolated in the test group's helper functions, the tests will also be easier to evolve. For example, we could completely change how the tests interact with the fake LightController and have to change only the helpers.

Complex Conditional Logic

The tests so far have been about EVERYDAY, so we have not even had to check the day setting in the production code yet. The next series of tests will help us drive the day-matching conditional logic one step at a time. Here is a first test:

tests/HomeAutomation/LightSchedulerTest.cpp
```
TEST(LightScheduler, ScheduleTuesdayButItsMonday)
{
    LightScheduler_ScheduleTurnOn(3, TUESDAY, 1200);
    setTimeTo(MONDAY, 1200);
    LightScheduler_WakeUp();
    checkLightState(LIGHT_ID_UNKNOWN, LIGHT_STATE_UNKNOWN);
}
```

This test will initially fail because there is no EVERYDAY check in the LightScheduler. So, we make the change:

src/HomeAutomation/LightScheduler.c
```
static void processEventDueNow(Time * time, ScheduledLightEvent * lightEvent)
{
    if (lightEvent->id == UNUSED)
        return;
    if (lightEvent->day != EVERYDAY)
        return;
    if (lightEvent->minuteOfDay != time->minuteOfDay)
        return;

    operateLight(lightEvent);
}
```

Now let's test-drive the exact day conditional with this test:

tests/HomeAutomation/LightSchedulerTest.cpp
```
TEST(LightScheduler, ScheduleTuesdayAndItsTuesday)
{
    LightScheduler_ScheduleTurnOn(3, TUESDAY, 1200);
    setTimeTo(TUESDAY, 1200);
    LightScheduler_WakeUp();
    checkLightState(3, LIGHT_ON);
}
```

The test fails until we add the exact day match:

src/HomeAutomation/LightScheduler.c
```
static void processEventDueNow(Time * time, ScheduledLightEvent * lightEvent)
{
    int reactionDay = lightEvent->day;
    if (lightEvent->id == UNUSED)
        return;
```

```
    if (reactionDay != EVERYDAY && reactionDay != today)
        return;
    if (lightEvent->minuteOfDay != time->minuteOfDay)
        return;

    operateLight(lightEvent);
}
```

Knowing what you know about the production code, do you need to test every day of the week? I say you don't, because each day's check uses the same code.

Now let's get the WEEKEND schedule behavior in place. I won't show each change to the code, but the conditional logic should grow incrementally by only adding the needed conditional clause in response to a failing test.

tests/HomeAutomation/LightSchedulerTest.cpp
```
TEST(LightScheduler, ScheduleWeekEndItsFriday)
{
    LightScheduler_ScheduleTurnOn(3, WEEKEND, 1200);
    setTimeTo(FRIDAY, 1200);
    LightScheduler_WakeUp();
    checkLightState(LIGHT_ID_UNKNOWN, LIGHT_STATE_UNKNOWN);
}
```

The first test case checks a boundary condition. No production code change was needed to make TEST(LightScheduler, ScheduleWeekEndItsFriday) pass, because it is not a WEEKEND.

tests/HomeAutomation/LightSchedulerTest.cpp
```
TEST(LightScheduler, ScheduleWeekEndItsSaturday)
{
    LightScheduler_ScheduleTurnOn(3, WEEKEND, 1200);
    setTimeTo(SATURDAY, 1200);
    LightScheduler_WakeUp();
    checkLightState(3, LIGHT_ON);
}
```

After watching TEST(LightScheduler, ScheduleWeekEndItsSaturday) fail, alter the production code to check for WEEKEND and for SATURDAY. Don't add the SUNDAY check yet.

tests/HomeAutomation/LightSchedulerTest.cpp
```
TEST(LightScheduler, ScheduleWeekEndItsSunday)
{
    LightScheduler_ScheduleTurnOn(3, WEEKEND, 1200);
    setTimeTo(SUNDAY, 1200);
    LightScheduler_WakeUp();
    checkLightState(3, LIGHT_ON);
}
```

TEST(LightScheduler, ScheduleWeekEndItsSunday) forces the addition of the SUNDAY clause in the conditional.

tests/HomeAutomation/LightSchedulerTest.cpp
```
TEST(LightScheduler, ScheduleWeekEndItsMonday)
{
    LightScheduler_ScheduleTurnOn(3, WEEKEND, 1200);
    setTimeTo(MONDAY, 1200);
    LightScheduler_WakeUp();
    checkLightState(LIGHT_ID_UNKNOWN, LIGHT_STATE_UNKNOWN);
}
```

TEST(LightScheduler, ScheduleWeekEndItsMonday) just passes. The boundary condition is already satisfied. You could add tests for every other weekday, but knowing the implementation, it's not really necessary.

Let's fast-forward a little to when we have completed the scheduler tests for all the day-matching conditions. You can see the rest of the tests in the book's code download.

Now we have a fairly complex conditional in processEventDueNow(). To isolate the complexity and improve the code's readability, extract the conditional logic into a helper function, DoesLightRespondToday(). With the extraction, the logic of processEventDueNow() is more clear.

src/HomeAutomation/LightScheduler.c
```
static void processEventDueNow(Time * time, ScheduledLightEvent * lightEvent)
{
    if (lightEvent->id == UNUSED)
        return;
    if (!DoesLightRespondToday(time, lightEvent->day))
        return;
    if (lightEvent->minuteOfDay != time->minuteOfDay)
        return;

    operateLight(lightEvent);
}
```

DoesLightRespondToday() is clear and focussed as well.

src/HomeAutomation/LightScheduler.c
```
static int DoesLightRespondToday(Time * time, int reactionDay)
{
    int today = time->dayOfWeek;

    if (reactionDay == EVERYDAY)
        return TRUE;

    if (reactionDay == today)
        return TRUE;
```

```c
    if (reactionDay == WEEKEND && (SATURDAY == today || SUNDAY == today))
        return TRUE;

    if (reactionDay == WEEKDAY && today >= MONDAY && today <= FRIDAY)
        return TRUE;

    return FALSE;
}
```

The series of if statements, in DoesLightRespondToday(), started out as one big compound if statement. It was a mess. You can see that by separating each logical area into its own if statement, it reads much easier. Strive to make the code readable, but don't believe your eyes. Make sure the conditional is fully tested.

Test the Wiring

We've been talking about TimeService invoking LightScheduler_WakeUp() once a minute. The relationship is shown in Figure 15, *Initial light scheduler design*, on page 120. The test case has been calling the function LightScheduler_WakeUp(). This callback was registered by the LightScheduler by passing a function pointer to the TimeService.

The following test assures that the system is wired properly:

tests/HomeAutomation/LightSchedulerTest.cpp
```c
TEST_GROUP(LightSchedulerInitAndCleanup)
{
};

TEST(LightSchedulerInitAndCleanup, CreateStartsOneMinuteAlarm)
{
    LightScheduler_Create();
    POINTERS_EQUAL((void *)LightScheduler_WakeUp,
                   (void *)FakeTimeService_GetAlarmCallback());

    LONGS_EQUAL(60, FakeTimeService_GetAlarmPeriod());
    LightScheduler_Destroy();
}
```

To test the registration, FakeTimeService needs to spy on the call to TimeService_SetPeriodicAlarmInSeconds(). This lets the test check that the proper callback was set.

Notice that this TEST() uses a new TEST_GROUP(). The initialization and cleanup tests have very different needs from the other LightScheduler tests. That's the reason for a new TEST_GROUP(). The TEST_GROUP() has nothing in it, because each TEST() is self-contained. There is no duplication to get rid of.

LightScheduler_Create() registers the callback like this:

src/HomeAutomation/LightScheduler.c
```
static ScheduledLightEvent scheduledEvent;
void LightScheduler_Create(void)
{
    scheduledEvent.id = UNUSED;

    TimeService_SetPeriodicAlarmInSeconds(60,
            LightScheduler_WakeUp);
}
```

This test checks that LightScheduler_Destroy() cancels the wakeup call:

tests/HomeAutomation/LightSchedulerTest.cpp
```
TEST(LightSchedulerInitAndCleanup, DestroyCancelsOneMinuteAlarm)
{
    LightScheduler_Create();
    LightScheduler_Destroy();
    POINTERS_EQUAL(NULL, (void *)FakeTimeService_GetAlarmCallback());
}
```

LightScheduler_Destroy() cancels the periodic alarm.

src/HomeAutomation/LightScheduler.c
```
void LightScheduler_Destroy(void)
{
    TimeService_CancelPeriodicAlarmInSeconds(60,
            LightScheduler_WakeUp);
}
```

The TimeService calls for creating and canceling the periodic wakeup look like this:

include/HomeAutomation/TimeService.h
```
typedef void (*WakeUpCallback)(void);

void TimeService_SetPeriodicAlarmInSeconds(
        int seconds, WakeUpCallback);

void TimeService_CancelPeriodicAlarmInSeconds(
        int seconds, WakeUpCallback);
```

The fake simply saves the callback function pointer and reports it on-demand.

tests/HomeAutomation/FakeTimeService.c
```
void TimeService_SetPeriodicAlarmInSeconds(int seconds, WakeUpCallback cb)
{
    callback = cb;
    period = seconds;
}
void TimeService_CancelPeriodicAlarmInSeconds(
        int seconds, WakeUpCallback cb)
{
```

```
        if (cb == callback && period == seconds)
        {
            callback = NULL;
            period = 0;
        }
    }
```

Let's review our progress. The production code for the LightScheduler and the interfaces it needs are wired together and evolving. The test fixture can effectively test the core application logic. We fast-forwarded through the day-matching conditional logic and are ready to do something different, making the LightScheduler handle multiple scheduled actions.

8.7 Make It Work for Many

To make the scheduler work for multiple scheduled items, we're going to need to be able to check the state of multiple lights, something our current LightControllerSpy cannot do. Let's evolve the LightControllerSpy to remember the state of each light like this:

tests/HomeAutomation/LightControllerSpyTest.cpp
```
TEST(LightControllerSpy, RememberAllLightStates)
{
    LightController_On(0);
    LightController_Off(31);
    LONGS_EQUAL(LIGHT_ON, LightControllerSpy_GetLightState(0));
    LONGS_EQUAL(LIGHT_OFF, LightControllerSpy_GetLightState(31));
}
```

Add a new accessor to LightControllerSpy's header file to allow any light's state to be checked:

tests/HomeAutomation/LightControllerSpy.h
```
int LightControllerSpy_GetLightState(int id);
int LightControllerSpy_GetLastId(void);
int LightControllerSpy_GetLastState(void);
```

In addition to remembering the last light change, now the LightControllerSpy keeps a record of the state of each light ID in an internal array. The test helper, checkLightState(), is modified to use LightControllerSpy_GetLightState(). This allows checkLightState() to work in the multiple-event case. Imagine all the editing needed if you decided to retrofit LightControllerSpy_GetLightState() into all the existing test cases.

The well-refactored test cases, with helper functions, can help minimize changes when there is a change in test strategy and fake interactions.

```
tests/HomeAutomation/LightSchedulerTest.cpp
```
```c
void checkLightState(int id, int level)
{
    if (id == LIGHT_ID_UNKNOWN)
    {
        LONGS_EQUAL(id, LightControllerSpy_GetLastId());
        LONGS_EQUAL(level, LightControllerSpy_GetLastState());
    }
    else
        LONGS_EQUAL(level, LightControllerSpy_GetLightState(id));
}
```

The spy is newly outfitted for its new mission, driving the code to handle multiple events. Starting with two events, here's the failing test case:

```
tests/HomeAutomation/LightSchedulerTest.cpp
```
```c
TEST(LightScheduler, ScheduleTwoEventsAtTheSameTime)
{
    LightScheduler_ScheduleTurnOn(3, SUNDAY, 1200);
    LightScheduler_ScheduleTurnOn(12, SUNDAY, 1200);

    setTimeTo(SUNDAY, 1200);

    LightScheduler_WakeUp();

    checkLightState(3, LIGHT_ON);
    checkLightState(12, LIGHT_ON);
}
```

As you add the code for multiple events, you can avoid breaking the existing tests by using the "Don't burn your bridges" principle. Add the new multi-event functionality alongside the support for a single event. See how the LightScheduler_Create() function handles both single- and multiple-event initializations like this:

```
src/HomeAutomation/LightScheduler.c
```
```c
static ScheduledLightEvent scheduledEvent;
static ScheduledLightEvent scheduledEvents[MAX_EVENTS];

void LightScheduler_Create(void)
{
    int i;

    scheduledEvent.id = UNUSED;

    for (i = 0; i < MAX_EVENTS; i++)
        scheduledEvents[i].id = UNUSED;
    TimeService_SetPeriodicAlarmInSeconds(60,
            LightScheduler_WakeUp);
}
```

With this careful approach, the single-event tests keep passing the whole time, unless you somehow make a mistake. When support for multiple events is in place, the single-event code can be deleted, one function at a time, and all tests should still pass. The same approach works for adding multiple event support to scheduleEvent(). The array is initialized in the for loop and the single event outside the loop.

src/HomeAutomation/LightScheduler.c
```c
static void scheduleEvent(int id, Day day, int minuteOfDay, int event)
{
    int i;

    for (i = 0; i < MAX_EVENTS; i++)
    {
        if (scheduledEvents[i].id == UNUSED)
        {
            scheduledEvents[i].day = day;
            scheduledEvents[i].minuteOfDay = minuteOfDay;
            scheduledEvents[i].event = event;
            scheduledEvents[i].id = id;
            break;
        }
    }

    scheduledEvent.day = day;
    scheduledEvent.minuteOfDay = minuteOfDay;
    scheduledEvent.event = event;
    scheduledEvent.id = id;
}
```

Bridges are intact, and all single event tests are passing. The multiple-event test still fails; we're almost done. Finally, when you add looping support to LightScheduler_WakeUp(), the new test passes. Now that old bridge can be torched.

src/HomeAutomation/LightScheduler.c
```c
void LightScheduler_WakeUp(void)
{
    int i;
    Time time;
    TimeService_GetTime(&time);

    for (i = 0; i < MAX_EVENTS; i++)
    {
        processEventDueNow(&time, &scheduledEvents[i]);
    }

    processEventDueNow(&time, &scheduledEvent);
}
```

Now the tests pass, we can delete the redundant single-event code from LightScheduler_Create(), scheduleEvent(), and LightScheduler_WakeUp(). It's best to delete the redundant implementation one function at a time, with a single editing command. Run the tests. You can get back to passing tests with a single UNDO when problems arise.

After deleting the single-event code, LightScheduler_WakeUp() looks like:

src/HomeAutomation/LightScheduler.c
```c
void LightScheduler_WakeUp(void)
{
    int i;

    Time time;
    TimeService_GetTime(&time);

    for (i = 0; i < MAX_EVENTS; i++)
    {
        processEventDueNow(&time, &scheduledEvents[i]);
    }
}
```

Let's finish this LightScheduler by dealing with the edge conditions and special cases. This test makes sure the code handles its design maximum of 128 scheduled events:

tests/HomeAutomation/LightSchedulerTest.cpp
```cpp
TEST(LightScheduler, RejectsTooManyEvents)
{
    int i;
    for (i = 0; i < 128; i++)
        LONGS_EQUAL(LS_OK,
                    LightScheduler_ScheduleTurnOn(6, MONDAY, 600+i));

    LONGS_EQUAL(LS_TOO_MANY_EVENTS,
                LightScheduler_ScheduleTurnOn(6, MONDAY, 600+i));
}
```

For this test to pass, we had to change LightScheduler_ScheduleTurnOn() and LightScheduler_ScheduleTurnOff() to return a result. It was a minor change to modify the header file and add condition checks to the implementation. You will notice that we also added a set of enum constants to the LightScheduler interface, allowing it to communicate each operation's result. We'll add others as we implement each error scenario.

This is a good opportunity to implement the test that removes a scheduled event. This test shows that the event slot is freed up when a scheduled item is removed.

```
tests/HomeAutomation/LightSchedulerTest.cpp
TEST(LightScheduler, RemoveRecyclesScheduleSlot)
{
    int i;
    for (i = 0; i < 128; i++)
        LONGS_EQUAL(LS_OK,
                    LightScheduler_ScheduleTurnOn(6, MONDAY, 600+i));

    LightScheduler_ScheduleRemove(6, MONDAY, 600);

    LONGS_EQUAL(LS_OK,
                LightScheduler_ScheduleTurnOn(13, MONDAY, 1000));
}
```

We'd also like to make sure the right event was removed. This test verifies the correct behavior:

```
tests/HomeAutomation/LightSchedulerTest.cpp
TEST(LightScheduler, RemoveMultipleScheduledEvent)
{
    LightScheduler_ScheduleTurnOn(6, MONDAY, 600);
    LightScheduler_ScheduleTurnOn(7, MONDAY, 600);
    LightScheduler_ScheduleRemove(6, MONDAY, 600);

    setTimeTo(MONDAY, 600);

    LightScheduler_WakeUp();

    checkLightState(6, LIGHT_STATE_UNKNOWN);
    checkLightState(7, LIGHT_ON);
}
```

Finally, we need to test LightScheduler rejects invalid light identifiers:

```
tests/HomeAutomation/LightSchedulerTest.cpp
TEST(LightScheduler, AcceptsValidLightIds)
{
    LONGS_EQUAL(LS_OK,
                LightScheduler_ScheduleTurnOn(0, MONDAY, 600));
    LONGS_EQUAL(LS_OK,
                LightScheduler_ScheduleTurnOn(15, MONDAY, 600));
    LONGS_EQUAL(LS_OK,
                LightScheduler_ScheduleTurnOn(31, MONDAY, 600));
}
TEST(LightScheduler, RejectsInvalidLightIds)
{
    LONGS_EQUAL(LS_ID_OUT_OF_BOUNDS,
                LightScheduler_ScheduleTurnOn(-1, MONDAY, 600));
    LONGS_EQUAL(LS_ID_OUT_OF_BOUNDS,
                LightScheduler_ScheduleTurnOn(32, MONDAY, 600));
}
```

You might think these condition checks are too simple to get wrong. Maybe they are, but my motto in this case is, if it's important enough to check a condition in the production code, it's important enough to test it.

8.8 Where Are We?

In this chapter, we created a seemingly target-dependent module by breaking the dependencies on the hardware and OS using link-time test doubles. We employed a spy and a fake. The tests are valid, and we made progress without hardware.

We started by composing a test list. This helps organize our thoughts. We don't expect to make a perfect test list. Start with whatever tests you can think of, and evolve the test list as you learn more.

We thought about how to implement the scheduler but did not implement it all at once. We let the tests drive us, but we did have a design goal in mind.

When there is collection behavior, use the 0-1-N TDD pattern. The 0 and 1 cases are usually easy to define and help clarify thoughts on interfaces, collaborators, and some boundary behaviors. They provide a stepping-stone to the more challenging behavior, and they help you get into the rhythm of TDD.

After you get a test to pass and come up for air, you may be disoriented and not know which way to go. Your test list will help you go in the right direction without treading much water.

Link-time test doubles are helpful, but sometimes you need more flexibility and configurability. Then you are going to need to convert some direct dependencies into runtime dependencies, the topic of the next chapter. Also, link-time test doubles means you may need multiple test builds if some builds need to include the code that is being overridden by the test double.

8.9 Put the Knowledge to Work

1. Build, run, and review the examples from the code/test directory.
2. Test-drive an alarm clock service that keeps a list of time callbacks. In production, the timer interrupt will ping the time service every 100 milliseconds. When a scheduled action is ready to run, call the callback function.
3. Your home automation system can notify you, via email, when your spouse's RFID tag has returned to or left the house. The RFID events (in

range, now out of range) are fed to your module. Test-drive the WhoIsHome module that emails changes in who is home to your email address. Email addresses are configurable by a person's RFID tag. You are not really sure how the email service works, but you do know the essential parts of an email: to, subject, and body.

Would ye both eat your cake and have your cake?
> John Heywood

CHAPTER 9

Runtime-Bound Test Doubles

In the previous chapter, we substituted test doubles using the linker. That approach works fine when the code being swapped out for the test double is not needed in the test build. What if the code being stubbed was needed for some of the tests but got in the way of some other tests? We need additional flexibility that the linker cannot provide. We will employ function pointers so that we can test a function and replace it too, in the same test build.

We happen to have a new feature that causes this problem in the LightScheduler. The scheduler right now does exactly what it is told; if a light is scheduled to turn on at 8 p.m., it does so at precisely 8 p.m. What's the problem? The system is supposed to make it look like someone is home even when they are not. If the neighborhood burglars are casing the house and they see the living room light turn on at 8 like clockwork, they will know that no one is home and may cause some mischief. What we need is a randomization feature.

9.1 Testing Randomness

When a particular light is being scheduled, the operator can select the randomize feature. What the randomize feature does is to randomly vary light controls up to thirty minutes early or thirty minutes late. For this we need a function that generates a random number in the range of +30 to -30.

If we randomize a light, how do we test it? When should it come on? Will we have to check a whole hour of possibilities and then not even be sure that the randomness is because of a bug or the random number generator?

It sounds like we have two separate problems. First, does the random minute generator produce an adequately random number, within the right range of values? Second, does the LightScheduler use the random minute generator appropriately?

This test needs the flexibility of runtime binding. We need tests for the random minute generator, and we need to get the random minute generator out of the way for some of the tests.

First, let's get the random minute generator working and tested. Here we will make sure that no generated values are outside the range:

t0/tests/HomeAutomation/RandomMinuteTest.cpp
```
TEST(RandomMinute, GetIsInRange)
{
    for (int i = 0; i < 100; i++)
    {
        minute = RandomMinute_Get();
        AssertMinuteIsInRange();
    }
}
```

Here's the TEST_GROUP test group that supports the previous test. The helper function, AssertMinuteIsInRange(), came from a little refactoring to make the test read a little easier.

t0/tests/HomeAutomation/RandomMinuteTest.cpp
```
enum { BOUND=30 };

TEST_GROUP(RandomMinute)
{
    int minute;
    void setup()
    {
        RandomMinute_Create(BOUND);
        srand(1);
    }
    void AssertMinuteIsInRange()
    {
        if (minute < -BOUND || minute > BOUND)
        {
            printf("bad minute value: %d\n", minute);
            FAIL("Minute out of range");
        }
    }
};
```

Notice that setup() initializes the standard library random number generator with a call to srand(). This keeps the random number generator from potentially causing random failures. This is done after RandomMinute_Create() to undo any seeding done in RandomMinute_Create().

We could get the previous test to pass just by returning a fixed in-range number. A better test makes sure that all the values in-range are generated.

```
t0/tests/HomeAutomation/RandomMinuteTest.cpp
```
```c
TEST(RandomMinute, AllValuesPossible)
{
    int hit[2*BOUND + 1];
    memset(hit, 0, sizeof(hit));
        int i;
    for (i = 0; i < 300; i++)
    {
        minute = RandomMinute_Get();
        AssertMinuteIsInRange();
        hit[minute + BOUND]++;
    }
    for (i = 0; i < 2* BOUND + 1; i++) {
        CHECK(hit[i] > 0);
    }
}
```

After a little experimentation with several platforms, I set the loop counter. If you were building a game that needed a specific random number distribution over many samples, a more thorough test would be needed. This is no slot machine, so this simple test will do.

9.2 Faking with a Function Pointer

Let's use our random minute generator for the randomized light schedule feature. The scheduler will have unpredictable results because of its unpredictable indirect input from RandomMinute_Get(). When production code depends on something unpredictable, it's time to substitute in a test double. We have a problem; the binding of the LightScheduler to RandomMinute_Get() is done by the linker, as you can see by looking at the interface of RandomMinute:

```
t0/include/HomeAutomation/RandomMinute.h
```
```c
void RandomMinute_Create(int bound);
int RandomMinute_Get(void);
```

Before we refactor the interface to allow function pointer substitution, let's design the test for the randomized schedule.

```
t0/tests/HomeAutomation/LightSchedulerRandomizeTest.cpp
```
```c
TEST(LightSchedulerRandomize, TurnsOnEarly)
{
    FakeRandomMinute_SetFirstAndIncrement(-10, 5);
    LightScheduler_ScheduleTurnOn(4, EVERYDAY, 600);
    LightScheduler_Randomize(4, EVERYDAY, 600);
    setTimeTo(MONDAY, 600-10);
    LightScheduler_WakeUp();
    checkLightState(4, LIGHT_ON);
}
```

The first line of the test calls to FakeRandomMinute_SetFirstAndIncrement() and establishes a *not so random* minute sequence. The random minute starts at -10 and increments by 5. The test schedules a turn on event and randomizes it. Then the test makes sure the light comes on at the scheduled time plus the random factor, minus ten.

Now that the test objective is clear, let's refactor the design so that we can substitute RandomMinute with FakeRandomMinute. The direct function call needs to be converted to a function pointer. The header file declaration looks like this:

t0/include/HomeAutomation/RandomMinute.h
```
void RandomMinute_Create(int bound);
extern int (*RandomMinute_Get)(void);
```

The pointer must be extern to avoid multiple definition errors at link time. The declaration says that there is a pointer to a function called RandomMinute_Get() that takes no arguments and returns an int.

In the .c file, we write the default production code implementation of the random minute generator. It's followed by the defining instance of the global function pointer RandomMinute_Get(). Notice that RandomMinute_Get() is initialized to point to RandomMinute_GetImpl().

t0/src/HomeAutomation/RandomMinute.c
```
int RandomMinute_GetImpl(void)
{
    return bound - rand() % (bound * 2 + 1);
}

int (*RandomMinute_Get)(void) = RandomMinute_GetImpl;
```

Any TEST() or TEST_GROUP() can override the default function pointer value with a pointer to the FakeRandomMinute. A good citizen always restores the original function pointer after running each test. setup() and teardown() are the most natural places to put the function pointer manipulations.

t0/tests/HomeAutomation/LightSchedulerRandomizeTest.cpp
```
TEST_GROUP(LightSchedulerRandomize)
{
    int (*savedRandomMinute_Get)();

    void setup()
    {
        LightController_Create();
        LightScheduler_Create();
        savedRandomMinute_Get = RandomMinute_Get;
        RandomMinute_Get = FakeRandomMinute_Get;
    }
```

```
    void teardown()
    {
        LightScheduler_Destroy();
        LightController_Destroy();
        RandomMinute_Get = savedRandomMinute_Get;
    }
};
```

Function pointer restoration is so common that CppUTest has a built-in macro for setting and restoring function pointers. When a function pointer is set with UT_PTR_SET() (during setup() or during any TEST()), it is automatically restored after teardown() completes.

t0/tests/HomeAutomation/LightSchedulerRandomizeTest.cpp
```
TEST_GROUP(LightSchedulerRandomize)
{
    void setup()
    {
        LightController_Create();
        LightScheduler_Create();
        UT_PTR_SET(RandomMinute_Get, FakeRandomMinute_Get);
    }

    void teardown()
    {
        LightScheduler_Destroy();
        LightController_Destroy();
    }

    void checkLightState(int id, int level)
     {
        if (id == LIGHT_ID_UNKNOWN)
        {
            LONGS_EQUAL(id, LightControllerSpy_GetLastId());
            LONGS_EQUAL(level, LightControllerSpy_GetLastState());
        }
        else
            LONGS_EQUAL(level, LightControllerSpy_GetLightState(id));
     }

    void setTimeTo(int day, int minute)
    {
        FakeTimeService_SetDay(day);
        FakeTimeService_SetMinute(minute);
    }
};
```

With function pointers, tests can intercept outgoing function calls from the code under test. It can be a very effective way to surgically isolate calls to particular functions. I've also seen this overused, where all of a sudden all functions are converted to function pointers. Use this, but only when it is called for. Like usual, it's a judgment call.

The code calling a function through a pointer better know it is calling through a pointer. This is easy enough to do; the calling code must see the function's declaration—if it hasn't, the compiler will issue a warning and make some assumptions. (You might not notice the warning if you tolerate warnings in your code.[1]) A call to a previously undeclared function is assumed to be a direct call. Calling a function pointer as a direct call is trouble. You can only hope it fails fast.

The function pointer allows very fine control over what is stubbed and what is not. Let's see how a single function can be faked out as we look at testing code with printed output.

9.3 Surgically Inserted Spy

When a system has printed output, it is usually manually inspected. Printed output can be very tedious to verify, so you probably don't want to reinspect the output as often as you should. We will never get totally away from manually inspecting printed output, but we can eliminate the re-inspections by locking in the desired behavior.

Let's say you already have a printf()-like function to produce printed output called FormatOutput(). As it is, FormatOutput() is a direct function call that is in a header file with many other utilities. You would like to create a spy for FormatOutput(), but you don't want to stub out all the functions in the file containing FormatOutput(). A more surgical approach is needed to intercept calls to just one function in a compilation unit. The prototype for the direct function call to FormatOutput() looks like this:

include/util/Utils.h
```
int FormatOutput(const char *, ...);
```

A function pointer is the right tool for surgically intercepting calls to FormatOutput(). To infiltrate the callers of FormatOutput(), first convert the FormatOutput() prototype to a function pointer.

include/util/Utils.h
```
extern int (*FormatOutput)(const char *, ...);
```

In the .c file, rename FormatOutput() to FormatOutput_Impl(). Then create the defining instance of the FormatOutput function pointer, initializing it to the address of

---

1. Shame on you :-)

FormatOutput_Impl(). To keep outsiders from calling FormatOutput_Impl() directly, you should also make it static:

src/util/Utils.c
```c
static int FormatOutput_Impl(const char * format, ...)
{
    /* snip */
}

int (*FormatOutput)(const char * format, ...) = FormatOutput_Impl;
```

With those changes to the .h and .c files, rebuild. There is no need to change the callers of FormatOutput(), because the calling syntax is the same for a direct call and a call through a function pointer.

If you are using printf() directly, you can do the same thing, initializing FormatOutput() like this:

src/util/Utils.c
```c
int (*FormatOutput)(const char * format, ...) = printf;
```

If your make does not use #include dependencies to decide what to rebuild, do a clean build. (Later invest in your build to do a proper incremental build based on dependencies.) If all callers to FormatOutput() are not recompiled, they will call the function pointer as a direct call; bad things will happen.

Let's write a test that shows how to use a FormatOutputSpy. The FormatOutputSpy captures whatever was to be printed so it can be retrieved and checked in the test case.

mocks/FormatOutputSpyTest.cpp
```cpp
TEST(FormatOutputSpy, HelloWorld)
{
    FormatOutputSpy_Create(20);
    FormatOutput("Hello, World\n");
    STRCMP_EQUAL("Hello, World\n", FormatOutputSpy_GetOutput());
}
```

When the spy is created, it is told how long of a string to capture. When calls to FormatOutput() have been overridden with FormatOutputSpy(), the output can be accessed by a call to FormatOutputSpy_GetOuput().

The TEST_GROUP() in the next code segment is responsible for overriding FormatOutput() and cleaning up after each test:

mocks/FormatOutputSpyTest.cpp
```cpp
extern "C"
{
#include "FormatOutputSpy.h"
}
```

```
TEST_GROUP(FormatOutputSpy)
{
    void setup()
    {
        UT_PTR_SET(FormatOutput, FormatOutputSpy);
    }

    void teardown()
    {
        FormatOutputSpy_Destroy();
    }
};
```

This test illustrates that the spy only captures the number of characters specified in FormatOutputSpy_Create():

mocks/FormatOutputSpyTest.cpp
```
TEST(FormatOutputSpy, LimitTheOutputBufferSize)
{
    FormatOutputSpy_Create(4);
    FormatOutput("Hello, World\n");
    STRCMP_EQUAL("Hell", FormatOutputSpy_GetOutput());
}
```

Like real FormatOutput(), the spy can be called multiple times. This test shows that the spy appends characters with each FormatOutput() call:

mocks/FormatOutputSpyTest.cpp
```
TEST(FormatOutputSpy, PrintMultipleTimes)
{
    FormatOutputSpy_Create(25);
    FormatOutput("Hello");
    FormatOutput(", World\n");
    STRCMP_EQUAL("Hello, World\n", FormatOutputSpy_GetOutput());
}
```

In this final test, the spy is called multiple times with more output than the spy can capture. This test assures that the output captured is limited to the specified maximum string length.

mocks/FormatOutputSpyTest.cpp
```
TEST(FormatOutputSpy, PrintMultipleOutputsPastFull)
{
    FormatOutputSpy_Create(12);
    FormatOutput("12345");
    FormatOutput("67890");
    FormatOutput("ABCDEF");
    STRCMP_EQUAL("1234567890AB", FormatOutputSpy_GetOutput());
}
```

Not all test doubles need tests. But in this case, with a more complex spy, tests are needed. The tests show how the spy behaves and makes sure it works. Here are the inner workings of the spy:

mocks/FormatOutputSpy.c
```c
#include <stdlib.h>
#include <stdarg.h>
static char * buffer = 0;
static size_t buffer_size = 0;
static int buffer_offset = 0;
static int buffer_used = 0;

void FormatOutputSpy_Create(int size)
{
    FormatOutputSpy_Destroy();
    buffer_size = size+1;
    buffer = (char *)calloc(buffer_size, sizeof(char));
    buffer_offset = 0;
    buffer_used = 0;
    buffer[0] = '\0';
}

void FormatOutputSpy_Destroy(void)
{
    if (buffer == 0)
        return;

    free(buffer);
    buffer = 0;
}

int FormatOutputSpy(const char * format, ...)
{
    int written_size;
    va_list arguments;
    va_start(arguments, format);
    written_size = vsnprintf(buffer + buffer_offset,
                buffer_size - buffer_used, format, arguments);
    buffer_offset += written_size;
    buffer_used += written_size;
    va_end(arguments);
    return 1;
}
const char * FormatOutputSpy_GetOutput(void)
{
    return buffer;
}
```

In the next section, we'll test-drive some production code that has to print something, using the spy to verify printed output.

9.4 Verifying Output with a Spy

In this section, we'll look at a utility module, the CircularBuffer. A CircularBuffer can be created with a specified capacity; it can have integers added to it and removed from it. It behaves as a first-in first-out data structure. Some of the situations a CircularBuffer might find itself in are shown in Figure 19, *Circular-Buffer*, on page 157.

The CircularBuffer also must print itself out, oldest entry to newest, and not disturb the contents of the buffer. Given all the special cases, this is not quite as easy as it sounds. We're coming into this problem with a working CircularBuffer and have to add the print capability. To get our test fixture in place, let's start with the simplest case, printing an empty buffer. When an empty buffer is printed, its output would look like this:

❰ Circular buffer content:
  <>

It seems like too simple of a case to test, but it is a boundary test that should not crash the system, and the simple case helps get the test fixture set up properly. Here is the test case that confirms that printing an empty CircularBuffer produces the desired output:

tests/util/CircularBufferPrintTest.cpp
```
TEST(CircularBufferPrint, PrintEmpty)
{
    expectedOutput = "Circular buffer content:\n<>\n";
    CircularBuffer_Print(buffer);
    STRCMP_EQUAL(expectedOutput, actualOutput);
}
```

The TEST_GROUP that supports CircularBuffer prints tests looks like this:

tests/util/CircularBufferPrintTest.cpp
```
TEST_GROUP(CircularBufferPrint)
{
    CircularBuffer buffer;
    const char * expectedOutput;
    const char * actualOutput;

    void setup()
    {
      UT_PTR_SET(FormatOutput, FormatOutputSpy);
      FormatOutputSpy_Create(100);
      actualOutput = FormatOutputSpy_GetOutput();
      buffer = CircularBuffer_Create(10);
    }
```

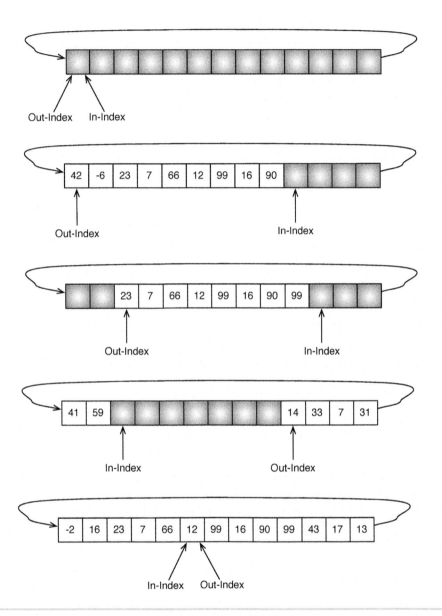

Figure 19— **CircularBuffer**

```
        void teardown()
        {
           CircularBuffer_Destroy(buffer);
           FormatOutputSpy_Destroy();
        }
};
```

Look at how actualOutput is assigned during setup() before the output has been captured. You might wonder, how can actualOutput be initialized now? FormatOutputSpy_GetOuput() simply returns a pointer to the beginning of its internal array that will hold the captured characters once the production code print function is called. The CircularBuffer_Create() parameter, 10, specifies the capacity of the buffer.

This TEST_GROUP tests just the print function of CircularBuffer. There is another TEST_GROUP (not shown) that drove the development of the other CircularBuffer operations. TEST_GROUP(CircularBufferPrint) is an example of organizing tests around a common setup.

This next test is another boundary test. It checks that a buffer containing a single item prints properly. When the buffer contains only the number 17, the output looks like this:

❰ Circular buffer content:
<17>

Here is the test that locks in that behavior:

tests/util/CircularBufferPrintTest.cpp
```
TEST(CircularBufferPrint, PrintAfterOneIsPut)
{
    expectedOutput = "Circular buffer content:\n<17>\n";
    CircularBuffer_Put(buffer, 17);
    CircularBuffer_Print(buffer);
    STRCMP_EQUAL(expectedOutput, actualOutput);
}
```

This test handles the case when there are a few items in the buffer, but it is not full and has not wrapped around to the first slot. Given that there are the values 10, 20, and 30 in the buffer, the output looks like this:

❰ Circular buffer content:
<10, 20, 30>

The TEST() looks like this:

tests/util/CircularBufferPrintTest.cpp
```
TEST(CircularBufferPrint, PrintNotYetWrappedOrFull)
{
    expectedOutput = "Circular buffer content:\n<10, 20, 30>\n";
    CircularBuffer_Put(buffer, 10);
    CircularBuffer_Put(buffer, 20);
    CircularBuffer_Put(buffer, 30);
    CircularBuffer_Print(buffer);
    STRCMP_EQUAL(expectedOutput, actualOutput);
}
```

Here is the test for another boundary case: the buffer is completely full, created with a capacity of five, but has not yet wrapped back around to the first location.

tests/util/CircularBufferPrintTest.cpp
```
TEST(CircularBufferPrint, PrintNotYetWrappedAndIsFull)
{
    expectedOutput = "Circular buffer content:\n"
                     "<31, 41, 59, 26, 53>\n";

    CircularBuffer b = CircularBuffer_Create(5);
    CircularBuffer_Put(b, 31);
    CircularBuffer_Put(b, 41);
    CircularBuffer_Put(b, 59);
    CircularBuffer_Put(b, 26);
    CircularBuffer_Put(b, 53);

    CircularBuffer_Print(b);

    STRCMP_EQUAL(expectedOutput, actualOutput);
    CircularBuffer_Destroy(b);
}
```

This test deals with the situation after wrap-around has occurred:

tests/util/CircularBufferPrintTest.cpp
```
TEST(CircularBufferPrint, PrintOldToNewWhenWrappedAndFull)
{
    expectedOutput =
        "Circular buffer content:\n"
        "<201, 202, 203, 204, 999>\n";

    CircularBuffer b = CircularBuffer_Create(5);
    CircularBuffer_Put(b, 200);
    CircularBuffer_Put(b, 201);
    CircularBuffer_Put(b, 202);
    CircularBuffer_Put(b, 203);
    CircularBuffer_Put(b, 204);
    CircularBuffer_Get(b);
    CircularBuffer_Put(b, 999);

    CircularBuffer_Print(b);

    STRCMP_EQUAL(expectedOutput, actualOutput);
    CircularBuffer_Destroy(b);
}
```

We could write some more tests, but I think you have the picture.

9.5 Where Are We?

We've seen a couple applications of the function pointer in making testable C code. First we saw that we use a function pointer to dynamically swap out troublesome code for some test cases as we did with the RandomMinute. Then we saw how to surgically insert a test double to substitute only one part of a compilation unit.

Any function call dependency can be converted to a function pointer. Maybe you wonder, is testability reason enough to convert a direct function call to a function pointer? Yes, it is. Should you turn *all* your direct function calls into function pointers? Of course not.

Like any tool, you want to use it when it's called for. If a link-time test double will do, use a link-time test double. It is the right tool for swapping out target platform dependencies and sometimes entire third-party libraries. The function pointer provides a more surgical tool for breaking dependencies at runtime. If you need the code in the test executable but you also need to get it out of the way for some tests, use a function pointer.

A function pointer is also a good tool for the job if you only want to stub out a subset of the functions in a compilation unit. But it's not the only tool. You could also split the compilation unit and use link-time binding. Choose the right tool for the job.

We're not done with function pointers. We employ them not only to make code more testable, but they can also be used to make code more flexible, as you will see when we get into the Chapter 11, *SOLID, Flexible, and Testable Designs*, on page 189.

Prior to the FormatOutputSpy, the test doubles have been pretty simple. There was only a single interaction with the test double during the test case. The FormatOutputSpy could record what happened over multiple interactions. In the next chapter, we'll look at the *mock object*. It lets the tests model more complex interactions between collaborating modules.

9.6 Put the Knowledge to Work

1. Extend the CircularBuffer so that it can print multiple lines of values in neat columns, allowing no more than sixty characters per line. It needs to handle only five-digit decimal numbers.

2. Evolve CircularBuffer print capabilities so that the column width adjusts to the two characters wider than the largest number in the buffer.

3. The *customer* can't decide how they want the CircularBuffer output. Separate print formatting from the CircularBuffer. A PrintFormatter function should be passed to the CircularBuffer, which gives each value in its correct order to the formatter.

4. The randomization implementation and tests for the LightScheduler that you can find in book's code download in directory code/t0 have just been barely started. Make a test list for the special cases, and test-drive the complete behavior. Two things to consider are that a random scheduled event should be operated only once a day, and a random scheduled event near midnight should handle the day change correctly.

Let's mock the midnight bell.
> *William Shakespeare*

CHAPTER 10

The Mock Object

While test-driving the LightScheduler, the test fixture intercepted calls to the TimeService and the LightController to verify the correct behavior of the LightScheduler. The test doubles employed were very simple and were made up of a few static variables along with some getters and setters. This works fine for those simple interactions. Unfortunately, not all interactions between software entities are so simple. Simple spies or stubs won't always work. For more complex interactions, we need a different tool, the *mock object*.

The mock object (or simply the *mock*) is a test double. It allows a test case to describe the calls expected from one module to another. During test execution the mock checks that all calls happen with the right parameters and in the right order. The mock can also be instructed to return specific values in proper sequence to the code under test. A mock is not a simulator, but it allows a test case to simulate a specific scenario or sequence of events.[1]

In this chapter, we'll use a mock to model and confirm the interactions between a device driver and the hardware. The mock intercepts commands to and from the device, simulating one usage scenario. In the "Endo-Testing: Unit Testing with Mock Objects" paper, the authors claim that using mock objects means that tests can be written for anything. This example shows that even something as hardware-dependent as a device driver can be thoroughly unit tested using a mock.

10.1 Flash Driver

When I talk to embedded developers about applying TDD to embedded systems, the statement often comes up, "Yeah, but you can't test-drive a device

---

1. Mock objects were first described in the paper *Endo-Testing: Unit Testing with Mock Objects [MFC01]*.

driver!" To that I reply, "Yes, you can." This example will kill two birds with one stone. We'll get right next to the silicon and develop part of a flash memory driver, and we'll use a mock object to model and confirm the complex interactions between the driver and the hardware.

For the example, we'll use the ST Microelectronics 16 Mb flash memory device (M28W160ECT). I chose this one for a number of reasons. The flash memory device requires a specific protocol, involving numerous device reads and device writes. There are also several failure modes, some of which would be very difficult to cause in the actual device. In addition, the device is well documented: its data sheet is fifty pages in length, including numerous flowcharts, tables, and detailed instructions. Finally, the vendor provides a reference design, so we can compare implementations.[2]

Figure 20, *Flash driver and its test fixture*, on page 165 shows the relationship between the test case, the mock, and the production code. The FlashDriver interacts with the hardware through two simple functions: IO_Read() and IO_Write().

src/IO/IO.c
```
#include "IO.h"
void IO_Write(ioAddress addr, ioData data)
{
    ioData * p = 0;
    *(p + addr) = data;
}
ioData IO_Read(ioAddress addr)
{
    ioData * p = 0;
    return *(p + addr);
}
```

These two functions are the gateway to the hardware from the driver. They are statically linked. Because there is no need for the production version of IO_Read() and IO_Write() during unit testing, a link-time test double works well. Function pointers would give additional flexibility to run unit tests in the target, along with test cases that actually interact with the hardware through the production versions of IO_Read() and IO_Write(). It's a small modification to convert to function pointers if we change our minds later.

MockIO is standing in for the hardware-dependent implementation of IO. The test case tells the mock which calls to IO_Read() and IO_Write() to expect. Then, during the exercise phase, the mock checks each actual call with the

---

2. You can find the device spec and code in the code download for the book in docs/STMicroelectronics.

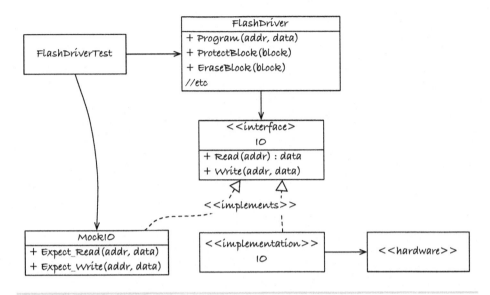

Figure 20— Flash driver and its test fixture

expected call. You can think of expectation setting as an additional step in the Four-Phase Test pattern: set up, establish expectations, exercise (and check), and check and clean up.

As shown in the flowchart in Figure 21, *Flash memory program—flowchart*, on page 166, flash operations can have many interactions. The flowchart shows how to program a specific location in the device. It also identifies the failures that can occur while programming a specific location in the flash.

Programming a memory location is initiated with two device writes. Then the driver goes into a *wait for ready* loop, waiting for the device to complete the operation. The flowchart shows that there are four possible outcomes, suggesting the need for at least four test cases. In addition to what the device flowchart suggests, our driver will read back the data from the device to confirm that the write was successful. That adds an additional test case. We'll also need a test case to simulate a device that never responds. The initial test list is shown in Figure 22, *Flash memory program—test list*, on page 166.

As shown in the sequence chart in Figure 23, *Flash_Write sequence chart—success case*, on page 167, multiple device interactions are needed to program a flash location. Simple spies and stubs cannot confirm the complex interaction needed. The mock object is the right tool for this job.

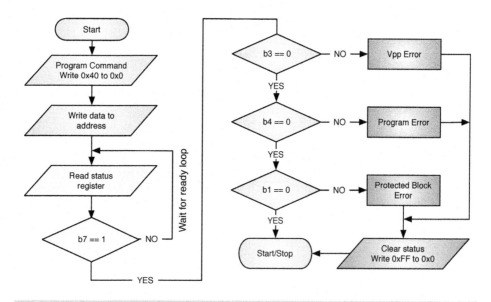

Figure 21— Flash memory program—flowchart

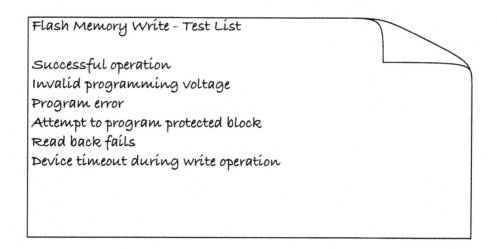

Figure 22— Flash memory program—test list

A common misconception is that a mock is a simulator; it is not. A mock is used to simulate and verify a series of interactions for a specific usage scenario. The mock has no idea what a flash device is. Each test case programs the mock for the needed scenario. The mock simulates a single scenario at a time, not the device in total. And it's good we don't have to create a flash

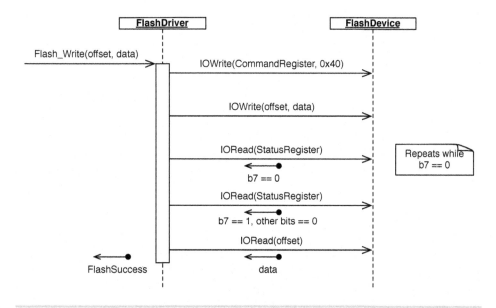

Figure 23— Flash_Write sequence chart—success case

simulator. Such a simulator would probably be more complicated than the device driver itself.

To be testable, all interactions from the driver to the hardware must go through a pair of functions, IO_Read() and IO_Write(). MockIO intercepts calls to those functions. The MockIO versions of IO_Read() and IO_Write() intercept and check each operation. In addition, IO_Read() is programmed to return specific values for each read operation in the usage scenario.

Let's see how to use MockIO. Treat MockIO as a black box; we'll look at its inner workings after that.

Tests with a mock object take a little getting used to. They are different in that they start with recording expectations rather than ending with checking expectations. This test shows how MockIO has its expectations *set up* for the scenario illustrated in Figure 23, *Flash_Write sequence chart—success case*, on page 167:

tests/IO/FlashTest.cpp
```
TEST(Flash, WriteSucceeds_ReadyImmediately)
{
    int result = 0;
    MockIO_Expect_Write(0, 0x40);
    MockIO_Expect_Write(0x1000, 0xBEEF);
    MockIO_Expect_ReadThenReturn(0, 1<<7);
```

```
    MockIO_Expect_ReadThenReturn(0x1000, 0xBEEF);
    result = Flash_Write(0x1000, 0xBEEF);
    LONGS_EQUAL(0, result);
    MockIO_Verify_Complete();
}
```

The test case is programming MockIO's behavior. Each call to MockIO identifies the I/O operations to expect and how to react to each. Ignoring the parameters for a second, this test says that Flash_Write() should do two IO_Write() calls followed by two IO_Read() calls. If the expectations are not met (in the specified order) by the end of the test case, the test fails. For the test to pass, the production code, Flash_Write(), should interact with the flash device as described by the expectations.

This test scenario represents a successful programming of location 0x1000 with the value 0xBEEF. Walking through the *establish expectations* phase of the test, the first call to MockIO_Expect_Write(0, 0x40) tells the mock that the first thing that should happen is a write to location 0x0 the value 0x40. As documented in the flowchart, this puts the device in program mode. The second thing the driver must do is write to location 0x1000 the value 0xBEEF. Then the call to MockIO_Expect_ReadThenReturn(0, 1<<7) tells the mock to expect a read from location 0x0 and that the mock should return a 1 in bit position 7, signaling the device's successful completion.

It's unlikely the device would really be ready on the first pass around the ready check loop, but the code better handle it properly at any rate. The error scenarios might be ready immediately. The magic numbers are straight from the flowchart on Figure 21, *Flash memory program—flowchart*, on page 166. After the device reports a successful program operation, the driver should read back the data written to confirm the successful write, which is programmed by the final MockIO_Expect_ReadThenReturn().

After all the expectations are set, the test calls the production code function Flash_Write(). Because Flash_Write() is linked to MockIO versions of IO_Read() and IO_Write(), each call is checked to see that it matches the expected call exactly. If calls are out of order or parameters are wrong, the test immediately fails. With a mock, the check phase is not as distinct as it is mingled with the execution of the production code.

In the final check phase, the test checks that Flash_Write() returns a 0, indicating successful programming of the flash memory location. By the time that check is made, all IO calls that happened were valid. The final line of the test case makes sure there are no unused expectations; if there are, MockIO_Verify_Complete() causes the test to fail.

Let's look at some of the errors MockIO generates as we test-drive the Flash_Write() function. Here's its first implementation:

src/IO/Flash.c
```c
int Flash_Write(ioAddress address, ioData data)
{
    return -1;
}
```

Because no expectations are met, we get this feedback from the mock:

```
mocks/MockIO.c:139: error: Failure in TEST(Flash, WriteSucceeds_ReadyImmediately)
     Expected 4 reads/writes but got 0
```

Now let's meet the first expectation with this implementation:

src/IO/Flash.c
```c
int Flash_Write(ioAddress address, ioData data)
{
    IO_Write(0x40, 0);
    return -1;
}
```

The IO_Write() call has the parameters reversed; we get this error:

```
mocks/MockIO.c:64: error: Failure in TEST(Flash, WriteSucceeds_ReadyImmediately)
     R/W 1: Expected IO_Write(0x0, 0x40)
            But was IO_Write(0x40, 0x0)
```

Aside from checking for unconsumed expectations and wrong parameters, MockIO checks that each operation matches its expectation. The test will fail under these conditions:

- IO_Read() called when expecting IO_Write()
- IO_Write() called when expecting IO_Read()
- IO_Write() called with the wrong address or data
- IO_Read() called with the wrong address

This code passes that test case:

src/IO/Flash.c
```c
int Flash_Write(ioAddress address, ioData data)
{
    IO_Write(0, 0x40);
    IO_Write(address, data);
    IO_Read(0);
    IO_Read(address);
    return FLASH_SUCCESS;
}
```

Notice we have not done the looping logic yet or checked for any of the error conditions. Those tests would come one by one as we have done in previous examples. Before we continue, let's refactor the test. Go ahead and eliminate the magic numbers and pull common items into the TEST_GROUP(). Now the test group looks like this:

tests/IO/FlashTest.cpp
```
TEST_GROUP(Flash)
{
    ioAddress address;
    ioData data;
    int result;

    void setup()
    {
        address = 0x1000;
        data = 0xBEEF;
        result = -1;

        MockIO_Create(10);
        Flash_Create();
    }

    void teardown()
    {
        Flash_Destroy();
        MockIO_Verify_Complete();
        MockIO_Destroy();
    }
};
```

And the magic numberless test case looks like this:

tests/IO/FlashTest.cpp
```
TEST(Flash, WriteSucceeds_ReadyImmediately)
{
    MockIO_Expect_Write(CommandRegister, ProgramCommand);
    MockIO_Expect_Write(address, data);
    MockIO_Expect_ReadThenReturn(StatusRegister, ReadyBit);
    MockIO_Expect_ReadThenReturn(address, data);
    result = Flash_Write(address, data);
    LONGS_EQUAL(FLASH_SUCCESS, result);
}
```

The refactored production code that passes this test looks like this:

src/IO/Flash.c
```
int Flash_Write(ioAddress address, ioData data)
{
    IO_Write(CommandRegister, ProgramCommand);
    IO_Write(address, data);
```

```
        IO_Read(StatusRegister);
        IO_Read(address);
        return FLASH_SUCCESS;
}
```

The literal constants are defined in a device-specific header file. I didn't add these to Flash.h because users of the driver don't need to know these constants.

include/IO/m28w160ect.h
```
typedef enum
{
        CommandRegister = 0x0,
        StatusRegister = 0x0
} Flash_Registers;

typedef enum
{
        ProgramCommand = 0x40,
        Reset = 0xff
} Flash_Command;
```

Because the header is used by both production and test code, errors in definitions won't be found by these tests. They could be found by code inspections and will certainly be found during hardware integration.

The flowchart shows that we need to loop while waiting for the device to finish the program command. Also, the error conditions must be interpreted and translated to return codes. The test fixture is in place, and we should be able to make good progress. But before we complete the Flash_Write()'s tests and production code, let's look deeper into MockIO.

10.2 MockIO

MockIO might seem like a mysterious thing. You might think that it's extra work that won't be needed and just takes time from the production code. Let's clear up some of the mystery around MockIO and look at its full interface and some of its implementation. I hope you will see that it's not that much trouble.

MockIO's public interface consists of the usual create/destroy functions, along with the functions for programming the expectations and assuring that all expectations are met.

mocks/MockIO.h
```
#ifndef D_MockIO_H
#define D_MockIO_H
#include "IO.h"
void MockIO_Create(int maxExpectations);
void MockIO_Destroy(void);
```

```
void MockIO_Expect_Write(ioAddress offset, ioData data);
void MockIO_Expect_ReadThenReturn(ioAddress  offset, ioData returnData);
void MockIO_Verify_Complete(void);
#endif
```

As you might expect, MockIO.c has an ordered table of expectations. It's made from an array of data structures and local variables.

mocks/MockIO.c
```
typedef struct Expectation
{
    int kind;
    ioAddress addr;
    ioData value;
} Expectation;

static Expectation * expectations = 0;
static int setExpectationCount;
static int getExpectationCount;
static int maxExpectationCount;
static int failureAlreadyReported = 0;
```

The expectations table and its associated local data are initialized and cleaned up like this:

mocks/MockIO.c
```
void MockIO_Create(int maxExpectations)
{
    expectations = calloc(maxExpectations, sizeof(Expectation));
    setExpectationCount = 0;
    getExpectationCount = 0;
    maxExpectationCount = maxExpectations;
    failureAlreadyReported = 0;
}

void MockIO_Destroy(void)
{
    if (expectations)
        free(expectations);
    expectations = 0;
}
```

As you saw in the test case, the expectations are recorded using these functions:

mocks/MockIO.c
```
void MockIO_Expect_Write(ioAddress addr, ioData value)
{
    failWhenNoRoomForExpectations(report_too_many_write_expectations);
    recordExpectation(FLASH_WRITE, addr, value);
}
```

```c
void MockIO_Expect_ReadThenReturn(ioAddress addr, ioData value)
{
    failWhenNoRoomForExpectations(report_too_many_read_expectations);
    recordExpectation(FLASH_READ, addr, value);
}
```

The failWhenNoMoreRoomForExpectations() function is a private file scope function that makes sure MockIO is initialized and has room for more expectations. If those checks are not satisfied, failWhenNoMoreRoomForExpectations() fails, never to return. When there is room, recordExpectation() makes an entry into the expectations table.

IO_Write() does not really write anything; it makes sure that whatever the caller is trying to write matches the expectations set in the corresponding MockIO_Expect_Write().

mocks/MockIO.c
```c
void IO_Write(ioAddress addr, ioData value)
{
    setExpectedAndActual(addr, value);
    failWhenNotInitialized();
    failWhenNoUnusedExpectations(report_write_but_out_of_expectations);
    failWhen(expectationIsNot(FLASH_WRITE), report_expect_read_was_write);
    failWhen(expectedAddressIsNot(addr), report_write_does_not_match);
    failWhen(expectedDataIsNot(value), report_write_does_not_match);
    getExpectationCount++;
}
```

IO_Write() can fail when MockIO has not been initialized, when there are no more unused expectations, when an IO_Read() was expected, or when there is a mismatch in the address or data written.

Likewise, IO_Read() does not really read anything—it makes checks similar to IO_Write(). In addition, it returns the return result specified in the second parameter of MockIO_Expect_ReadThenReturn().

mocks/MockIO.c
```c
ioData IO_Read(ioAddress addr)
{
    setExpectedAndActual(addr, NoExpectedValue);
    failWhenNotInitialized();
    failWhenNoUnusedExpectations(report_read_but_out_of_expectations);
    failWhen(expectationIsNot(FLASH_READ), report_expect_write_was_read);
    failWhen(expectedAddressIsNot(addr), report_read_wrong_address);

    return expectations[getExpectationCount++].value;
}
```

With this mechanism we can rig a series of return values so we can get Flash_Write() to loop, waiting for a specific bit setting from IO_Read().

Finally, MockIO_Verify_Complete() confirms that all the preprogrammed expectations have been met. MockIO_Verify_Complete() should be called after the exercise phase of the TEST(). It can be called in teardown().

mocks/MockIO.c
```c
void MockIO_Verify_Complete(void)
{
    if (failureAlreadyReported)
        return;
    failWhenNotAllExpectationsUsed();
}
```

Notice that MockIO_Verify_Complete() checks the mock has not reported any other errors. Any mock failure terminates the test case but not the running of teardown(). This makes sure that MockIO_Verify_Complete() does not report another error during teardown().

Now that you've seen how the mock works, let's go back and finish Flash_Write(). You can find the full listing of MockIO and its tests in the online code download.

10.3 Test-Driving the Driver

Before we looked under the hood of MockIO, Flash_Write() passed a simple test where the device is immediately ready. It is not likely that the device would be ready right away. According to its specification, this device has a typical write time of ten microseconds. When the driver runs in a real device, the StatusRegister may be read hundreds or thousands of times. The driver needs to loop, waiting for the operation to complete, though we can prove the looping logic with just a few reads:

tests/IO/FlashTest.cpp
```cpp
TEST(Flash, WriteSucceeds_NotImmediatelyReady)
{
    MockIO_Expect_Write(CommandRegister, ProgramCommand);
    MockIO_Expect_Write(address, data);
    MockIO_Expect_ReadThenReturn(StatusRegister, 0);
    MockIO_Expect_ReadThenReturn(StatusRegister, 0);
    MockIO_Expect_ReadThenReturn(StatusRegister, 0);
    MockIO_Expect_ReadThenReturn(StatusRegister, ReadyBit);
    MockIO_Expect_ReadThenReturn(address, data);

    result = Flash_Write(address, data);
    LONGS_EQUAL(FLASH_SUCCESS, result);
}
```

Here's the error that drives us to add the looping logic to IO_Read():

```
IO/FlashTest.cpp:78: error: Failure in
                             TEST(Flash, WriteSucceeds_NotReadyImmediately)
../mocks/MockIO.c:83: error:
    R/W 4: Expected IO_Read(0x0) returns 0x0;
           But was IO_Read(0x1000)
```

Now add the loop to Flash_Write():

src/IO/Flash.c
```c
int Flash_Write(ioAddress address, ioData data)
{
    ioData status = 0;

    IO_Write(CommandRegister, ProgramCommand);
    IO_Write(address, data);

    while ((status & ReadyBit) == 0)
        status = IO_Read(StatusRegister);

    IO_Read(address);

    return FLASH_SUCCESS;
}
```

Flash_Write() handles the happy path through the function. So now let's get to the error conditions. The first error on our flowchart is the V_{pp} error. The V_{pp} bit is set when the programming voltage on the device is incorrect. To test this in the target, we'd have to damage the hardware, which means the error detection code might never run until there is a board failure. We'll set VppErrorBit along with ReadyBit. Note that the flowchart shows that the driver must reset the device for each error case.

tests/IO/FlashTest.cpp
```cpp
TEST(Flash, WriteFails_VppError)
{
    MockIO_Expect_Write(CommandRegister, ProgramCommand);
    MockIO_Expect_Write(address, data);
    MockIO_Expect_ReadThenReturn(StatusRegister, ReadyBit | VppErrorBit);
    MockIO_Expect_Write(CommandRegister, Reset);

    result = Flash_Write(address, data);

    LONGS_EQUAL(FLASH_VPP_ERROR, result);
}
```

We'll need similar test cases for each of the other two possible device errors (tests for EraseErrorBit and BlockProtectionErrorBit are not shown). Here is the tested implementation that handles all the errors in the spec:

src/IO/Flash.c
```c
int Flash_Write(ioAddress offset, ioData data)
{
    ioData status = 0;
    IO_Write(CommandRegister, ProgramCommand);
    IO_Write(offset, data);

    while ((status & ReadyBit) == 0)
        status = IO_Read(StatusRegister);

    if (status != ReadyBit)
    {
        IO_Write(CommandRegister, Reset);

        if (status & VppErrorBit)
            return FLASH_VPP_ERROR;
        else if (status & ProgramErrorBit)
            return FLASH_PROGRAM_ERROR;
        else if (status & BlockProtectionErrorBit)
            return FLASH_PROTECTED_BLOCK_ERROR;
        else
            return FLASH_UNKNOWN_PROGRAM_ERROR;
    }
    IO_Read(address);

    return FLASH_SUCCESS;
}
```

Our driver requirements say that the driver must read back the written data to confirm a successful write. Add the scenario where the data read back does not match the data written:

tests/IO/FlashTest.cpp
```cpp
TEST(Flash, WriteFails_FlashReadBackError)
{
    MockIO_Expect_Write(CommandRegister, ProgramCommand);
    MockIO_Expect_Write(address, data);
    MockIO_Expect_ReadThenReturn(StatusRegister, ReadyBit);
    MockIO_Expect_ReadThenReturn(address, data-1);

    result = Flash_Write(address, data);

    LONGS_EQUAL(FLASH_READ_BACK_ERROR, result);
}
```

One other thing: the device specification says that until ReadyBit is set, other status bits may change and should be ignored. This test assures that the driver terminates the loop only when ReadyBit is set.

tests/IO/FlashTest.cpp
```cpp
TEST(Flash, WriteSucceeds_IgnoresOtherBitsUntilReady)
{
    MockIO_Expect_Write(CommandRegister, ProgramCommand);
    MockIO_Expect_Write(address, data);
    MockIO_Expect_ReadThenReturn(StatusRegister, ~ReadyBit);
    MockIO_Expect_ReadThenReturn(StatusRegister, ReadyBit);
    MockIO_Expect_ReadThenReturn(address, data);

    result = Flash_Write(address, data);

    LONGS_EQUAL(FLASH_SUCCESS, result);
}
```

The Flash_Write() device driver function is almost done. Before we add timeout detection, let's refactor Flash_Write() by extracting the error processing. Here's the refactored Flash_Write():

src/IO/Flash.c
```c
int Flash_Write(ioAddress offset, ioData data)
{
    ioData status = 0;
    IO_Write(CommandRegister, ProgramCommand);
    IO_Write(offset, data);

    while ((status & ReadyBit) == 0)
        status = IO_Read(StatusRegister);
    if (status != ReadyBit)
        return writeError(status);
    if (data != IO_Read(offset))
        return FLASH_READ_BACK_ERROR;
    return FLASH_SUCCESS;
}
```

Extracting the error handling helper function helps keep Flash_Write() concise.

src/IO/Flash.c
```c
static int writeError(int status)
{
    IO_Write(CommandRegister, Reset);
    if (status & VppErrorBit)
        return FLASH_VPP_ERROR;
    else if (status & ProgramErrorBit)
        return FLASH_PROGRAM_ERROR;
    else if (status & BlockProtectionErrorBit)
        return FLASH_PROTECTED_BLOCK_ERROR;
    else
        return FLASH_UNKNOWN_PROGRAM_ERROR;
}
```

Now let's get the code to handle the timeout.

10.4 Simulating a Device Timeout

It's possible for the flash memory device to never become ready, probably because of some transient or permanent hardware error. Testing the timeout with a real device would be difficult. Like V_{pp} error, we might even need to hack up a board. However, with an addition to our test fixture, we can reliably test the error case.

The device specification says that the device has a typical response time of ten microseconds. Let's give the driver five milliseconds before ending in an error. In terms of implementation, the driver can read a real-time clock tick to get the current rolling μs counter during the ready wait loop. If it makes sense with your system's context switch time, you could also consider a delay or processor yield during the loop. After the timeout period expires, Flash_Write returns FLASH_TIMEOUT_ERROR. We can control this timeout if we take control of the RTC tick with a link-time fake. It looks like this:

mocks/FakeMicroTime.c
```c
void FakeMicroTime_Init(uint32_t start, uint32_t incr)
{
    time = start;
    increment = incr;
    totalDelay = 0;
}
uint32_t MicroTime_Get(void)
{
    uint32_t t = time;
    time += increment;
    return t;
}
```

Using FakeMicroTime_Init(), the fake is started at a particular μs and increments by the supplied value each time MicroTime_Get() is called. This test case forces a timeout.

tests/IO/FlashTest.cpp
```cpp
TEST(Flash, WriteFails_Timeout)
{
    FakeMicroTime_Init(0, 500);
    Flash_Create();
    MockIO_Expect_Write(CommandRegister, ProgramCommand);
    MockIO_Expect_Write(address, data);
    for (int i = 0; i < 10; i++)
        MockIO_Expect_ReadThenReturn(StatusRegister, ~ReadyBit);
    result = Flash_Write(address, data);
    LONGS_EQUAL(FLASH_TIMEOUT_ERROR, result);
}
```

First, we initialize FakeMicroTime to start at 0 and increment by 500 μs. Using 500 as the upper limit results in breaking out of the loop with a timeout after ten laps. Ten I/O reads are expected before declaring a timeout.

Once we have everything compiling, the test fails as it runs out of expectations; it looks like this:

```
IO/FlashTest.cpp:210: error: Failure in TEST(Flash, WriteFails_Timeout)
../mocks/MockIO.c:83: error:
        R/W 13: No more expectations but was IO_Read(0x0)
```

Now we'll add the needed timeout detection:

src/IO/Flash.c
```c
int Flash_Write(ioAddress offset, ioData data)
{
    ioData status = 0;
    uint32_t timestamp = MicroTime_Get();

    IO_Write(CommandRegister, ProgramCommand);
    IO_Write(offset, data);

    status = IO_Read(StatusRegister);
    while ((status & ReadyBit) == 0)
    {
        if (MicroTime_Get() - timestamp >= FLASH_WRITE_TIMEOUT_IN_MICROSECONDS)
            return FLASH_TIMEOUT_ERROR;
        status = IO_Read(StatusRegister);
    }

    if (status != ReadyBit)
        return writeError(status);

    if (data != IO_Read(offset))
        return FLASH_READ_BACK_ERROR;

    return FLASH_SUCCESS;
}
```

When clocks roll over, as this one will every 136 years, you'd like the code to continue working. Maybe it won't matter in 136 years, but maybe your hardware only has a 16-bit timer: then a μs timer rolls over in just about 18 hours. We can test it like this:

tests/IO/FlashTest.cpp
```cpp
TEST(Flash, WriteFails_TimeoutAtEndOfTime)
{
    FakeMicroTime_Init(0xffffffff, 500);
    Flash_Create();
    MockIO_Expect_Write(CommandRegister, ProgramCommand);
```

```
    MockIO_Expect_Write(address, data);
    for (int i = 0; i < 10; i++)
        MockIO_Expect_ReadThenReturn(StatusRegister, ~ReadyBit);
    result = Flash_Write(address, data);
    LONGS_EQUAL(FLASH_TIMEOUT_ERROR, result);
}
```

As far as we know, we have all the scenarios covered. We're ready when the hardware is ready to integrate.

10.5 Is It Worth It?

Unlike the test doubles supporting the development of the LightScheduler, MockIO is much more complex. The mock is more than 200 lines of code. There are about 150 lines of Flash test code on top of that, all to test about 70 lines of production code. It seems like that might be a lot of investment.

It *is* worth it. For one thing, MockIO won't just be used for the flash driver. It is a handy tool for testing anything that does I/O reads and writes. That investment will be leveraged across many drivers. Looking at the reference implementation from the manufacturer, there are almost 900 lines of C code. Much of this code is not as simple as Flash_Write()—there is much looping and conditional logic. Given that, the effort to put the mock together is not big compared to the overall flash driver size and the value of avoiding Debug on Hardware (DOH!).

When the driver meets the hardware, we are likely to bump into integration problems. We could also write some hardware integration tests intended to be run only on the hardware. As we find integration problems where the tests don't agree with the hardware, the tests and production code need to be revised to be compatible with the real world.

I think the case for writing these tests is strong. The work in progress is well tested. The regression test safety net is in place for future driver modifications. Yes, there is more typing to do, but typing is not the limiting factor when programming. It's thinking, understanding, problem solving, experimenting, proving concepts, and keeping the code working that takes time.

10.6 Mocking with CppUMock

CppUTest has an extension library to support writing of mocks called CppUMock. You may anticipate that mocks for different modules might have considerable duplication between them. That led Bas Vodde, one of CppUTest's authors, to create CppUMock.

Let's see how to use CppUTest Mock Support to test-drive the Flash driver. This test is equivalent to the first Flash test earlier in the chapter.

t1/tests/IO/FlashTest.cpp
```cpp
TEST(Flash, WriteSucceeds_Immediately)
{
    mock().expectOneCall("IO_Write")
            .withParameter("addr", CommandRegister)
            .withParameter("value", ProgramCommand);
    mock().expectOneCall("IO_Write")
            .withParameter("addr", (int) address)
            .withParameter("value", data);

    mock().expectOneCall("IO_Read")
            .withParameter("addr", StatusRegister)
            .andReturnValue((int) ReadyBit);
    mock().expectOneCall("IO_Read")
            .withParameter("addr", (int) address)
            .andReturnValue((int) data);

    int result = Flash_Write(address, data);

    LONGS_EQUAL(FLASH_SUCCESS, result);
}
```

The first statement in the test sets the first expectation. The mock should expect a call to IO_Write() with two parameters. The first parameter's name is addr, and its value is CommandRegister. The second parameter's name is value, and its value should be ProgramCommand.

Notice that the two IO_Read() calls also specify a return value for the call. IO_Write has a void return type, so there is no .andReturnValue() clause.

Now for mock versions of IO_Write() and IO_Read(). You write the mock version of IO_Write() like this:

t1/tests/IO/FlashTest.cpp
```cpp
void IO_Write(ioAddress addr, ioData value)
{
    mock_c()->actualCall("IO_Write")
            ->withIntParameters("addr", addr)
            ->withIntParameters("value", value);
}
```

The mock setup code used to set expectations is C++, but the mock_c code in the .c file is pure C, though a unique style. IO_Write() simply informs mock_c() of the name of the function called and each of the parameters' names and values. IO_Read() is similar.

t1/tests/IO/FlashTest.cpp
```
ioData IO_Read(ioAddress addr)
{
    mock_c()->actualCall("IO_Read")
            ->withIntParameters("addr", addr);

    return mock_c()->returnValue().value.intValue;
}
```

Like IO_Write(), IO_Read() checks the function name and each parameter. Additionally, it returns the associated value.

Here is the TEST_GROUP:

t1/tests/IO/FlashTest.cpp
```
TEST_GROUP(Flash)
{
    ioAddress address;
    ioData data;
    int result;

    void setup()
    {
        address = 0xfeed;
        data = 0x1dea;
    }

    void teardown()
    {
        mock().checkExpectations();
        mock().clear();
    }
};
```

The teardown() call to mock().checkExpectations() makes sure all expectations have been met. .clear() cleans up after the mock. There is a plug-in that can be installed into CppUTest that makes these calls after teardown().

If we ran the test with a skeleton of Flash_Write() that does no I/O, we'd get the following output:

```
t1/tests/IO/FlashTest.cpp:105: error: Failure in
    TEST(Flash, WriteSucceeds_ReadyImmediately)
        Mock Failure: Expected call did not happen.
        EXPECTED calls that did NOT happen:
                IO_Write -> int addr: <0>, int value: <64>
                IO_Write -> int addr: <65261>, int value: <7658>
                IO_Read -> int addr: <0>
                IO_Read -> int addr: <65261>
        ACTUAL calls that did happen:
                <none>
```

If the production code didn't put the device in *command mode*, CppUMock will generate this error:

```
t1/tests/IO/FlashTest.cpp:105: error: Failure in
    TEST(Flash, WriteSucceeds_ReadyImmediately)
        Mock Failure: Expected call did not happen.
        EXPECTED calls that did NOT happen:
                IO_Write -> int addr: <0>, int value: <64>
        ACTUAL calls that did happen:
                IO_Write -> int addr: <65261>, int value: <7658>
                IO_Read -> int addr: <0>
                IO_Read -> int addr: <65261>
```

Unlike the handcrafted mock, this version of CppUTest mock does not reject calls that are not in the same order as the expect calls. This makes for a more flexible test if there is no order dependency in the interactions, but it is a problem when there is an order dependency.

CppUMock takes a lot of the pain and repetition out of creating mocks. It has more capabilities than we've discussed here, so give it a test-drive to see what else it does.[3] In the next section we'll look at Unity's mock support, CMock, that generates mocks from header files.

10.7 Generating Mocks

CMock[4] is a mock generator that is a companion to Unity. CMock generates test double functions that conform to the interface specified in a header file. Let's see what CMock will generate if we give it IO.h:

include/IO/IO.h
```
#ifndef D_IO_H
#define D_IO_H
#include <stdint.h>

typedef uint32_t ioAddress;
typedef uint16_t ioData;

ioData IO_Read(ioAddress offset);
void IO_Write(ioAddress offset, ioData data);

#endif
```

CMock generates a header file and a mock implementation. The .h file looks a lot like the mock we handcrafted.

---

3. You can find CppUMock documentation at http://www.cpputest.org/node/30.
4. You can find CMock at http://sourceforge.net/projects/cmock/.

mocks/cmock/MockIO.h
```
/* AUTOGENERATED FILE. DO NOT EDIT. */
#ifndef _MOCKIO_H
#define _MOCKIO_H

#include "IO.h"

void MockIO_Init(void);
void MockIO_Destroy(void);
void MockIO_Verify(void);

void IO_Read_ExpectAndReturn(ioAddress offset, ioData toReturn);
void IO_Write_Expect(ioAddress offset, ioData data);

#endif
```

The .c file is about 255 lines of generated code. Essentially, the generated mock is doing the same job as the handcrafted mock. A tool like CMock can be very helpful for testing complex interactions between collaborating C modules. Here is the generated IO_Read():

mocks/cmock/MockIO.c
```
ioData IO_Read(ioAddress offset)
{
  Mock.IO_Read_CallCount++;
  if (Mock.IO_Read_CallCount > Mock.IO_Read_CallsExpected)
  {
    TEST_FAIL("Function 'IO_Read' called more times than expected");
  }

  if (Mock.IO_Read_Expected_offset != Mock.IO_Read_Expected_offset_Tail)
  {
    ioAddress* p_expected = Mock.IO_Read_Expected_offset;
    Mock.IO_Read_Expected_offset++;
    TEST_ASSERT_EQUAL_MEMORY_MESSAGE(
        (void*)p_expected, (void*)&(offset), sizeof(ioAddress),
        "Function 'IO_Read' called with unexpected value for argument 'offset'.");
  }

  if (Mock.IO_Read_Return != Mock.IO_Read_Return_Tail)
  {
    ioData toReturn = *Mock.IO_Read_Return;
    Mock.IO_Read_Return++;
    return toReturn;
  }
  else
  {
    return *(Mock.IO_Read_Return_Tail - 1);
  }
}
```

With a little extra work, CMock allows you to customize the generated mocks. You can add the ability to ignore some calls and override others with function pointers.

10.8 Where Are We?

In this chapter, we saw how MockIO is used for testing complex interactions between a driver and the hardware, testing code that would appear to be too hardware-dependent to test off the hardware. Mocks are not just for testing at the hardware level. Mocks are helpful whenever the interactions are complex. Mocks help when you need the test double to be involved in checking for correct behavior as it happens.

In this example we chose a link-time mock. Mocks can also be substituted via a function pointer. A function pointer would be appropriate if you wanted to use the real IO_Read() and IO_Write() functions for some tests. You would go the function pointer route if some tests actually interact with the hardware.

Mocks enforce a strict ordering of interactions, which can lead to fragile tests when the precise ordering of interactions is not critical to correctness. This is not the case in the flash driver examples, where orderings are essential. CppUMock and CMock can take some of the repetition out of creating mocks. Don't put learning the tool in front of trying the concept. Hand-crafting is OK too. As usual, choose the right tool for the job. Simple interactions should lead to using simple test doubles. More complex interactions suggest using mocks.

10.9 Put the Knowledge to Work

1. Use MockIO to implement the CFI command in Appendix B of the device specification in docs/STMicroelectronics/m28w160ect.pdf. Compare your implementation to the vendor's reference driver in docs/StMicroelectronics.

2. Read include/IO/m28w160ect.pdf and implement the *Erase Suspend & Resume Flowchart*.

3. Implement a mock equivalent to MockIO using the CppUMock in CppUTest/include/CppUTestExt.

4. Yeah, I know, you have real work to do. Take one of your device drivers, get it into the test harness, and write characterization tests for a driver you need to change using MockIO, CppUMock, or CMock.

Part III

Design and Continuous Improvement

If you think good architecture is expensive, try bad architecture.
> Brian Foote and Joseph Yoder

CHAPTER 11

SOLID, Flexible, and Testable Designs

To build good designs, it is important to change the usual way of design evaluation from NIH[1] to using SOLID design principles. The five design principles, described in Bob Martin's book (*Agile Software Development, Principles, Patterns, and Practices [Mar02]*), spell the word SOLID.

S   Single Responsibility Principle
O   Open Closed Principle
L   Liskov Substitution Principle
I   Interface Segregation Principle
D   Dependency Inversion Principle

This chapter has two major topics. First we'll look at the SOLID design principles, which are a handful of tried-and-true principles that help build better designs. We'll reflect on how some of the earlier examples in the book follow these principles. In the second major topic of the chapter we will look at advanced C programming approaches as we apply the SOLID principles to C modules. We'll look at some more advanced usage of function pointers to build SOLID, flexible, and testable designs.

Building SOLID designs is important because over the life of a software system, there will be many changing needs for the system and many changing ideas of how to best implement the system. Awareness of SOLID will help us organize our code into modules that have high internal cohesion and are loosely coupled to other modules. They compartmentalize ideas so that code changes tend to be more localized and designs are more testable.

Why is this in a book about TDD? TDD helps drive design. TDD helps you see when a good design starts to go bad. Let's say you can see the code change

---

1. Not Invented Here.

you want to make, but you can't find a decent way to test it. The tests are warning you. The design is starting to deteriorate. TDD is a code-rot radar, and the SOLID design principles help you envision a better design so you can avoid the rot.

11.1 SOLID Design Principles

Let's look at each principle. We'll look at the SOLID influence on the design of some of the examples you've already seen in this book, as well as some new designs.

Single Responsibility Principle

The Single Responsibility Principle (SRP) states that a module should have a single responsibility—it should do one thing, and it should have a single reason to change. Applying SRP leads to modules with good cohesion, modules that are made up of functions and data with a unified purpose—in a nutshell, modules that do a job and do it well.

We've seen SRP at work in the modules in this book. The CircularBuffer, found in Section 9.3, *Surgically Inserted Spy*, on page 152, is responsible for maintaining the integrity of a FIFO data structure holding integers. The LightScheduler, found in Chapter 8, *Spying on the Production Code*, on page 117, turns lights on or off at a scheduled time.

When modules and their functions are well-named, their responsibilities should be clear. There should be little need for complex explanations. The modules, along with their tests, tell their story.

We also applied SRP to functions in a module. Well-focused responsibilities help you recognize where changes should be made as requirements evolve. When this principle is not followed, you get those 1,000-line functions participating in global function and data orgies.

Open Closed Principle

The Open Closed Principle (OCP), described by Meyer in *Object-Oriented Software Construction [Mey97]* and interpreted by Bob Martin, says a module should be "open for extension but closed for modification."

Let me explain OCP by metaphor: a USB port can be extended (you can plug any compliant USB devices into the port) but does not need to be modified to accept a new device. So, a computer that has a USB port is open for extension but closed for modification for compliant USB devices.

When some aspect of a design follows the OCP, it can be extended by adding new code, rather than modifying existing code. We can say that the LightScheduler (from Chapter 8, *Spying on the Production Code*, on page 117) is open for extension for new kinds of LightControllers. Why? If the interface is obeyed, the calling code (the client) does not care about the type of the called code (the server). OCP supports substitution of service providers in such a way that no change is needed to the client to accommodate a new server.

Liskov Substitution Principle

The Liskov Substitution Principle (LSP) was defined by Barbara Liskov in her paper *Data Abstraction and Hierarchy [Lis88]*. Paraphrasing her work, LSP says that client modules should not care which kind of server modules they are working with. Modules with the same interface should be substitutable without any special knowledge in the calling code.

We have seen LSP at work with the test doubles. For example, the client code, LightScheduler, did not have to behave differently when interacting with the server's test double, LightControllerSpy. The client cannot tell the difference.

The Liskov Substitution Principle may sound a lot like the Open Closed Principle. That's because OCP and LSP are two sides of the same coin. But there is more to LSP than just having an interface that links or a compatible function pointer type. The meaning of the calls must be the same. The expectations of both the client and the server must be met.

Nothing additional is required from the LightScheduler when it interacts with a LightControllerSpy or a production LightController. No additional preconditions must be established, and no postconditions are weakened. The LightControllerSpy and LightController are not only syntactically substitutable but are semantically substitutable from the LightScheduler perspective.

In Appendix 5, *Example OS Isolation Layer*, on page 313, you will find an example that illustrates LSP in the design of a operating system isolation layer.

Interface Segregation Principle

The Interface Segregation Principle (ISP) suggests that client modules should not depend on fat interfaces. Interfaces should be tailored to the client's needs. For example, the TimeService, from Section 8.3, *Link-Time Substitution*, on page 119, has a very focused interface. There may be many more time-related functions in the target operating system. Although the target OS tries to be everything for every application, the TimeService is focused on the needs of this system. By tailoring interfaces, we limit dependencies, make code more easily ported, and make it easier to test the code that uses the interface.

Dependency Inversion Principle

In the Dependency Inversion Principle (DIP), Bob Martin tells us that high-level modules shouldn't depend on low-level modules. Both should depend on abstractions. He also says that abstractions should not depend on the details. Details should depend on abstractions. We can break dependencies with abstractions and interfaces.

We often implement DIP In C by using a function pointer to break an unwanted direct dependency. On the left in Figure 24, *Inverting a dependency with a function pointer*, on page 193, the LightScheduler depends directly on *RandomMinute_Get*. The arrow points to the dependency. The high level depends directly on the details. The right side of the figure shows an inverted dependency. Here the high level depends on an abstraction, which is an interface in the form of a function pointer. The details also depend on the abstraction; RandomMinute_Get() implements the interface.

Operating systems use the same mechanism to keep the OS code from depending directly on your code. A callback function is a form of dependency inversion.

When we introduce an abstract data type, like CircularBuffer, we are applying DIP, because the CircularBuffer does not reveal its inner workings. Clients of the CircularBuffer depend on the idea, the abstraction, and not the details.

Dependency inversion in C does not have to involve function pointers or ADTs. In C, it's almost more a state of mind. We applied DIP when the Flash driver called the functions IO_Read() and IO_Write() in Section 10.1, *Flash Driver*, on page 163. We could have interacted with the memory-mapped I/O device directly but abstracted the direct access into the interface.

We are using DIP when:

- implementation details hide behind an interface,
- the interface does not reveal the implementation details,
- a client calls a server through a function pointer,
- a server calls a client back through a function pointer, and
- an ADT hides the details of a data type.

These interrelated principles can give some guidance for avoiding the data structure function call free-for-all all too prevalent in C programming. In the next section, we'll look at more techniques for applying these ideas in C.

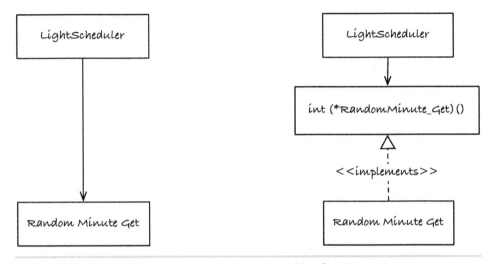

Figure 24—Inverting a dependency with a function pointer

11.2 SOLID C Design Models

In the following sections, we will look at several design models for applying the SOLID principles to C modules. All the examples illustrate SRP and DIP, so I won't call those out. The first two models will be familiar because they have appeared in prior example code. The last two models show how to implement OCP and LSP with C function pointers.

Each model is more complex than the previous model. Each solves some specific design problem at the cost of some added complexity. You can decide whether the complexity is worth it as we work through some examples. Here are the four models we'll look at:

Single-instance module
  Encapsulates a module's internal state when only one instance of the module is needed

Multiple-instance module
  Encapsulates a module's internal state and lets you create multiple instances of the module's data

Dynamic interface
  Allows a module's interface functions to be assigned at runtime

Per-type dynamic interface
  Allows multiple types of modules with the same interface to have unique interface functions

We'll do a quick review of the first two models and relate them to some of the examples earlier in the book. Then we'll go in-depth on the last two models.

Single-Instance Module

You have already seen this model in action in the LightScheduler in Chapter 8, *Spying on the Production Code*, on page 117. Aside from a stand-alone function with no state, this is the simplest module form and will probably be the most often used. Let's review the LightScheduler interface:

```
t0/include/HomeAutomation/LightScheduler.h
#include "TimeService.h"

enum { LS_OK=0, LS_TOO_MANY_EVENTS, LS_ID_OUT_OF_BOUNDS };

void LightScheduler_Create(void);
void LightScheduler_Destroy(void);
int LightScheduler_ScheduleTurnOn(int id, Day day, int minuteOfDay);
int LightScheduler_ScheduleTurnOff(int id, Day day, int minuteOfDay);
void LightScheduler_Randomize(int id, Day day, int minuteOfDay);
void LightScheduler_ScheduleRemove(int id, Day day, int minuteOfDay);
void LightScheduler_WakeUp(void);
```

For single-instance modules, the header file defines everything needed to interact with the module, including the enum for specifying time constants, as well as the function prototypes.

The data structures that the scheduler needs to do its job are hidden as file scope variables in the .c file. The scheduler's data is not needed in the header because no other modules should care. This makes it impossible for other modules to depend on the structure and assures its integrity is the scheduler's responsibility.

Multiple-Instance Module

Sometimes an application needs several instances of a module that contain different data and state. For example, an application might need several first-in first-out data structures. The CircularBuffer, explored in Section 9.3, *Surgically Inserted Spy*, on page 152, is an example of a multiple-instance module. Each instance of CircularBuffer may have its own unique capacity and current contents. Here is what the interface to the CircularBuffer looks like:

```
include/util/CircularBuffer.h
#ifndef D_CircularBuffer_H
#define D_CircularBuffer_H

typedef struct CircularBufferStruct * CircularBuffer;
```

```
CircularBuffer CircularBuffer_Create(int capacity);
void CircularBuffer_Destroy(CircularBuffer);
int CircularBuffer_IsEmpty(CircularBuffer);
int CircularBuffer_IsFull(CircularBuffer);
int CircularBuffer_Put(CircularBuffer, int);
int CircularBuffer_Get(CircularBuffer);
int CircularBuffer_Capacity(CircularBuffer);
void CircularBuffer_Print(CircularBuffer);
#endif  /* D_CircularBuffer_H */
```

This is a well-established design model based on Liskov's abstract data type, introduced in Section 3.1, *Elements of a Testable C Module*, on page 27. As we saw earlier, the members of the CircularBufferStruct are not revealed in the header file. The typedef statement declares that there is a struct of a given name but hides the members of the struct to users of the interface. This prevents users of the CircularBuffer from directly depending upon the data in the struct. The struct is defined in the .c file, hidden from view.

11.3 Evolving Requirements and a Problem Design

Before we go in-depth into the two dynamic interface models, we'll look at a requirements change that led to a problematic design. We'll then see how the dynamic interface models can help create a better design.

So far in the home automation system design, we have not looked at the light-controlling hardware. The LightScheduler and its tests drove the design of the LightController interface introduced in Section 8.2, *Dependencies on Hardware and OS*, on page 118. The interface is intention-revealing and hardware-independent. Creating a test double for the interface allowed us to make concrete progress on the LightScheduler.

Now the product manager and hardware designers have refined some of the requirements. The system must be able to handle different light-controlling technologies in one shipped binary. Also, the light operations will be expanded to support brightening, dimming, and strobe. During system configuration, the administrator of the home automation system selects from one of the supported light-controlling hardware products. Let's look at a not so great, but common, way to handle this situation, and then we'll look at a SOLID design.

A common, though problematic, way to handle hardware variations in C is to use conditional logic during runtime. A design that relies on runtime conditional logic often results in code that is difficult to understand and maintain. The application problem being solved is buried in a mass of conditional logic, making virtually everything a special case. Let's look at the LightController interface and how a runtime choice of light-controlling hardware was shoehorned into the code. Before we get to the problematic part of this design, let's look at the reasonable parts to set the stage.

LightController Interface

t1/include/HomeAutomation/LightController.h
```c
void LightController_Create(void);
void LightController_Destroy(void);
BOOL LightController_Add(int id, LightDriver);
void LightController_TurnOn(int id);
void LightController_TurnOff(int id);
```

Most of the interface is not surprising. Notice that LightController_Add() takes a LightDriver ADT as a parameter and adds it to its internal storage.

A Specific LightDriver

t1/include/devices/LightDriver.h
```c
typedef struct LightDriverStruct * LightDriver;

typedef enum  LightDriverType
{
    TestLightDriver,
    X10,
    AcmeWireless,
    MemoryMapped
} LightDriverType;

typedef struct LightDriverStruct
{
    LightDriverType type;
    int id;
} LightDriverStruct;
```

Each specific type of LightDriver needs to define a struct that begins with an instance of LightDriverStruct, like this:

t1/src/devices/X10LightDriver.c
```c
typedef struct X10LightDriverStruct * X10LightDriver;
typedef struct X10LightDriverStruct
{
    LightDriverStruct base;
    X10_HouseCode house;
    int unit;
    char message[MAX_X10_MESSAGE_LENGTH];
} X10LightDriverStruct;
```

This is a fairly common technique for managing a family of related data structures. By putting LightDriverStruct at the beginning, each member of the family will have the same memory layout for the common data. Don't accidentally use LightDriver in place of LightDriverStruct. The LightDriverStruct is contained by value, not by pointer.

After the LightDriverStruct comes the hardware-specific parameters; in this example, we use the X10 implementation.[2] The X10-specific data includes the house code and the unit number. The house code is set to a value from X10_A to X10_P inclusive. The unit number ranges from 0 to 15. The combination of the two values identifies a specific light. These constants are part of the X10 driver interface.

Here is a representative specific interface, again for X10:

t1/include/devices/X10LightDriver.h
```
#include "LightDriver.h"

typedef enum X10_HouseCode
{
    X10_A,X10_B,X10_C,X10_D,X10_E,X10_F,
    X10_G,X10_H,X10_I,X10_J,X10_K,X10_L,
    X10_M,X10_N,X10_O,X10_P
} X10_HouseCode;

LightDriver X10LightDriver_Create(int id, X10_HouseCode code, int unit);
void X10LightDriver_Destroy(LightDriver);
void X10LightDriver_TurnOn(LightDriver);
void X10LightDriver_TurnOff(LightDriver);
```

The specific LightDriver create functions return a LightDriver ADT. All their driver functions accept the ADT too.

The create function looks like this:

t1/src/devices/X10LightDriver.c
```
LightDriver X10LightDriver_Create(int id, X10_HouseCode house, int unit)
{
    X10LightDriver self = calloc(1, sizeof(X10LightDriverStruct));
    self->base.type = X10;
    self->base.id = id;
    self->house = house;
    self->unit = unit;
    return (LightDriver)self;
}
```

---

2. X10 is an industry standard for device communication used in home automation.

X10LightDriver_Create() takes the common id parameter as well as parameters specific to X10. It allocates memory for the X10 data structure and then populates it. Finally, X10LightDriver_Create() returns the X10LightDriverStruct as LightDriver base type.

X10 driver functions look like this:

t1/src/devices/X10LightDriver.c
```
void X10LightDriver_TurnOn(LightDriver base)
{
    X10LightDriver self = (X10LightDriver)base;
    formatTurnOnMessage(self);
    sendMessage(self);
}

void X10LightDriver_TurnOff(LightDriver base)
{
    X10LightDriver self = (X10LightDriver)base;
    formatTurnOffMessage(self);
    sendMessage(self);
}
```

Drivers start by casting the generic LightDriver pointer into their specific driver type. Then they do whatever detailed work is necessary, which for X10 means formatting a message and sending it to the device.

The Problematic switch Statement

The data structures and X10LightDriver functions we've seen so far in this design are fine. But this design breaks down in the next function. Looking into the LightController, we find a switch statement that knows the type of the currently configured hardware and chooses the implementation to match the type of the hardware.

t1/src/HomeAutomation/LightController.c
```
void LightController_TurnOn(int id)
{
    LightDriver driver = lightDrivers[id];
    if (NULL == driver)
        return;

    switch (driver->type)
    {
    case X10:
        X10LightDriver_TurnOn(driver);
        break;
    case AcmeWireless:
        AcmeWirelessLightDriver_TurnOn(driver);
        break;
```

```c
        case MemoryMapped:
            MemMappedLightDriver_TurnOn(driver);
            break;
        case TestLightDriver:
            LightDriverSpy_TurnOn(driver);
            break;
        default:
            /* now what? */
            break;
    }
}
```

The problem is that the switch statement is going to be repeated, as you can probably anticipate. We will come back to discuss that further after we look at a little more of the design.

The previous code used lightDrivers, an array internal to the LightController that holds all the LightDriver instances. It is created like this:

t1/src/HomeAutomation/LightController.c
```c
static LightDriver lightDrivers[MAX_LIGHTS] =
{ NULL };

void LightController_Create(void)
{
    memset(lightDrivers, 0, sizeof lightDrivers);
}
```

LightController_Create() initializes the driver pointers to NULL. LightController_Destroy() dispatches to the destroy function for each specific LightDriver type.

t1/src/HomeAutomation/LightController.c
```c
static void destroy(LightDriver driver)
{
    if (!driver)
        return;

    switch (driver->type)
    {
    case X10:
        X10LightDriver_Destroy(driver);
        break;
    case AcmeWireless:
        AcmeWirelessLightDriver_Destroy(driver);
        break;
    case MemoryMapped:
        MemMappedLightDriver_Destroy(driver);
        break;
    case TestLightDriver:
        LightDriverSpy_Destroy(driver);
        break;
```

```
        default:
            /* now what? */
            break;
    }
}

void LightController_Destroy(void)
{
    int i;
    for (i = 0; i < MAX_LIGHTS; i++)
    {
        LightDriver driver = lightDrivers[i];
        destroy(driver);
        lightDrivers[i] = NULL;
    }
}
```

Now, back to the problem duplication.

The switch statement's conditional logic is repeated in LightController_TurnOn(), LightController_TurnOff(), and LightController_Destroy().[3] There are other LightDriver requirements coming. We'll need to brighten, dim, and strobe controlled lights as well. This pattern will be duplicated at least three more times.

There is another problem with this code. There is test code, LightDriverSpy_TurnOn(), mixed in with production code. It's good the code can be tested; it's not good that the production code has knowledge of the test code.

The duplicate switch statement is exactly the problem that the Open Closed Principle is designed to address. In Figure 25, *Coupled light driver design*, on page 201, we can see that the LightController knows each of the devices it must manage. Adding a new kind of LightDriver means touching all the switch statements. Adding a new operation results in the need for yet another switch. If the LightController were open for extension for new kinds of LightDrivers, a new driver would plug into the design without the usual slicing and stitching needed for duplicate switch statement *Shotgun Surgery*.[4] We can do better with a SOLID design.

The Test Safety Net

Before we improve this design, let's look at some of the tests that drove the current design; they will be our safety net during the refactoring. Here is the test for LightController_TurnOn() along with its TEST_GROUP:

---

3. You can look for yourself in the code download.
4. Shotgun Surgery is one of Martin Fowler's code smells.

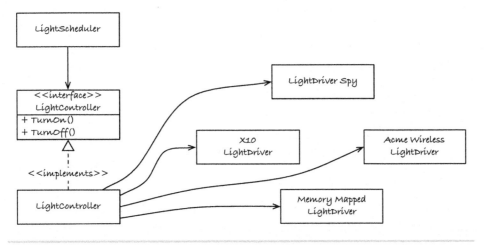

Figure 25— Coupled light driver design

t1/tests/HomeAutomation/LightControllerTest.cpp
```
TEST_GROUP(LightController)
{
    LightDriver spy;

    void setup()
    {
      LightController_Create();
      LightDriverSpy_AddSpiesToController();
    }

    void teardown()
    {
       LightController_Destroy();
    }
};

TEST(LightController, TurnOn)
{
        LightController_TurnOn(7);
        LONGS_EQUAL(LIGHT_ON, LightDriverSpy_GetState(7));
}
```

The TurnOn test shows that the callers of LightController_TurnOn() don't have to concern themselves with LightDrivers; they are hidden from view. The test indirectly confirms the LightController() is working by checking the LightDriverSpy. The LightController is populated with spies, one for each light ID, by LightDriverSpy_AddSpiesToController().

One more thing about the LightController—when a new LightDriver is added on top of a previously added LightDriver, LightController_Add() destroys the old driver before installing the new driver, as this test illustrates:

t1/tests/HomeAutomation/LightControllerTest.cpp
```cpp
TEST(LightController, AddingDriverDestroysPreviousAndDoesNotLeak)
{
    LightDriver spy = LightDriverSpy_Create(1);
    LightController_Add(1, spy);
    LightController_Destroy();
}
```

The test would fail with a leak if the old driver is just overwritten.

Here is the LightDriverSpy interface. You can pretty easily figure out its operation from its interface. The tests in t1/mocks/LightDriverSpyTest.cpp show the behavior explicitly.

t1/mocks/LightDriverSpy.h
```c
#include "LightDriver.h"
#include "LightController.h"

LightDriver LightDriverSpy_Create(int id);
void LightDriverSpy_Destroy(LightDriver);
void LightDriverSpy_TurnOn(LightDriver);
void LightDriverSpy_TurnOff(LightDriver);

/* Functions just needed by the spy */
void LightDriverSpy_Reset(void);
int LightDriverSpy_GetState(int id);
int LightDriverSpy_GetLastId(void);
int LightDriverSpy_GetLastState(void);
void LightDriverSpy_AddSpiesToController(void);

enum {
    LIGHT_ID_UNKNOWN = -1, LIGHT_STATE_UNKNOWN = -1,
    LIGHT_OFF = 0, LIGHT_ON = 1
};
```

Like any LightDriver, LightDriverSpy can be created, destroyed, turned on, and turned off. You can see that in the first part of the spy's interface. The second part of the interface is for debriefing the spy after its mission.

In terms of the SOLID design principles, the previous design does not follow OCP for adding new kinds of drivers. The LightController knows each LightDriver type. You can anticipate Shotgun Surgery whenever a new driver type is added. The fact that there are already several types of drivers (in the online code base) is evidence that the design should be improved.

11.4 Improving the Design with Dynamic Interface

Now that we've reviewed the existing design with its duplicate conditional logic, let's improve the design and eliminate the duplication with a dynamic interface.

A dynamic interface uses one or more function pointers to allow the implementation of a given function to be chosen at runtime. This single level of indirection provides runtime flexibility.[5] Function pointers are a powerful language feature that allow the caller of a function to avoid a compile or link-time dependency on a particular function.

Applying OCP and LSP

We can apply the Open Closed and the Liskov Substitution Principles to eliminate the redundant conditional logic. The design vision is illustrated in Figure 26, *Extendable light driver design*, on page 204. In this design, the LightController is open for extension for new LightDrivers while being closed for modification. Unlike the previous design, the LightController has no knowledge of any specific LightDrivers.

We'll keep most of the existing design and refactor out the duplicate switch statements to a design that uses function pointers. This will eliminate the direct dependencies on specific driver functions such as X10LightDriver_TurnOn() or LightDriverSpy_TurnOn().

We could change all the LightDriver prototypes into function pointers; you have seen how to do that with the RandomMinute example found in Section 9.1, *Testing Randomness*, on page 147. I prefer to keep the function pointers behind the scenes as private data, so we will implement the function pointers under the hood of the LightDriver. It makes for a cleaner interface and less global data to abuse.

I won't show each refactoring step but enough to get the idea of the incremental transformation of the design. If you are following along in the code, make sure you build with every small change.

Envision the Change in the Test

Recall that the administrator can choose the supported light-controlling technology during system configuration. Let's test-drive the interface of the LightDriver using the LightDriverSpy as an example.

---

5. This is the basis of *polymorphism* in object-oriented programming.

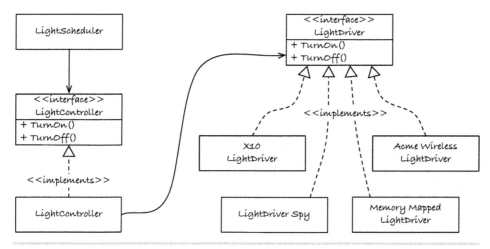

Figure 26— **Extendable light driver design**

t1/mocks/LightDriverSpyTest.cpp
```
TEST_GROUP(LightDriverSpy)
{
    LightDriver lightDriverSpy;

    void setup()
    {
        LightDriverSpy_Reset();
        lightDriverSpy = LightDriverSpy_Create(1);
        // LightDriverSpy_InstallInterface();
    }

    void teardown()
    {
        LightDriverSpy_Destroy(lightDriverSpy);
    }
};

TEST(LightDriverSpy, On)
{
    //LightDriver_TurnOn(lightDriverSpy);
    LightDriverSpy_TurnOn(lightDriverSpy);
    LONGS_EQUAL(LIGHT_ON, LightDriverSpy_GetState(1));
}
```

There are two commented-out lines. We need two new functions to try the idea. LightDriverSpy_InstallInterface() tells the spy to install its function pointers into the LightDriver. LightDriver_TurnOn() dispatches through the installed function pointer. Once we make LightDriver_TurnOn() work, we can apply the same idea to the other two functions.

Function Pointer Interface

The following code shows the struct that holds the function pointers for each driver function:

t2/include/devices/LightDriverPrivate.h
```
typedef struct LightDriverInterfaceStruct
{
    void (*TurnOn)(LightDriver);
    void (*TurnOff)(LightDriver);
    void (*Destroy)(LightDriver);
} LightDriverInterfaceStruct;
```

Notice the name of the file holding the data structures. By naming the file LightDriverPrivate.h, we're letting the world know that they should ignore the details of the data structures. Unlike CircularBuffer, we could not define the struct in the .c file; multiple files need to know the struct layout.

The interface is set on the LightDriver like this:

t2/src/devices/LightDriver.c
```
static LightDriverInterface interface = NULL;

void LightDriver_SetInterface(LightDriverInterface i)
{
    interface = i;
}
```

The generic LightDriver_TurnOn() function calls the specific driver through this interface struct, passing a pointer to the LightDriver ADT.

t2/src/devices/LightDriver.c
```
void LightDriver_TurnOn(LightDriver self)
{
    interface->TurnOn(self);
}
```

Drivers Don't Change

The LightDriver functions themselves do not change, just how the LightController gets to them. Here is the existing LightDriverSpy_TurnOn() function:

t2/mocks/LightDriverSpy.c
```
void LightDriverSpy_TurnOn(LightDriver base)
{
    LightDriverSpy self = (LightDriverSpy)base;
    states[self->base.id] = LIGHT_ON;
    lastId = self->base.id;
    lastState = LIGHT_ON;
}
```

Here the spy initializes its TurnOn() function pointer to point to LightDriver-Spy_TurnOn(), while leaving the other two pointers NULL.

t2/mocks/LightDriverSpy.c
```
static LightDriverInterfaceStruct interface =
{
    LightDriverSpy_TurnOn,
    0,
    0
};
```

Once we have LightDriver_TurnOn() passing its tests, we can follow the same approach to LightDriver_TurnOff() and LightDriver_Destroy().

When we've finished, the LightDriver interface looks like this:

t2/include/devices/LightDriver.h
```
typedef struct LightDriverStruct * LightDriver;

typedef struct LightDriverInterfaceStruct * LightDriverInterface;

void LightDriver_SetInterface(LightDriverInterface);
void LightDriver_Destroy(LightDriver);
void LightDriver_TurnOn(LightDriver);
void LightDriver_TurnOff(LightDriver);
const char * LightDriver_GetType(LightDriver);
int LightDriver_GetId(LightDriver);

#include "LightDriverPrivate.h"
```

Protect Against NULL Pointers

Before we change LightController to call the new LightDriver functions, let's protect the LightDriver functions from NULL pointers. We'll have to test for NULL interface and NULL driver instances. It might seem trivial to test these cases, but if it is important enough to go in the production code, it is important enough to test.

This interface structure that will help us test the NULL conditions.

t2/tests/devices/LightDriverTest.cpp
```
#define NONSENSE_POINTER (LightDriver)~0
static LightDriver savedDriver = NONSENSE_POINTER;
static void shouldNotBeCalled(LightDriver self) { savedDriver = self ;}

LightDriverInterfaceStruct interface =
{
    shouldNotBeCalled,
    shouldNotBeCalled,
    shouldNotBeCalled
};
```

```
LightDriverStruct testDriver =
{
    "testDriver",
    13
};
```

In the next test, we don't expect the stub function shouldNotBeCalled() to be called. If it is, the savedDriver will be changed from the NONSENSE_POINTER value of all ones to NULL. Here is the test that checks for the NULL pointer being passed to the driver functions:

t2/tests/devices/LightDriverTest.cpp
```
TEST(LightDriver, NullDriverDoesNotCrash)
{
    LightDriver_SetInterface(&interface);
    LightDriver_TurnOn(NULL);
    LightDriver_TurnOff(NULL);
    LightDriver_Destroy(NULL);
    POINTERS_EQUAL(NONSENSE_POINTER, savedDriver);
}
```

So, you can see in the previous test that a valid interface is set, but NULL LightDriver instances are passed to the driver functions.

This next test protects against an uninitialized interface, which is set to NULL by default. The test resets the interface to NULL and makes sure that no drivers are called.

t2/tests/devices/LightDriverTest.cpp
```
TEST(LightDriver, NullInterfaceDoesNotCrash)
{
    LightDriver_SetInterface(NULL);
    LightDriver_TurnOn(&testDriver);
    LightDriver_TurnOff(&testDriver);
    LightDriver_Destroy(&testDriver);
    POINTERS_EQUAL(NONSENSE_POINTER, savedDriver);
}
```

Those tests drove the addition of the validity check on each of the LightDriver functions. Here is LightDriver_TurnOn(), for example:

t2/src/devices/LightDriver.c
```
void LightDriver_TurnOn(LightDriver self)
{
    if (isValid(self))
        interface->TurnOn(self);
}
```

isValid() was extracted into its own helper function to eliminate the duplicate conditional clause in each of the driver functions.

```
t2/src/devices/LightDriver.c
static BOOL isValid(LightDriver self)
{
    return interface && self;
}
```

With the NULL checks done by LightDriver, none of the specific drivers need to do NULL checks.

Eliminating the Switch

We are almost ready to eliminate the switch statements from LightController for destroy, turn on, and turn off. But first, add a call to LightDriverSpy_AddSpiesTo-Controller() and LightDriverSpy_InstallInterface() to the LightController and LightScheduler tests' setup() functions.

Here is the updated TEST_GROUP(LightController):

```
t2/tests/HomeAutomation/LightControllerTest.cpp
TEST_GROUP(LightController)
{
    void setup()
    {
        LightController_Create();
        LightDriverSpy_AddSpiesToController();
        LightDriverSpy_InstallInterface();
        LightDriverSpy_Reset();
    }

    void teardown()
    {
        LightController_Destroy();
    }
};

TEST(LightController, TurnOn)
{
    LightController_TurnOn(7);
    LONGS_EQUAL(LIGHT_ON, LightDriverSpy_GetState(7));
}
```

Test should still pass. Now, one at a time, remove the switch statement and add a call to the appropriate LightDriver function. After refactoring, the turn-on and turn-off functions look like the following:

```
t2/src/HomeAutomation/LightController.c
void LightController_TurnOn(int id)
{
    LightDriver_TurnOn(lightDrivers[id]);
}
```

```c
void LightController_TurnOff(int id)
{
    LightDriver_TurnOff(lightDrivers[id]);
}
```

After that change, you might feel the LightController is not really pulling its weight, but its main job is to map from the light ID to the associated driver. It's pulling its weight with that single responsibility.

Hide the Details

With the driver function calls going through the function pointers, the Light-Driver implementations should be converted to file scope, making it impossible to call them directly. The driver functions should be called only through their associated function pointer.

t2/mocks/LightDriverSpy.c
```c
static void destroy(LightDriver base)
{
    free(base);
}
static void update(int id, int state)
{
    states[id] = state;
    lastId = id;
    lastState = state;
}
static void turnOn(LightDriver base)
{
    LightDriverSpy self = (LightDriverSpy)base;
    update(self->base.id, LIGHT_ON);
}
static void turnOff(LightDriver base)
{
    LightDriverSpy self = (LightDriverSpy)base;
    update(self->base.id, LIGHT_OFF);
}
```

Here is the fully initialized struct, pointing to the file scope implementations:

t2/mocks/LightDriverSpy.c
```c
static LightDriverInterfaceStruct interface =
{
    turnOn,
    turnOff,
    destroy
};
```

This style of data structure initialization is error prone; the initializer order must match the struct member declaration order. Being ANSI compliant, it's the most portable way to initialize the structure. If you have a C99-compatible compiler, you could use this approach:

```
t2/mocks/LightDriverSpy.c
static LightDriverInterfaceStruct interface =
{
    .Destroy = destroy,
    .TurnOn = turnOn,
    .TurnOff = TurnOff,
};
```

The advantage of this approach is that it's harder to mess up the initialization. Also, any unmentioned fields are set to zero. Think of this as applying the DRY principle.[6] Only one place in the code cares about the ordering of the structure members. If all you have is ANSI C, don't worry; you have the tests to help keep you safe. Also, if you had functions that are not supported by all drivers, those drivers cannot even mention the unsupported operations, and the default do-nothing behavior can be implemented like this:

```
t2/src/devices/LightDriver.c
void LightDriver_SetBrightness(LightDriver self, int level)
{
    if(isValid(self) && interface->setBrightness)
        interface->setBrightness(self, level);
}
```

We've converted the design to be open for extension for new kinds of drivers. Each of the specific drivers is also changed to meet the LightControllers interface expectations. We have a flexible enough design for today's requirements. But what happens when those requirements change, as they always do?

11.5 More Flexibility with Per-Type Dynamic Interface

Good news from marketing—we just sold 1,000 units. Supporting other manufacturers has really opened the market!

The bad news is that someone in marketing did not get the memo that we handle a homogeneous manufacturer's equipment at only one installation. They sold systems claiming our machine can work with any combination of supported vendor hardware. It's already printed on the packaging materials and user's guide.

---

6. Don't Repeat Yourself

Why is opportunity usually followed by a design change? No worries. It's great to have the opportunity, and our clean design can evolve the design to handle the market need.

Let's look at how we can evolve the design to meet the new need. To customize the driver type per light, each driver struct needs an associated set of function pointers. Instead of just one interface pointer, as in the dynamic interface model, each LightDriverStruct has a pointer to a table of interface functions. This is the same mechanism used in C++ for implementing virtual functions. Calling a function declared as virtual in C++ means the function is called through a virtual function table (*vtable*). We'll convert our design to use a vtable.

A Test with Two Different Drivers

First let's design a test to drive the work. To show that the design can simultaneously handle more than one set of function pointers, we will need another test double module to use along with the LightDriverSpy. Let's add a simple test double that counts calls to TurnOn() and TurnOff(). With a CountingLightDriver, we can write this test:

```
t3/tests/HomeAutomation/LightControllerTest.cpp
TEST(LightController, turnOnDifferentDriverTypes)
{
    LightDriver otherDriver = CountingLightDriver_Create(5);
    LightController_Add(5, otherDriver);
    LightController_TurnOn(7);
    LightController_TurnOn(5);
    LightController_TurnOff(5);

    LONGS_EQUAL(LIGHT_ON, LightDriverSpy_GetState(7));
    LONGS_EQUAL(2, CountingLightDriver_GetCallCount(otherDriver));
}
```

The test creates a CountingLightDriver, with an id of 5, and adds it to the LightController, replacing one of the LightDriverSpy instances. When the test case turns on light number 7, it is using a LightDriverSpy installed during setup(). Turning on light 5, and then off, results in the CountingLightDriver reporting two calls.

Let's look at the new test double.

Call Counting Test Double

The CountingLightDriver follows the same conventions as any other driver.

```
t3/mocks/CountingLightDriver.c
typedef struct CountingLightDriverStruct * CountingLightDriver;

typedef struct CountingLightDriverStruct
```

```
{
    LightDriverStruct base;
    int counter;
} CountingLightDriverStruct;
```

This function increments a counter for each CountingLightDriver.

t3/mocks/CountingLightDriver.c
```
static void count(LightDriver base)
{
    CountingLightDriver self = (CountingLightDriver)base;
    self->counter++;
}
```

count() will be installed into the interface table for the CountingLightDriver. The initial create function looks like the others and is compatible with the other already defined drivers.

t3/mocks/CountingLightDriver.c
```
LightDriver CountingLightDriver_Create(int id)
{
    CountingLightDriver self = calloc(1, sizeof(CountingLightDriverStruct));
    self->base.type = "CountingLightDriver";
    self->base.id = id;
    return (LightDriver)self;
}
```

Here is an accessor function for getting the count out of the CountingLightDriver.

t3/mocks/CountingLightDriver.c
```
int CountingLightDriver_GetCallCount(LightDriver base)
{
    CountingLightDriver self = (CountingLightDriver)base;
    return self->counter;
}
```

Test-Driving in the Vtable

Our new test continues to fail as the changes are made. Now we can rewire the code to meet the new requirement. First let's add a vtable field into the LightDriverStruct. This will let each LightDriver instance point to the LightDriverInterface for that type.

t3/include/devices/LightDriverPrivate.h
```
typedef struct LightDriverStruct
{
    LightDriverInterface vtable;
    const char * type;
    int id;
} LightDriverStruct;
```

Let's go back to the CountingLightDriver and install the interface into the vtable. Here is the interface struct:

t3/mocks/CountingLightDriver.c
```c
static LightDriverInterfaceStruct interface =
{
        count, count, destroy
};
```

CountingLightDriver_Create() initializes the vtable member. Notice that all instances of the same type point to the same function table.

t3/mocks/CountingLightDriver.c
```c
LightDriver CountingLightDriver_Create(int id)
{
    CountingLightDriver self = calloc(1, sizeof(CountingLightDriverStruct));
    self->base.vtable = &interface;
    self->base.type = "CountingLightDriver";
    self->base.id = id;
    return (LightDriver)self;
}
```

So far, we have not changed the LightDriver to dispatch through the vtable. Before we change the LightDriver, let's set the vtable field for LightDriverSpy.

t3/mocks/LightDriverSpy.c
```c
LightDriver LightDriverSpy_Create(int id)
{
    LightDriverSpy self = calloc(1, sizeof(LightDriverSpyStruct));
    self->base.vtable = &interface;
    self->base.type = "Spy";
    self->base.id = id;
    return (LightDriver)self;
}
```

After a clean compile, make the LightDriver functions dispatch through the vtable member of LightDriver instead of the LightDriver's single interface pointer. It's best to try them one at a time. That way, if there is a problem, we won't have a lot of work to do to get back to working code. As long as we leave the interface pointer alone, dispatches to LightDriverSpy will continue to work.

Here is LightDriver_TurnOn():

t3/src/devices/LightDriver.c
```c
void LightDriver_TurnOn(LightDriver self)
{
    if (self)
        self->vtable->TurnOn(self);
}
```

Notice the validity check is simpler. It only has to check that the driver is not NULL, because all drivers are responsible for initializing a vtable.

If you run the tests with just LightDriver_TurnOn() dispatching through the vtable, there will be one failing test. CountingLightDriver_GetCallCount() reports a single call when in the end there should be two.

Here are the unsurprising implementations of the other two dynamically called driver functions. You can brave and change both, knowing the first one worked. But if anything goes wrong, try them one at a time.

t3/src/devices/LightDriver.c
```c
void LightDriver_TurnOff(LightDriver self)
{
    if (self)
        self->vtable->TurnOff(self);
}

void LightDriver_Destroy(LightDriver self)
{
    if (self)
        self->vtable->Destroy(self);
}
```

You might decide that you don't want to trust all the drivers to initialize their pointers. In that case, you would want to have this implementation and the associated tests. (Again, if it is important enough to go into the production code, it is important enough to test.)

t3/src/devices/LightDriver.c
```c
void LightDriver_TurnOn(LightDriver self)
{
    if (self && self->vtable && self->vtable->TurnOn)
        self->vtable->TurnOn(self);
}
```

At this point, the per-type dynamic interface design works! All that is left is to apply the same changes to the other driver types and throw out the interface setting and installing functions from LightDriver and the specific light drivers.

11.6 How Much Design Is Enough?

At the start of a new development effort, there is considerable uncertainty. There are unknowns in hardware, software, product goals, and *requirements*. How can we get started with all this uncertainty? Isn't it better to wait? If you wait, there really is no end to the waiting, because certainty will never come. So, it's better to get started sooner even though some things will change later.

I am not suggesting that you shouldn't think ahead—it's impossible not to. But you *can* choose what you will act on now vs. what you will act on later. There is a thin line between thinking ahead and analysis paralysis. When you start piling guesses on top of guesses, consider that you've gone too far ahead, and it's time to try the ideas in code.

When there is uncertainty in the hardware/software boundary, you can start from the inside by solving the application problem, working your way to where application code can articulate what it wants from the hardware. Create an interface that provides exactly the services the application needs from the hardware. The LightScheduler/LightController relationship is an example of this. The LightController became part of our *hardware abstraction layer*.

A nice side effect of the application driving the interface is that hardware implementation details are less likely to pollute the application's core. The LightScheduler knows nothing about X10 or any of the other drivers, and that's a good thing.

We saw that the design had to evolve as requirements became more clear during the LightController to LightDriver evolution. That's no failure; that's good news that we've learned more. The problem with much of the legacy code out there today is that as requirements evolved, designs were not improved to more naturally accept the changes.

We can't anticipate all the coming product changes; that is why we have to get good at design evolution. Underlying many of these ideas are the Extreme Programming *Rules of Simple Design* (from http://c2.com/xp/XpSimplicityRules.html). Let's look at them and see how they help us keep the design good for today's requirements.

XP Rules of Simple Design

1. **Runs all the tests.**
   The code must do what is needed. Why bother if it does not?

2. **Expresses every idea that we need to express.**
   The code should be self-documenting, communicating the intention of the programmer.

3. **Says everything once and only once.**
   Duplication must be removed so that as things change, the same idea does not have to be changed in numerous places.

4. **Has no superfluous parts.**
   This final rule prevents us from putting in things that are not yet needed.

The rules are evaluated in order. Rule 1 rules them all. If the code does not meet its intended purpose, demonstrated by passing tests, the code is not valuable to anyone. Rules 2 and 3 help with the maintainability of the code, keeping it clean with a design fit for today's requirements. The first three rules speak for themselves but rule 4 is a little more difficult to understand.

The fourth rule tells us to not over-engineer the design. It should be perfect for the currently implemented features. Adding complexity early delays features and integration opportunities. It wastes time when the premature design is wrong. Living with unused or unneeded design elements slows progress. Designs always evolve. We need to be good at keeping the design right for the currently supported features.

That fourth rule may be the hardest to follow for people new to TDD. Like I said before, it's OK to think ahead; just try to act on the design vision only when the tests pull it in. Having the tests as a safety net makes this a very practical and productive way to work.

11.7 Where Are We?

In this chapter, we looked at the SOLID design principles and four design models for keeping C modules flexible and when to use them. We looked at how designs earlier in the book were influenced by SOLID. We also went beyond the earlier examples and looked at how to effectively use function pointers to reduce coupling between C modules.

The function pointer is an important C capability that is often overlooked by programmers. It plays a very important role in the application of SOLID in C, making code more flexible and testable. It's a helpful tool for eliminating duplicate conditional logic.

With a dynamic interface, the system can choose a specific implementation of a function at runtime. For example, as the system initializes itself the software can interrogate the hardware to determine the hardware environment. Then driver functions can be installed based on the kind of hardware discovered. Instead of spreading the decisions making around the system, the decision is made once, and the system is configured to support the situation.

As I've suggested, and the XP Rules of Simple Design reinforce, choose an appropriate model for the job. Don't add complexity before it is needed. Choose the simplest option that passes all tests, expresses the programmer's intent, and has no duplication.

11.8 Put the Knowledge to Work

1. Look at the application of OCP and LSP in MyOS in Appendix 5, *Example OS Isolation Layer*, on page 313. Evolve MyOS to support Mutex and Event. A Mutex can be acquired and released. One thread can wait for a signal from another thread.

2. Add an accessor function to get the return result from a joined thread by calling Thread_Result(). (You can find my work on that in t1/tests/MyOS, t1/include/MyOS, and t1/src/MyOS.)

3. Make a list of all the changes needed to add LightDriver functions for brighten, dim, and strobe to the LightDriver in the code/t1 code base.

4. Add LightDriver functions for brighten, dim, and strobe to the LightDriver and LightDriverSpy in the code/t3 code base. Test-drive this, of course. Compare the work needed in code/t1 to code/t3.

5. Some interfaces do not support brighten and dim. Such a device's driver should do nothing when those operations are called. Test-drive your design change.

6. Other modules need their own instance of RandomMinute. Evolve RandomMinute to allow its random number generator to be seeded (see srand() in the C library). Convert RandomMinute, FakeRandomMinute, and tests to use the per-type dynamic interface.

Humpty Dumpty sat on a wall,
Humpty Dumpty had a great fall.
All the king's horses and all the king's men
couldn't put Humpty together again.
> *Traditional English Nursery Rhyme*

CHAPTER 12

Refactoring

A well-designed system won't stay well-designed unless there is constant care and energy put back into the code to avoid software entropy.[1] As a multitude of little and big changes are applied to the code, it is natural for disorder to grow if you don't take the time to counteract the disorganization.

Many of the ideas in this chapter come from Martin Fowler's book *Refactoring, Improving the Design of Existing Code [FBBO99]*. It is an excellent resource to get a greater understanding of refactoring.

Martin Fowler says, "Any fool can write code that the compiler understands, but it takes real skill to write code other programmers can understand." With the potential long life of code we write, writing code that other programmers can understand is critical to our product's success.

So, what is refactoring? Refactoring is the modifying of a computer program's structure, without modifying its behavior. Why would anyone want to do that? Isn't it all about behavior? Who really cares about a program's structure besides idealist software developers? Let's look at software's inherent values to answer those questions.

12.1 Two Values of Software

Software systems have two inherent values—one obvious, one not so obvious. The obvious value is in what the software does. When you place a phone call with your cell phone, software does a lot of the work. It makes the call possible. Software keeps your car's engine running smoothly. Software keeps your bank accounts in order. The internal structure of the code does not matter

---

1. Entropy is the measure of a system's disorganization.

as long as the code behaves itself, right? No, that's wrong. Code structure is the key to the less obvious value of software.

Software must be soft; it must be easy to change. Easy to change has huge business value. Think back to that marketing request that seemed so trivial, but it had to wait for next year's release to make it into the product. Was it caused by hard-to-understand, overly complex, and inconsistent code? Some of you might be nodding right now.

What happened to that beautiful design? How did it rot? Well, it slowly degraded because changes in functionality were not accompanied by changes in design. Code rots one line at a time.

If marketing would only make their mind up, we could have beautiful code. This is flawed thinking. The world is ever-changing; why should your *requirements* not change? Fighting requirements changes is usually a losing battle. Compare today's requirements to last year's or to five year ago. Would it have been possible to anticipate those requirements and build the code to handle them? Probably not, but even if you could, that would have wasted precious time to market for earlier products.

With refactoring, we accept change as a given and get good at dealing with change. We enhance the critical, but not so visible, value of software by keeping code clean. What is clean code? You can find many answers to that question in Bob Martin's book *Clean Code [Mar08]*. Simply put, in my own words, code should be easy for someone to understand and modify.

12.2 Three Critical Skills

The relationship between the three critical skills needed to be successful in keeping code clean is illustrated in Figure 27, *Three critical refactoring skills*, on page 221. First, the developer needs a good nose for code smells, but that is not enough. The developer also needs to envision a better design, a bright idea. The final skill is to transform the design from one structure to another, keeping it running and passing its tests the whole time.

Let's talk a little more about each of these critical skills.

A Nose for Bad Code

There is a tendency in our profession to apply the *Not Invented Here* (NIH) factor when evaluating design and code. It goes something like this: code invented by me, I like; code invented by someone else, I don't like. Although an easy-to-learn code evaluation technique, it is not really that useful.

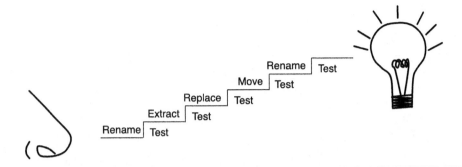

Figure 27— Three critical refactoring skills

Instead of "that code stinks," we must develop a keen sense of code smells. Like a chef or a gardener, we should be able to identify different smells. If we can identify a particular code smell, we have a better chance of eliminating the bad smell. In Fowler's book, he describes a number of code smells. We'll be exploring code smells in Section 12.3, *Code Smells and How to Improve Them*, on page 222.

A Vision of Better Code

Once we sense what's wrong with the code, next we draw on our knowledge of code and design to envision a better solution. The SOLID design principles provide some guidance for structure and coupling. This skill takes the longest to master, requiring study and experience. Other design envisioning comes more easily, like choosing better names and seeing segments of code to extract.

Transform the Code

Given the current state of the code and a vision of the destination, we perform a series of code changes, or *refactorings*, that move the code toward the improved design. For simple changes, maybe the series requires only a single refactoring. More complex changes may require many steps and incremental change over time.

Without the ability to transform one working design into another, you incur great risk, the same risk the Humpty Dumpty faced while sitting on that high wall, described in Figure 28, *Refactoring vs. Humpty Dumpty design change*, on page 222.[2]

---

2. Humpty Dumpty from *The Book of Knowledge*, p. 968, Vol. III, The Grolier Society, New York, 1911. Public domain image found at http://commons.wikimedia.org/wiki/File:Humpty-Dumpty.jpg.

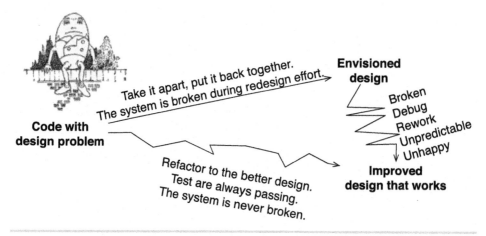

Figure 28— Refactoring vs. Humpty Dumpty design change

You are likely to discover that the envisioned design and the improved design that works are different, once you get into the code and understand the details better.

Notice that refactoring is used as either a noun or a verb. I could say, "I am refactoring the LightScheduler" or "I think we should use the extract function refactoring."

12.3 Code Smells and How to Improve Them

In this section, we'll look at many of the code smells found in C code. We'll also envision some design changes that can make the situation better. As I mentioned, Fowler has a list of code smells, but his list is more suitable for the smells found in code written in an object-oriented programming language. Some apply to C, but then C also has its own common smells.

Duplicate Code

Duplicate code is essentially the root cause of most code smells. The problems of duplication are well known and were discussed earlier in *DRY: Don't Repeat Yourself*, on page 69.

Bad Names

Good names make code easier to understand; bad names make code obscure. Sometimes you'd think there is a penalty for using vowels or whole words in C code.

Tim Ottinger has some good advice for naming in his chapter in *Clean Code* [Mar08]. The advice is written from an object-oriented perspective but is still applicable to C. My brief advice on names is about making code easier to come back to or read the first time:

- Make names readable. Avoid abbreviations and acronyms. Use LightScheduler, not lht_sched.

- Reveal intended outcome in function names, not internal workings: Find(), not BinarySearch()

BinarySearch() might be fine for a library function, where several search algorithms are available. But in the context of solving some domain-specific problem, a function like FindScheduledEvent() is much better than BinarySearchForScheduledEvent().

Bad Pasta

We've all heard of spaghetti code, but it's not the only pasta in the programming pantry. Besides spaghetti, there's ravioli, lasagna, and meatballs with the spaghetti code.[3]

We all know spaghetti code—it's that snarled mess of code that keeps you from knowing what is going on. This kind of code is typified by high *Cyclomatic Complexity*.[4]

Ravioli code, on the other hand, consists of small self-contained packets loosely coupled with a tomato-based sauce. When it comes to code, ravioli is a good pasta. Some people say that if the ravioli packets get too small, you can't see what is going on because processing is spread over too many packets. I suspect you don't have that problem. Large mounds of spaghetti is usually the problem.

Lasagna code[5] is typified in a layered architecture, with cohesion in the layer and loose coupling between layers. Again, it's a more desirable pasta-based code structure than spaghetti. Sometimes lasagna code comes with spaghetti in the layers; that's better than just spaghetti but not as good as just lasagna.

Finally, there is spaghetti and meatball code. It's a tangled mess, with some modular code that depends on the tangled mess. This is ideally a code base in transition to greater modularity, but it could go both ways.

---

3. http://en.wikipedia.org/wiki/Spaghetti_code
4. Cyclomatic Complexity is the number of paths through a function. A big number is bad.
5. The term was coined by database guru Joe Celko in 1982.

The transition from spaghetti code can be a long one. It usually starts by extracting small functions from big functions and grouping related data together. After several rounds of extractions, function dependencies on subsets of data become evident. The data groupings and the functions that operate on them can be extracted to form new modules or form layers. You'll increase the ravioli and lasagna and rely less on a strict spaghetti diet. Your code structure will be moving in the right direction.

Long Function

The *Long Function* is the offspring of most C coding smells. "How long should a function be?" Should it be one screen, twenty-five lines, fifty lines, or a hundred lines?

That first answer, one screen, is reportedly in a lot of coding standards. That coding standard is routinely violated, but it's a hard one to measure when you have these high-res screens and tiny fonts.

A function is too long if it cannot quickly fit in your head. Sometimes that is one line but rarely a screenful at any font size. A hundred-line switch statement that simply dispatches to one of N workers is not a problem. You can quickly understand why it is the way it is.

There is some evidence that allowing code to spread to more than one screen is probably very bad for quick comprehension. The study by Hidetake Uwano et al. in *Analyzing Individual Performance of Source Code Review Using Reviewers' Eye Movement [UNMM07]*, used eye movement to better understand a programmer's cognitive action while trying to understand a segment of source code. In Figure 29, *Tracking eye movement during code review*, on page 225, we can see where the eye, and consequently the mind, focuses attention during the act of understanding code.

The researchers found that code reviewers first performed an initial scan of the code and then focused in on some detail. You can see the quick scan in the first sixty eye fixations followed by the deep dive beyond the 60th fixation. If the code did not fit on a page, there would be a lot scrolling and searching for variable declarations, references, and manipulations.

I conclude from Dr. Uwano's data that there is a penalty paid when trying to understand a long function. Letting a function spread beyond one screenful will definitely make it difficult to fit the code in your head. On the other hand, a twenty-five line function with complex conditionals and looping and global data references probably won't fit too quickly into your head either.

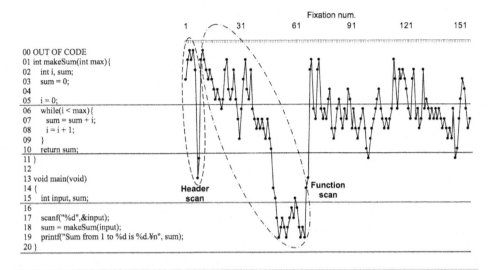

Figure 29— Tracking eye movement during code review

With the next code example, imagine that we inherited the LightScheduler rather than building it ourselves as we did in Chapter 8, *Spying on the Production Code*, on page 117. It has tests, but it has problems.

t2/src/HomeAutomation/LightScheduler.c
```
void LightScheduler_WakeUp(void)
{
    int i;
    Time time;
    TimeService_GetTime(&time);
    Day td = time.dayOfWeek;
    int min = time.minuteOfDay;

    for (i = 0; i < MAX_EVENTS; i++)
    {
        ScheduledLightEvent * se = &eventList[i];
        if (se->id != UNUSED)
        {
            Day d = se->day;
            if ( (d == EVERYDAY) || (d == td) || (d == WEEKEND &&
                    (td == SATURDAY || td == SUNDAY)) ||
                    (d == WEEKDAY && (td >= MONDAY
                                        && td <= FRIDAY)))
            {
                /* it's the right day */
                if (min == se->minuteOfDay + se->randomMinutes)
                {
                    if (se->event == TURN_ON)
                        LightController_TurnOn(se->id);
```

```
            else if (se->event == TURN_OFF)
                LightController_TurnOff(se->id);

            if (se->randomize == RANDOM_ON)
                se->randomMinutes = RandomMinute_Get();
            else
                se->randomMinutes = 0;

            }
          }
        }
      }
}
```

It's hard to see what is going on. There are short and cryptic names and five levels of nesting. How many responsibilities does LightScheduler_WakeUp() have? Quite a few. A function with a single responsibility will tell its story much better.

t2/src/HomeAutomation/LightScheduler.c
```
void LightScheduler_WakeUp(void)
{
    int i;
    Time time;

    TimeService_GetTime(&time);

    for (i = 0; i < MAX_EVENTS; i++)
    {
        processEventsDueNow(&time, &eventList[i]);
    }
}
```

By extracting the contents of the for loop into a well-named function, the responsibility of LightScheduler_WakeUp() is clear—it for processes scheduled events that are due now.

Higher-level functions should look high level and read like a use case, inasmuch as that is possible in C. High-level functions delegate to lower-level functions to do the work. I don't mean there are only two levels; this pattern repeats as we get to the code that does the dirty work. Code like this acts as an index on the underlying implementation, making it so the programmer can find the part of the code they are interested in.

Intention-revealing names are much easier to relate to than the nitty-gritty detail found in long C functions. As evidence, see how main() (shown in Figure 29, *Tracking eye movement during code review*, on page 225) is visited only once and the low-level C is studied with nearly a hundred eye fixations?

Enough ranting on about long functions; what should we do about it? The obvious answer is the right answer—make them smaller. As a function grows, it should be broken into pieces.

When you add new functionality and the function starts to get *too long*, split out a new function. If you are tempted to put in a comment for a block of code, instead create a new function with a descriptive name and move the code there.

This refactoring has a name. Fowler calls it *Extract Method*. It's a rather object-oriented name where functions that are part of an object are called *methods*. In C let's just call it *Extract Function*.

Long functions do too much, violating the Single Responsibility Principle. They obscure potentially useful ideas and hide duplication. To get rid of long functions, we need a nose that can detect the root causes. The next few smells often contribute to long functions.

Abstraction Distraction

Each function should have a consistent level of abstraction. C functions tend to exhibit a code smell Fowler calls *Primitive Obsession*. The high-level ideas are lost in the noise produced by primitive types and operations.

The roller coaster of abstraction levels is distracting. Shifting levels of abstraction should happen with purpose. Code exhibiting *Abstraction Distraction* is often fixed like a long function is fixed, with some function extractions.

Bewildering Boolean

You are staring at the code. The ANDs, ORs, and parentheses are making your mind numb. You ask, "What is this conditional for?" You are bewildered, and your brain has recognized the *Bewildered Boolean* code smell. How much more time do you have to spend interpreting this code:

```
if (!(day == EVERYDAY || day == today
    ||(day == WEEKEND && (SATURDAY == today
    || SUNDAY == today)) || (day == WEEKDAY
    && today >= MONDAY && today <= FRIDAY)))
    return;
```

compared to code that is intention-revealing like this:

```
if (!matchesToday(day))
    return;
```

With the refactored code segment, the dependent variable is obvious. The intention of the conditional is obvious. If you're interested in the day-matching logic, look into matchesToday(). If you are not, there is no need to waste time interpreting the complex conditional.

Switch Case Disgrace

The switch/case goes on for pages; some cases have nested switch or if statements. This code won't quickly fit into anyone's head.

Functions with switch/case statements should follow the Single Responsibility Principle. The function should be about determining the case and then doing something simple or delegating to something to do the work.

Duplicate Switch Case

When the switch/case logic is duplicated but with different actions, it's time to think of replacing the need for duplicate switch/case logic by applying the Open/Closed Principle and using a design that employs one of the patterns in the previous chapter.

Nefarious Nesting

Deeply nested code is hard to understand, especially when there are hanging else statements that have to be matched up or loops within loops. Even having just a couple levels of nesting, with its beautiful cascading curly braces look, is hard to understand.

If the code has a loop, with nested conditional logic, consider making it a function that is only about the loop, with a helper function that does the work each iteration through the loop. An interesting consequence of this is that the helper function could be tested separately from the loop. This is important to making code testable.

Feature Envy

Martin Fowler describes feature envy from a object-oriented design perspective. To paraphrase, one object is envious of another if it grabs the other's data, operates on it, and then puts it back into the other object or produces some derived output.

In C, this is basically what happens when a data structure is passed around or globally accessed. It may not be obvious which module owns a given struct that is part of a data structure/function call free-for-all.

Feature envy often leads to a lot of duplication. When there is no place to put code that manipulates a particular data structure, each function that wants to use the struct is likely to have to do the same work as other users of the struct. Just to illustrate how out of control this can get, consider the Y2K reengineering that consumed so much effort at the end of the 1990s. Too much code had to deal with years that contained two digits.

We can improve modularity, improve coupling, and reduce duplication by using the OO concepts and data abstraction discussed in *Multiple-Instance Module*, on page 194.

Long Parameter List

How many parameters are too many? That depends on the context. When a common parameter is duplicated in many function signatures, it's a pretty good indication that a new data structure is needed.

Like many code problems, *Long Parameter List* tends to happen over time. Initially, just a couple parameters are needed. Then another is added and later another. Functions start to get long, so someone tries to do the right thing and extract a helper function. In doing so, the long parameter list is copied. A few more cell divisions, and you have a duplicate long parameter list mess.

To improve the situation, we need a new module. The duplicate parameter list becomes the core of a new module. One of the calls with the long parameter list becomes the module's initialization function. The other functions replace their long parameter list with a pointer to the newly defined struct.

Willy-Nilly Initialization

The *Willy-Nilly Initialization* smell tickles your nostrils when you start adding tests to existing legacy code. You find that a lot of manual initialization of data is needed before a test can run without crashing the tests.

A likely root cause to this problem is that there are no distinct initialization functions for the data structures involved; the data structures tend to get initialized willy-nilly.[6] The code shows no real distinction made between initialization and running.

Improving this smell involves collecting related initialization code into one place and making initialization obvious. You might find that if you start developing tests for legacy code that you will write these functions out of necessity in the test cases. Once you have them there, consider migrating the initialization code back into the production code and eliminate some Willy-Nilly Initialization.

---

6. Willy-nilly: in a haphazard or spontaneous manner

Global Free-for-All

A *Global Free-for-All* is made of numerous global variables and data structures. There is no clear ownership of the data. Any function can access any global data. Globals often suffer from Willy-Nilly Initialization. They also are a strong coupling force. Adding tests to code with lots of globals is a challenge, because one test might leave state information in the globals that break other tests or, just as bad, that other tests start to depend upon.

File scope variables can have a negative impact on testability too. Data held in static variables is retained between test runs. A test that might work fine one minute is broken the next because a static (or global) is not in the right state for the test. The single-instance module relies on static variables but does not suffer from data retention when initialization functions are provided.

To combat the global free-for-all, consider encapsulating globals in protective function calls. One of the calls should be for properly initializing the global data. If global data is a struct, consider converting its use to an abstract data type.

Comments

Comments sometimes are necessary but are more often a weakness. The goal of refactoring is to have well-structured code where the code speaks for itself. Save comments for when there is no other way. Martin Fowler suggests that "Comments are often used as a deodorant."

Why am I disparaging comments? Comments tend to get stale. Over time, comments tend to fall into disrepair and become lies. Programmers don't trust comments. Fowler also says, "Comments are a code smell when they are out-of-date."

Well-structured code won't need many comments. Also, some comments are duplication. Why maintain the same idea twice? I've seen plenty of comment headers like this where comments are mandated. Have a look at the code in Figure 30, *A Mandated Comment Block*, on page 231. Is this mandated comment worth the effort to maintain it? No. It adds no value and took time to create.

When should we use comments? Use them when the code cannot be made clear through good names and structure. They should be used when code cannot speak for itself, like working around a problem API or for code that *had* to be optimized and is no longer as clear as it could be. Use comments to describe why a particular implementation is chosen over some other. Use comments at the module level to establish context and describe responsibility.

```
/*******************************************
 * Function:
 *   BOOL Time_IsLeapYear(int year)
 *
 * Parameters
 *   year - the year to test for leap year
 *
 * Returns
 *   TRUE - for leap years
 *   FALSE - for non-leap years
 *
 * Process
 *   years evenly divisible by 4 but not
 *   divisible by 100, except when divisible by
 *   400 return TRUE, otherwise FALSE
 *******************************************/
BOOL Time_IsLeapYear(int year)
{
    if (year % 400 == 0)
        return TRUE;
    if (year % 100 == 0)
        return FALSE;
    if (year % 4 == 0)
        return TRUE;
    return FALSE;
}
```

Figure 30—A Mandated Comment Block

What should we do with our existing comments? Use your existing comments as hints to how to restructure the code. Try to replace a comment with an extracted and well-named function. Delete valueless comments.

Your code can speak for itself much better when a module has a single responsibility, is well named, and has functions that reveal intention. When you are tempted to add a comment, see whether you can get the code to speak for itself by extracting a function and naming it well. If after following this advice a comment is still needed, add it.

Commented-Out Code

Source files littered with commented-out code are an ugly mess. New or returning programmers are faced with questions about what the code is supposed to do. "Should the code be uncommented?" "Is it no longer needed?" "When will it be needed and under what circumstances is it needed?" "What's that for?!"

The solution to this code smell is simple; delete the commented-out code. It can always be recovered from your source repository.

Conditional Compilation

Code littered with conditional compilation is hard to follow. Sometimes conditional compilation is unavoidable, but it should be considered the tool of last choice when dealing with platform variations. Conditional compilation used in a focused way might not be so bad, but often the conditional compilation approach spreads platform dependencies around the code.

When looking through a client's code, I saw a lot of conditional compilation. Large chunks of their code were bracketed by #ifdef BOARD_V1 or #ifdef BOARD_V2. I got curious and listed all occurrences of BOARD_V2. There were thousands of them. The code was out of control. The code size basically doubled from version 1 to version 2. I guess the code only going up by 50 percent on the next board could be viewed as an improvement, but not to me. They told me they knew it was a bad idea, but they were in a hurry. I doubt this brute-force method of incorporating BOARD_V2 cost them more than an approach that improved the design and brought together the commonality of the boards and separated the differences.

I prefer using the linker or function pointers to isolate platform dependencies, like we did with TimeService and LightDriver, respectively. We grouped platform-dependent code, bounding the work of changing platforms. And we kept the platform-dependent and independent code separate. The independent code is your long-term investment. There's another example of this in CppUTest. Look at PlatformSpecificFunctions.h and the implementations in the Platforms directory.

12.4 Transforming the Code

About half of Martin Fowler's book is a catalog of refactorings. Each refactoring has a name, a problem that it solves, and a series of detailed steps that guide you through a code transformation. Fowler uses Java in his examples, but there is still plenty of useful advice for embedded C programmers.

To give you the feel of refactoring, we'll refactor a long function. As we refactor, I'll introduce some helpful techniques and a guiding principle.

Like in the real world, most of your time will be spent extracting functions from long functions. Aside from Rename, Extract Function is the most often used refactoring. Extracting functions reveals the work the long function is doing, raising its level of abstraction. In the process, *I suspect* we'll discover a function that is out of place; we'll move it.

We saw this code earlier, when it was part of LightScheduler_WakeUp(). In addition to extracting this function, the cryptic names have been replaced by better names.

`t2/src/HomeAutomation/LightScheduler.c`
```c
static void processEventsDueNow(Time * time, ScheduledLightEvent * event)
{
    Day today = time->dayOfWeek;
    int minuteOfDay = time->minuteOfDay;

    if (event->id != UNUSED)
    {
        Day day = event->day;
        if ( (day == EVERYDAY) || (day == today) || (day == WEEKEND &&
                (today == SATURDAY || today == SUNDAY)) ||
                (day == WEEKDAY && (today >= MONDAY
                                    && today <= FRIDAY)))
        {
            /* it's the right day */
            if (minuteOfDay == event->minuteOfDay + event->randomMinutes)
            {
                if (event->event == TURN_ON)
                    LightController_TurnOn(event->id);
                else if (event->event == TURN_OFF)
                    LightController_TurnOff(event->id);

                if (event->randomize == RANDOM_ON)
                    event->randomMinutes = RandomMinute_Get();
                else
                    event->randomMinutes = 0;
            }
        }
    }
}
```

What's that smell? It's a long function, of course, with root causes in bewildering boolean and nefarious nesting. Now we need to identify which ideas to pull out of this code and put in their own functions.

Envision the Code You Wish You Had

When envisioning a better code structure, it's helpful to add a comment before the offending code that represents the code you wish you had, like this:

`t2/src/HomeAutomation/LightScheduler.c`
```c
static void processEventsDueNow(Time * time, ScheduledLightEvent * event)
{
    Day today = time->dayOfWeek;
    int minuteOfDay = time->minuteOfDay;
```

```
    if (event->id != UNUSED)
    {
        Day day = event->day;
        /* if (isEventDueNow()) */
        if ( (day == EVERYDAY) || (day == today) || (day == WEEKEND &&
                (today == SATURDAY || today == SUNDAY)) ||
                (day == WEEKDAY && (today >= MONDAY
                                && today <= FRIDAY)))
        {
            if (minuteOfDay == event->minuteOfDay + event->randomMinutes)
            {
                /* operateLight(); */
                if (event->event == TURN_ON)
                    LightController_TurnOn(event->id);
                else if (event->event == TURN_OFF)
                    LightController_TurnOff(event->id);
                /* resetRandomize(); */
                if (event->randomize == RANDOM_ON)
                    event->randomMinutes = RandomMinute_Get();
                else
                    event->randomMinutes = 0;
            }
        }
    }
}
```

I added several comments for the functions I wished I had. These are not permanent comments; they are comments that help envision better code. It's more common to add the comments one at a time, especially in a really long function. I'm showing several because it would have been fine to start with any one of them.

Choose a name that reveals the intention of the function from the caller's perspective. Try to make in-function comments unnecessary; code should read like a story—well, a story that a computer geek can read.

Evaluate Signatures

When you are about to extract a function, evaluate the needed parameters and return types. Let's consider the parameters needed for each of these extraction candidates, and I'll justify my decisions. You might arrive at a different conclusion.

- Should isEventDueNow() be passed the time or does it get it? Should it know about events or just the day and minute of interest?

    Let's pass in the time because we want all events to be evaluated against the same time.

Let's also pass in the event. That keeps isEventDueNow() at a higher level of abstraction.

isEventDueNow() takes the place of the Bewildering Boolean, so it must return a BOOL.

- Should operateLight() know about event or just the light operation and ID?

    We'll pass in the event; two struct members are needed, and the function is useful only in this .c file.

    operateLight() has no return value.

- It looks like resetRandomize() needs to know the event; not only is it queried, it is modified.

    Also, resetRandomize() has no return value.

Now that we have a good idea of the parameters, let's extract the functions using an important principle.

Don't Burn Bridges Principle

Let's start by extracting an easy one, operateLight(). Notice the comment now includes the parameter event like we decided while evaluating the signature needed:

t2/src/HomeAutomation/LightScheduler.c
```c
/* operateLight(event); */
if (event->event == TURN_ON)
    LightController_TurnOn(event->id);
else if (event->event == TURN_OFF)
    LightController_TurnOff(event->id);
```

Copy, don't cut, from the start of the comment to the end of the code to be included in operateLight(). Paste it into the file before processEventsDueNow(); add the return type, parameter, and curly braces. Get it to compile. It will look like this:

t2/src/HomeAutomation/LightScheduler.c
```c
static void operateLight(ScheduledLightEvent * event)
{
    if (event->event == TURN_ON)
        LightController_TurnOn(event->id);
    else if (TURN_OFF == event->event)
        LightController_TurnOff(event->id);
}
```

Only after the extracted function compiles do you delete the old code and call the new. The edit to go from the old working code to the newly extracted code should be easy to undo. I like to uncomment the call to the extracted function and then select and delete old code. If tests pass, processEventsDueNow() is a little better. If they fail, a couple undos will restore the code that passes all your tests.

A natural instinct for programmers who are not used to working with comprehensive automated unit tests is to cut the code being extracted out of its original home. Then create a new function, paste in the cut code, modify it so it compiles, and finally call the extracted function. As soon as you have cut the code out of its original home, the code is broken. The code might compile, but it won't pass its tests. Your new bridge is incomplete; your old bridge is burning.

Keep your working bridge intact during construction of the new bridge. Watch the tests run one final time before cutting over to the new code. When something goes wrong, resist the urge to debug. Restore the original code, and look for what went wrong with the safety of passing tests.

Ignore this advice at your own peril. If you choose to try a fix or two, be aware of the bridge back to working code.

Avoid Abstraction Distraction

After pulling out isEventDueNow(), operateLight(), and resetRandomize() into static functions, the processEventsDueNow() looks like the following:

t2/src/HomeAutomation/LightScheduler.c
```
static void processEventsDueNow(Time * time, ScheduledLightEvent * event)
{
    if (event->id != UNUSED)
    {
        if (isEventDueNow(time, event))
        {
            operateLight(event);
            resetRandomize(event);
        }
    }
}
```

You can't really call this function long, in the sense of the number of lines of code, but something is still wrong; there are two levels of abstraction. Asking if (event->id != UNUSED) is notably different from the other lines in this function. scheduleEvent() (which we last saw in Section 8.6, *Make It Work for None, Then One*, on page 127) makes a similar comparison. Let's DRY this code; extract the conditional into a new function:

```
t2/src/HomeAutomation/LightScheduler.c
static BOOL isInUse(ScheduledLightEvent * event)
{
    return event->id != UNUSED;
}
```

Once the extract function compiles, replace the conditional with the new function, and run the tests.

```
t2/src/HomeAutomation/LightScheduler.c
static void processEventsDueNow(Time * time, ScheduledLightEvent * event)
{
    if (isInUse(event))
    {
        if (isEventDueNow(time, event))
        {
            operateLight(event);
            resetRandomize(event);
        }
    }
}
```

With isInUse(), the abstraction is consistent. Let's flatten the function by replacing nesting with a guard clause.

```
t2/src/HomeAutomation/LightScheduler.c
static void processEventsDueNow(Time * time, ScheduledLightEvent * event)
{
    if (!isInUse(event))
        return;

    if (isEventDueNow(time, event))
    {
        operateLight(event);
        resetRandomize(event);
    }
}
```

Now, let's get rid of the duplicate conditional.

Remove Duplication

We'll come back to isEventDueNow() after we make scheduleEvent() use isInUse(), eliminating the duplicate conditional.

```
t2/src/HomeAutomation/LightScheduler.c
static void scheduleEvent(int id, Day day, long int minuteOfDay, int control,
        int randomize)
{
    int i;
```

```c
    for (i = 0; i < MAX_EVENTS; i++)
    {
        if (!isInUse(&eventList[i]))
        {
            eventList[i].id = id;
            eventList[i].day = day;
            eventList[i].minuteOfDay = minuteOfDay;
            eventList[i].event = control;
            eventList[i].randomize = randomize;
            resetRandomize(&eventList[i]);
            break;
        }
    }
}
```

scheduleEvent() is not reading so well. It is really two ideas: finding an open slot in the event table and populating the slot.

Separate Ideas

Let's separate the finding of a vacant slot from saving the schedule data. Finding a vacant slot should be its own function. But, the code is not ready to extract a find function unless we want it to return the index. I'd prefer it to return a pointer to an available slot. So for starters, let's get rid of the clutter of all the array indexing.

t2/src/HomeAutomation/LightScheduler.c
```c
static void scheduleEvent(int id, Day day, long int minuteOfDay, int control,
        int randomize)
{
    int i;
    ScheduledLightEvent * event = 0;
    for (i = 0; i < MAX_EVENTS; i++)
    {
        if (!isInUse(&eventList[i]))
        {
            event = &eventList[i];
            event->id = id;
            event->day = day;
            event->minuteOfDay = minuteOfDay;
            event->event = control;
            event->randomize = randomize;
            resetRandomize(event);
            break;
        }
    }
}
```

We introduced a pointer and changed from array to pointer syntax. Run the tests. (I made an editing mistake during that last "too simple to fail" step. The tests caught it.)

Now we can separate the find loop from the event data initialization:

t2/src/HomeAutomation/LightScheduler.c
```c
static void scheduleEvent(int id, Day day, long int minuteOfDay, int control,
        int randomize)
{
    int i;
    ScheduledLightEvent * event = 0;

    for (i = 0; i < MAX_EVENTS; i++)
    {
        if (!isInUse(&eventList[i]))
        {
            event = &eventList[i];
            break;
        }
    }

    if (event)
    {
        event->id = id;
        event->day = day;
        event->minuteOfDay = minuteOfDay;
        event->event = control;
        event->randomize = randomize;
        resetRandomize(event);
    }
}
```

With that change, we can copy the loop code into findUnusedEvent() and make it compile:

t2/src/HomeAutomation/LightScheduler.c
```c
static ScheduledLightEvent * findUnusedEvent(void)
{
    int i;
    ScheduledLightEvent * event = 0;
    for (i = 0; i < MAX_EVENTS; i++)
    {
        if (!isInUse(&eventList[i]))
        {
            event = &eventList[i];
            return event;
        }
    }
    return NULL;
}
```

After the clean compile, we change scheduleEvent() to call findUnusedEvent().

t2/src/HomeAutomation/LightScheduler.c
```c
static void scheduleEvent(int id, Day day, long int minuteOfDay, int control,
        int randomize)
{

    ScheduledLightEvent * event = findUnusedEvent();

    if (event)
    {
        event->id = id;
        event->day = day;
        event->minuteOfDay = minuteOfDay;
        event->event = control;
        event->randomize = randomize;
        resetRandomize(event);

    }
}
```

That's better, but there are now two levels of abstraction represented in scheduleEvent(). Extracting the event initialization would level the abstraction.

t2/src/HomeAutomation/LightScheduler.c
```c
static void setEventSchedule(ScheduledLightEvent * event,
        int id, Day day, long int minute, int control, int randomize)
{
        event->id = id;
        event->day = day;
        event->minuteOfDay = minute;
        event->event = control;
        event->randomize = randomize;
        resetRandomize(event);
}
```

Here's scheduleEvent() with a consistent level of abstraction:

t2/src/HomeAutomation/LightScheduler.c
```c
static void scheduleEvent(int id, Day day, long int minute, int control,
        int randomize)
{

    ScheduledLightEvent * event = findUnusedEvent();

    if (event)
        setEventSchedule(event, id, day, minute, control, randomize);
}
```

Tests are passing, so now clean up findUnusedEvent() like this:

```
t2/src/HomeAutomation/LightScheduler.c
static ScheduledLightEvent * findUnusedEvent(void)
{
    int i;
    ScheduledLightEvent * event = eventList;

    for (i = 0; i < MAX_EVENTS; i++, event++)
    {
        if (!isInUse(event))
            return event;
    }
    return NULL;
}
```

Notice in the previous refactoring that we introduced a temporary variable to help the code read a little better.

We have scheduleEvent() and its helpers in order; let's go back to isEventDueNow().

Organizing a Bewildering Boolean

We swept the big messy conditional under the rug:

```
t2/src/HomeAutomation/LightScheduler.c
static BOOL isEventDueNow(Time * time, ScheduledLightEvent * event)
{
    Day today = time->dayOfWeek;
    int minuteOfDay = time->minuteOfDay;
    Day day = event->day;
    if ( (day == EVERYDAY) || (day == today) || (day == WEEKEND &&
        (today == SATURDAY || today == SUNDAY)) ||
         (day == WEEKDAY && (today >= MONDAY
                          && today <= FRIDAY)))
    {
        if (minuteOfDay == event->minuteOfDay + event->randomMinutes)
            return TRUE;
    }
    return FALSE;
}
```

The essential questions being asked are "Is it the scheduled day, and is it the scheduled minute?"

Let's separate the nested conditional from the body of the compound conditional. If it's not the right minute, the day is irrelevant.

```
t2/src/HomeAutomation/LightScheduler.c
static BOOL isEventDueNow(Time * time, ScheduledLightEvent * event)
{
    Day today = time->dayOfWeek;
    int minuteOfDay = time->minuteOfDay;
```

```
    Day day = event->day;

    if (minuteOfDay != event->minuteOfDay + event->randomMinutes)
        return FALSE;

    if ( (day == EVERYDAY) || (day == today)
            || (day == WEEKEND &&
                (today == SATURDAY || today == SUNDAY))
            || (day == WEEKDAY && (today >= MONDAY
            && today <= FRIDAY)))
        return TRUE;

    return FALSE;
}
```

Copy the complex conditional, and put it in its new home.

t2/src/HomeAutomation/LightScheduler.c
```
static BOOL daysMatch(Day scheduledDay, Day today)
{
    if ((day == EVERYDAY) || (day == today)
            || (day == WEEKEND &&
                (today == SATURDAY || today == SUNDAY))
            || (day == WEEKDAY && (today >= MONDAY
            && today <= FRIDAY)))
        return TRUE;
    return FALSE;
}
```

This compiles but is still messy. Before we cut over to the extracted daysMatch(), let's clean it up.

t2/src/HomeAutomation/LightScheduler.c
```
static BOOL daysMatch(Day scheduledDay, Day today)
{
    if (scheduledDay == EVERYDAY)
        return TRUE;
    if (scheduledDay == today)
        return TRUE;
    if (scheduledDay == WEEKEND && (today == SATURDAY || today == SUNDAY))
        return TRUE;
    if (scheduledDay == WEEKDAY && (today >= MONDAY && today <= FRIDAY))
        return TRUE;
    return FALSE;
}
```

It looks nicer and compiles, but many tests fail. Something is wrong with the extracted code. Get back to passing tests by restoring isEventDueNow() with a couple undos.

While we figure this out, we might have to change code in existing isEvent-DueNow() and new daysMatch() functions. Undo on error might be kind of cumbersome. Let's try the *quick swap* technique.

Quick Swap

Quick swap lets you swap between two implementations quickly. It preserves the old working code while you try to get the new broken code to pass the tests. Quick swap uses conditional compilation to switch between the pre- and postrefactored code, like this:

t2/src/HomeAutomation/LightScheduler.c
```c
static BOOL isEventDueNow(Time * time, ScheduledLightEvent * event)
{
    Day today = time->dayOfWeek;
    int minuteOfDay = time->minuteOfDay;
    Day day = event->day;

    if (minuteOfDay != event->minuteOfDay + event->randomMinutes)
        return FALSE;

#if 1
    if (daysMatch(today, day))
        return TRUE;
#else
    if ( (day == EVERYDAY) || (day == today)
            || (day == WEEKEND &&
            (today == SATURDAY || today == SUNDAY))
            || (day == WEEKDAY && (today >= MONDAY
            && today <= FRIDAY)))
        return TRUE;
#endif
    return FALSE;
}
```

After finding the silly mistake, tests pass. Here's the working daysMatch:

t2/src/HomeAutomation/LightScheduler.c
```c
static BOOL daysMatch(Day today, Day scheduledDay)
{
    if (scheduledDay == EVERYDAY)
        return TRUE;
    if (scheduledDay == today)
        return TRUE;
    if (scheduledDay == WEEKEND && (today == SATURDAY || today == SUNDAY))
        return TRUE;
    if (scheduledDay == WEEKDAY && (today >= MONDAY && today <= FRIDAY))
        return TRUE;
    return FALSE;
}
```

I accidentally reversed the parameters to daysMatch() during the extraction. The safety net caught the mistake. (It would have been better to call daysMatch() from isEventDueNow() before cleaning it up.)

We could take the refactoring further and extract each conditional. If these checks were duplicated (which they are not), it would be best to extract them, eliminating the duplication. It's a judgment call. We'll stop here.

Don't forget the final step of the quick swap. Delete the conditional compilation used in the quick swap. Don't leave it in case you need it again; you won't. It will only confuse future programmers who look at this code.

t2/src/HomeAutomation/LightScheduler.c
```c
static BOOL isEventDueNow(Time * time, ScheduledLightEvent * event)
{
    Day today = time->dayOfWeek;
    int minuteOfDay = time->minuteOfDay;
    Day day = event->day;

    if (minuteOfDay != event->minuteOfDay + event->randomMinutes)
        return FALSE;
    if (!daysMatch(today, day))
        return FALSE;
    return TRUE;
}
```

Now that we've isolated daysMatch(), it seems a little out of place. That function has an obvious case of *Feature Envy*. This sounds like a job for *Move Function*.

Move Function

daysMatch() has more to do with TimeService than LightScheduler. All the constants are part of TimeService, and one of the parameters comes from the Time data structure. It is likely that daysMatch() functionality is or will be duplicated in other TimeService clients that need to compare days and metadays. TimeService is not doing its job. This is the essence of Feature Envy.

Before we move daysMatch(), let's let it know more about TimeService by passing time to it, rather than today. This eliminates LightScheduler's knowledge of the dayOfWeek member of Time.

After testing the changed signature, make a copy of daysMatch(). Name it so that it will fit in well in TimeService and get it to compile.

t2/src/HomeAutomation/LightScheduler.c
```c
BOOL Time_MatchesDayOfWeek(Time * time, Day day)
{
    int today = time->dayOfWeek;
    if (day == EVERYDAY)
```

```
        return TRUE;
    if (day == today)
        return TRUE;
    if (day == WEEKEND && (today == SATURDAY || today == SUNDAY))
        return TRUE;
    if (day == WEEKDAY && today >= MONDAY && today <= FRIDAY)
        return TRUE;
    return FALSE;
}
```

I named the new function with the prefix Time because the function is all about interrogating the Time structure. After a clean compile, modify isEventDueNow() to use Time_MatchesDayOfWeek(). The test should pass.

t2/src/HomeAutomation/LightScheduler.c
```
static BOOL isEventDueNow(Time * time, ScheduledLightEvent * event)
{
    int minuteOfDay = time->minuteOfDay;
    Day day = event->day;

    if (minuteOfDay != event->minuteOfDay + event->randomMinutes)
        return FALSE;
    if (!Time_MatchesDayOfWeek(time, day))
        return FALSE;
    return TRUE;
}
```

Your compiler should be warning you now that daysMatch() is not used. Delete it now.

To be consistent, the minute matching conditional should also be moved to TimeService. This relieves LightScheduler of any knowledge of the internals of Time. We extract the helper in the same usual way.

t2/src/HomeAutomation/LightScheduler.c
```
BOOL Time_MatchesMinuteOfDay(Time * time, int minuteOfDay)
{
    return time->minuteOfDay == minuteOfDay;
}
```

With tests passing, isEventDueNow() looks like this:

t2/src/HomeAutomation/LightScheduler.c
```
static BOOL isEventDueNow(Time * time, ScheduledLightEvent * event)
{
    int todaysMinute = event->minuteOfDay + event->randomMinutes;
    Day day = event->day;
    if (!Time_MatchesMinuteOfDay(time, todaysMinute))
        return FALSE;
    if (!Time_MatchesDayOfWeek(time, day))
        return FALSE;
```

```
    return TRUE;
}
```

Tests are running, and we're almost ready to move the new functions. First add the function prototypes to TimeService.h and then build.

Obviously, when we move functions, we have to delete the original or we'll have a duplication function in our system. So, when we build after the move and see a problem, we immediately suspect that we left the original behind.

```
❮ make
[...]
Linking t2_tests
ld: duplicate symbol _TimeService_Create in lib/libt2.a(TimeService.o)
                                    and mocks/FakeTimeService.o
```

We have a *duplicate symbol* error but not because of the newly moved functions. TimeService production code and the test double are colliding. Before proceeding, we better revert to when the tests pass.

Splitting the Source File

The LightScheduler test fixture uses the linker to substitute a test double for the OS-dependent TimeService functions. With the latest change, the TimeService has both platform-dependent and independent functions. The tests should use the platform-independent implementations of Time_MatchesDayOfWeek() and Time_MatchesMinuteOfDay() but use the test-double version of TimeService_GetTime(). In object-oriented programming this would be called an *abstract class* or a *partial abstraction*. To mimic the concept of a partial abstraction in C using a link-time test double, we need to split the production code into two files. We end up with these three files:

- Time.c: Holds the platform-independent Time functions.
- TimeService.c: Holds the platform-specific functions that can be overridden by the linker.
- FakeTimeService.c: Holds the test double functions that override the platform-specific functions.

Earlier in Chapter 9, *Runtime-Bound Test Doubles*, on page 147, we used function pointers to override one (but not all) of the functions in the RandomMinute. Function pointers let you be selective about which functions to override and when. Splitting the source file is another dependency management tool in your toolbox. We split the source file so that the operating system–dependent code can be overridden at link time, while keeping the time comparison functions.

Why didn't we use function pointers? First, the OS-dependent code will never need to be swapped in during host-based testing. Second, and more significantly, it is likely that the target-dependent code would not even compile on the development system. So, splitting target-dependent from target-independent code would have been needed anyway.

Add Tests for Moved Function

With Time_MatchesDayOfWeek() moved to Time.c, it should have its own tests. The existing tests provide the safety net for the refactoring, but for the long-term the new functions need their own tests. The tests document the code's responsibility and make sure any future failures of the Time functions are caught directly by its own tests and not as a side effect of some other test.

With time checking now in the Time module, we can do exhaustive tests:

```
t2/tests/util/TimeTest.cpp
TEST_GROUP(Time)
{
    Time time;
     void setup()
    {
      TimeService_Create();
    }
    void givenThatItIs(Day day)
    {
        FakeTimeService_SetDay(day);
    }
    void CheckThatTimeMatches(Day day)
    {
        TimeService_GetTime(&time);
        CHECK(Time_MatchesDayOfWeek(&time, day));
    }
    void CheckThatTimeDoesNotMatch(Day day)
    {
        TimeService_GetTime(&time);
        CHECK(!Time_MatchesDayOfWeek(&time, day));
    }
};

TEST(Time, ExactMatch)
{
    givenThatItIs(MONDAY);
    CheckThatTimeMatches(MONDAY);
    givenThatItIs(TUESDAY);
    CheckThatTimeMatches(TUESDAY);
    givenThatItIs(WEDNESDAY);
    CheckThatTimeMatches(WEDNESDAY);
    givenThatItIs(THURSDAY);
```

```
    CheckThatTimeMatches(THURSDAY);
    givenThatItIs(FRIDAY);
    CheckThatTimeMatches(FRIDAY);
    givenThatItIs(SATURDAY);
    CheckThatTimeMatches(SATURDAY);
    givenThatItIs(SUNDAY);
    CheckThatTimeMatches(SUNDAY);
}

TEST(Time, WeekendDays)
{
    givenThatItIs(SATURDAY);
    CheckThatTimeMatches(WEEKEND);
    givenThatItIs(SUNDAY);
    CheckThatTimeMatches(WEEKEND);
}

TEST(Time, NotWeekendDays)
{
    givenThatItIs(MONDAY);
    CheckThatTimeDoesNotMatch(WEEKEND);
    givenThatItIs(TUESDAY);
    CheckThatTimeDoesNotMatch(WEEKEND);
    givenThatItIs(WEDNESDAY);
    CheckThatTimeDoesNotMatch(WEEKEND);
    givenThatItIs(THURSDAY);
    CheckThatTimeDoesNotMatch(WEEKEND);
    givenThatItIs(FRIDAY);
    CheckThatTimeDoesNotMatch(WEEKEND);
}
```

In the code download, you can find the tests for WEEKDAY and EVERYDAY.

You can also see that this refactoring, along with adding Time tests, means that many of the scheduled-day centric tests could (and should) be eliminated. Ideally, any single production code problem should only cause a single test failure that points right at the problem. By the way, this ideal does not really happen much in practice but should not stop us from having focused tests.

Incremental Cutover

In a code base that had a lazy module like TimeService, it is likely that there are other places in the code that can use the new time-matching functions. This would be a good time to seek them out and incrementally change them. You also want to delete no longer needed test cases as you transition the code to use the newly moved functions. This can eliminate a lot of duplicate tests.

Encapsulate Data Structure

From the LightScheduler's perspective, Time could be an abstract data type, as we discussed in *Multiple-Instance Module*, on page 194. LightScheduler no longer accessed any members of Time. If no other clients directly access the members of Time, we can hide its internals. The internals of Time become opaque.

Hiding data is important. The Y2K problem at the end of the last millennium illustrates the point. Too much code depended upon the date's representation. When a well-known data representation changes, there will be some serious Shotgun Surgery to perform.

12.5 But What About Performance and Size?

Some of you may be concerned over the *extra* functions and function calls that are the result of refactoring, maybe for speed, maybe for memory size. You may have such constrained environments that you have to squeeze every last *bit* of space and performance out of it. My advice, as well as that of many others, is to first structure code for clarity and optimize only when measurements support the optimizations.

Make It Work, Then Right, Then Fast

In *Extreme Programming Explained [Bec00]*, Kent Beck promotes this motto:

- Make it work.
- Make it right.
- Make it fast.

What would you rather do, debug some optimized tricky code or optimize some clean and well-factored code? It's not a trick question. Making clean code fast is much easier than making tricky code work.

The first statement, *make it work*, is all about getting the code to perform the correct behavior. Your tests help you get the code to have the right behavior and to keep the right behavior while making it right and fast. To get the tests to pass, do whatever it takes, including cut/paste/hack. Breaking a good design is fair in this game, as long as you don't skip the *make it right* step.

Make it right means clean up the code. Make the code follow the Rules of Simple Design that are discussed at the end of Chapter 11, *SOLID, Flexible, and Testable Designs*, on page 189. Refactor the code: make the names right, make the code's intention clear, remove duplication, and keep the design simple. Removing duplication is likely to be highly aligned with keeping the code's footprint small. The tests developed during TDD allow you to make the code right, without breaking it.

The final step is *make it fast* (enough). I like to add *enough* because any effort to make it faster than is needed is effort that could be used to add more functionality. Again, the tests support this effort by holding the external behavior steady. How do you know what is fast enough? You need to know where the code spends its time; you need metrics.

The sequence does not mean we should not avoid stupid or wasteful things. But it suggests that some design attributes, such as functionality and clean code, may be more valuable than sheer speed. Sure, some places need the sheer speed but not every line of code.

Let's hear what an expert has to say about optimizing code.

An Optimization Expert's Opinion

Dr. Joseph M. Newcomer's is an expert in optimization. In his article "Optimization: Your Worst Enemy," he says, "But always, and I repeat, always, my experience has been that no programmer has ever been able to predict or analyze where performance bottlenecks are without data. No matter where you think the time is going, you will be surprised to discover that it is going somewhere else."[7]

Newcomer tells of yearlong efforts to redesign key system components and resulted in slower code. He tells of a silly low-level optimizations that sent developers on long bug hunts while migrating code to a different platform.

In an email discussion with Dr. Newcomer, he added, "Along the lines of 'well-structured code is not efficient,' I often get 'all those function calls add unnecessary overhead.' The truth is that first-class optimizing compilers will often automatically inline short code fragments, and in a modern computer, function call is close to zero cost."

Not all of you are in the modern processors Dr. Newcomer refers to, but the bottom line is the same. Keep code clean and expressive and optimize with data.

Beware of Micro-optimizations

Favor macro-optimizations over micro-optimizations. For example, it may take more space and time to call a function through a function pointer than directly, but eliminating multiple switch statements in favor of one switch

---

7. http://www.flounder.com/optimization.htm

statement and dispatching through function pointers may be an overall savings in both space and execution time. If you are sweating the little stuff, you probably have bigger problems.

Performance Tests

If there are time critical areas of code, try to isolate them so you can measure them. You can write tests that will fail if a function exhausts its time budget.

```
TEST(Performance, PostEventDeadline)
{
    Voltage v;
    unsigned long start = get_tic();
    for (int i = 0; i < 1000; i ++)
        QueueVoltageReading(v);
    unsigned long end = get_tic();

    CHECK(DEADLINE * 1000 >= end - start);
}
```

A test like the one shown previously is machine-dependent and won't be very useful when run on the development system. This is a target-dependent test.

System-level performance tests, though outside the scope of this book, should be part of your toolkit. If you follow the ideas for testability at the unit level, you will find that you have plenty of hooks for doing higher-level component, subsystem, and system tests.

> **Fourth of July Test**
>
> The radio system had a requirement to be able to handle the load on the Fourth of July in a major U.S. city, a big day for radio calls. The manufacturer of the system had done a study a few years earlier, so they had an accurate traffic model for that busy day.
>
> The system's technical reviewers were concerned about the design and threading model we were planning. They wanted to do more analysis on the design. But because we had test hooks in all the right places, I proposed we build a test, the Fourth of July test.
>
> The main traffic concern was the push-to-talk events. We devised a test script that fed push-to-talk events into the system, loading it to capacity and beyond. Initially the test uncovered some concurrency problems, and these problems resisted detection at the unit level. With the concurrency problems cleared up, we could measure the system idle time during peak load. The data showed that we were well within performance margins. We continued with confidence in the chosen architecture with measurements rather than opinion. As rocket scientist Wernher von Braun said, "One test result is worth 1,000 expert opinions."

12.6 Where Are We?

Refactoring is a big topic. To learn more, definitely look into Martin Fowler's book and online resources such as the c2 wiki.[8]

Generally speaking, refactoring should be part of everyday development. It's not on your schedule, and you don't ask for permission to refactor. You do it to keep the code clean, you do it to help you understand code you've never looked at before, you do it to pay for sins of the past.

The refactoring mind-set insists that programming is not only about instructing the computer what to do but that programming is also about telling other programmers what you are telling the computer to do.

In this chapter, we refactored without fear because we had tests acting as a safety net. But many of you have significant amounts of *legacy code*, or bad code without tests. Changing legacy code is risky. The next chapter is about improving legacy code safely.

12.7 Put the Knowledge to Work

1. Now that TimeService is responsible for comparing days and metadays, there are many redundant LightScheduler tests. You are not paid by the test. Remove the redundant tests from LightScheduler.

2. Refactor the LightScheduler found in code/t0/src/HomeAutomation in the book code distribution. Compare your result with mine.

3. Convert Time into an *abstract data type* by getting the structure declaration out of the public header file. You can use your refactored code from the previous exercise or the work in progress in code/t1/src/HomeAutomation.

---

8. http://www.c2.com/cgi/wiki?ExtremeProgrammingRoadmap

Let us change our traditional attitude to the construction of programs. Instead of imagining that our main task is to instruct a computer what to do, let us concentrate rather on explaining to human beings what we want a computer to do.
➤ Donald Knuth

CHAPTER 13

Adding Tests to Legacy Code

Refactoring without tests is dangerous; with all the details we must keep straight, a mistake is easy to make. How many code reviews have you been in where the design changes are not made because "We already tested it"? You already know it is dangerous to change code without tests.

You'll find that adding tests to existing C code is no easy task. The existing code is likely to suffer from functions and modules that know too much about each other and have grown beyond sensible limits (remember that coding standard that said all functions must fit on a screen?). Before TDD, you may have had no strong motivation to keep code testable. So, it should be no surprise that legacy code resists being tested the way we've tested code throughout this book.

Michael Feathers' book *Working Effectively with Legacy Code [Fea04]* is a great source for a deep dive into legacy code issues and refactoring techniques. Feathers defines *legacy code* as "code without tests." I can't justify the definition better than Michael:

> "Code without tests is bad code. It doesn't matter how well written it is; it doesn't matter how pretty or object-oriented or well-encapsulated it is. With tests, we can change the behavior of our code quickly and verifiably. Without them, we really don't know if our code is getting better or worse."

Let's start by looking at a policy to help guide improving a legacy code base.

13.1 Legacy Code Change Policy

Here is a policy for a team adopting TDD that has a legacy code base:

- Test-drive new code.
- Add tests to legacy code before modification.
- Test-drive changes to legacy code.

You've been learning TDD, so the first line of the policy should be no surprise. New code should be test-driven. Whole new functions, modules, and subsystems can be developed with TDD.

In *Working Effectively with Legacy Code*, Michael describes *sprouting*. When there is a need to change some legacy code, see whether you can sprout a new function or module to do the new behavior. Test-drive it, and call it from the legacy code. Michael says, "You might not be able to get all those call points under test easily, but at the very least, you can write tests for this new code." This approach means we always work to make the code a little better than we found it.

Sprouting can be very safe when operations done by the sprouted code do not impact the flow of control of the calling code. When return results are used in conditionals and data structures are modified, then sprouting might not be enough; some behavior-preserving tests for the legacy code might be needed too.

Where did this policy come from? Good policies come from good principles like the *Boy Scout Principle*.

13.2 Boy Scout Principle

The Boy Scouts follow this simple principle: leave the camp cleaner than you found it. This does not mean that all the trash has to be cleaned up now, but you can't let it get worse, and it must get at least a little better. In *Clean Code [Mar08]*, Bob Martin asks, "What if code got a little better every time you changed it?" I'll answer this: the industry would not find itself in the mess it's in. The industry norm is for code to incrementally worsen with each change. We need to reverse that.

Much of the time, following the Boy Scout rule won't be hard. It suggests an incremental strategy, which is a mind-set that we will continue to make things better. It's not to deny that we'll face some large and serious legacy code situations where the incremental changes may not be enough. Every day we will find opportunities to be a Boy Scout.

Adding to a Long Function

Extract something; there are plenty of opportunities to pull out some idea and name it. You want to add three lines; take out five—the net improvement leaves the function two lines shorter, but I bet you can do better. Fix another complex conditional nearby to start a pattern of improvement. Remember, add tests first to preserve behavior.

Adding to a Complex Conditional

Extract the conditional into a well-named helper function. Write a few tests for it. That's picking up the obvious beer cans. Look at the new code carefully. Does the conditional really belong with some other module? If so, the complex conditional is likely to be duplicated, and the newly extracted function should be moved. Do the work or add it to your technical debt list.

Copy/Paste/Tweak Temptation

Maybe you're tempted by a copy/paste/tweak opportunity that meets the functional requirements. Don't do it, except maybe to test your hypothesis. Before or after the change, do what the code is telling you: extract the common code into a helper function. Generalize and parameterize it so it handles both cases. Write tests around the code to be extracted to guard against breaking existing functionality. Make a list of the other previous cut/paste/tweaks of the same code for conversion.

Cryptic Local Variable Name

Once you figure out what the variable is for, rename it to help you, and your teammates, on the next code visit.

Deep Nesting

Pull out a nesting level or two into a helper function. Flatten nested conditionals with guard clauses.

13.3 Legacy Change Algorithm

Michael defines the legacy code change algorithm as:

1. Identify change points.
2. Find test points.
3. Break dependencies.
4. Write tests.
5. Make changes and refactor.

1. Identify Change Points

One bit of good news: Michael's algorithm starts the way you always start to change legacy code; you have to find the parts of the existing code that you think you need to change.

2. Find Test Points

Once the change points are identified, consider how to test it. Where are the natural points to sense what is happening in the code, and where does the code get its inputs? Test points are most often evident in the *seams* formed by function calls.

Test points don't have to be seams, as we will see in Section 13.4, *Test Points*, on page 257. Global variables, as much as we dislike them, can provide test points. A data structure passed to a function can provide a test point.

3. Break Dependencies (or Not)

To get legacy code into a test harness or to gain access to some test points we have to break dependencies. We've seen how to do this on new code during the TDD process using linker, function pointer, or preprocessor test doubles. We'll use these techniques in legacy code.

In monolithic functions, the function call boundaries are not there. We'll need to employ some *safe* function extractions before you can employ the test double. When you are modifying *legacy code*, you must be very careful and favor very safe code changes. Working with a colleague will also help avoid the little mistakes that can happen.

Sometimes the risk of breaking dependencies is too high. In the next section, we'll look at a couple alternative approaches to breaking dependencies: sensing variables, using existing debug output as a sense point, and inserting inline monitors.

To break dependencies on global data, you can encapsulate access to a problem global in an accessor function. Then during the test you can override the accessor to give you better control over the global.

4. Write Tests

With test points in place, write some tests to characterize and help preserve the behavior of the legacy code. This step can be very involved, especially if the code under test has never been in a test harness before. In Section 13.6, *Crash to Pass*, on page 263, we'll look at a common pattern used to get the code into the test harness.

5. Make Changes and Refactor

Finally, when some behavior preserving tests are in place, it should be safe to apply some of the refactoring transformations, getting the code ready for the change we'd like to make. With the legacy behavior held steady with tests, it is safe to test-drive the new behavior.

In the next section, we'll look at some test point options for legacy code.

13.4 Test Points

We need test points to confirm our understanding of what the code is doing. Sometimes they are easier to get to than others.

Seams

Function calls form *seams* between different parts of the code. These seams make the best test points. Seams let us see and influence what the code under test is doing.

Michael defines a seam as follows: "A seam is a place where you can alter the behavior in your program without editing in that place."

Seams are where we can employ test doubles to spy on data passed to collaborators, allowing the test case to make sure the code under test is giving its collaborator the right instructions. Function call seams are also where the test double can provide indirect inputs to the code under tests through a test double's return results.

Your code probably has many function seams already. The exception to this is the monolithic function. Creating seams in a monolithic function can be dangerous; adding a *sensing variable* might be safer.

Global Variables

I am not going to make a case for global variables here, but maybe you already have some. Global variables can serve as test points as well as mechanisms to get specific test values into the code under test. Once the code is under test, you can start to encapsulate globals.

Sensing Variables

Michael Feathers describes sensing variables in his book. A sensing variable is helpful for getting access to hard-to-reach data or intermediate results in a long function.

You have a big monolithic function you need to change. You think you know where changes are needed, but the risks and unknowns are too great to start with any structural changes. Adding one or more sensing variables is a low-risk option.

A sensing variable can be used to inspect an intermediate value in a series of computations, a value of a state variable, or maybe a count of the number of times through a loop.

A sensing variable is a global variable that tests can inspect. Tests can vary some inputs to the code under test and see the impact on the sensing variable.

Are you objecting to the idea of adding a global for test? When you are adding tests to legacy code, it's not the right time to get all purist about global variables. Given already compromised legacy code, we will make compromises for the sake of gaining a test point. I'd like to think that introducing a sensing variable is not a permanent change to the code but rather an intermediate step used in the process of trying to untangle long functions. If we were test-driving production code, we'd look to exploit a function seam instead of a sensing variable.

Debug Output Sense Point

In Debug-Later Programming, code often gets sprinkled with calls to a debug output function. Often the debug output can be switched on and off either through conditional compilation or through runtime control. You can use this existing debug output instrumentation as a *debug output sense point* to get at hard-to-access information about the behavior of the code.

In Section 9.3, *Surgically Inserted Spy*, on page 152, we saw how a test can capture printed output. We could use a similar idea for intercepting and monitoring debug output. Long-term, I'd like to rely less on debug output, but again, we're working in legacy code and may not be able to solve all problems in one day.

For test, you could create a debug output spy that captures debug output much like FormatOutputSpy(). I expect that this spy might need some other capabilities such as asking for the number of entries, finding specific entries by output line number or specific content, or finding adjacent entries.

Inline Monitor

The *Debug Output Sense Point* is a special case of an *inline monitor* test point. With an inline monitor, we can insert a special function call into the code to report on any information to test cases. This is like a sensing variable, with a couple differences. An inline monitor allows multiple readings of a particular sense point while the test is running. It also allows checks to be made while the test is running, much as the mock object did in Chapter 10, *The Mock Object*, on page 163.

Back in Section 1.1, *Why Do We Need TDD?*, on page 2, we looked at the case of the Zune bug. We could have applied an inline monitor to the code to break out of the infinite loop like this. We'll declare and insert a call to an inline monitor called monitorLoop():

src/zune/RtcTime.c
```
void monitorLoop(int days);
static void SetYearAndDayOfYear(RtcTime * time)
{
    int days = time->daysSince1980;
    int year = STARTING_YEAR;
    while (days > 365)
    {
        if (IsLeapYear(year))
        {
            if (days > 366)
            {
                days -= 366;
                year += 1;
            }
        }
        else
        {
            days -= 365;
            year += 1;
        }
        monitorLoop(days);
    }
    time->dayOfYear = days;
    time->year = year;
}
```

monitorLoop() will look at each passed-in value of days and make sure that no two monitorLoop() calls have the same days value. That would indicate the loop won't end by itself. Insert a call to monitorLoop() inside the suspected loop. Declare the monitorLoop() function to avoid warnings. If the call to monitorLoop() is going to be in the production code for a while, I'd probably put it in a header file to keep the signatures in sync with the test code.[1]

In the test case, define monitorLoop():

tests/zune/RtcTimeTest.cpp
```
extern "C"
{
#include "RtcTime.h"
```

---

1. Because of copyright concerns, this code is not from the Zune but has the same problem as the Zune 30G.

```
static int lastMonitoredDays;
void monitorLoop(int days)
{
    CHECK(lastMonitoredDays != days);
    lastMonitoredDays = days;
}
}
```

The lastMonitoredDays variable has to be reset in setup() to avoid potential false positives if the tests accidentally talk to each other through stale values in lastMonitoredDays.

tests/zune/RtcTimeTest.cpp
```
void setup()
{
    lastMonitoredDays = -1;
}
```

Running this test breaks out of the loop and avoids the test harness hanging like a Zune.

Getting legacy code into a test harness can be quite a challenge in itself. The next section should help you see what to expect while adding tests to legacy code.

13.5 Two-Stage struct Initialization

Code that has dependencies on public data structures has its own unique initialization problems. Data structures with manual initialization or, worse, willy-nilly initialization makes keeping duplication out of tests difficult.

Let's say we're integrating a digital video recorder into the home automation system. The DVR functions use a publicly known data structure to hold the programming information. The structure is first initialized with DvRecorder_Create(). But it is possible for programs to be stored in the DVR's nonvolatile memory. So, initializing the recorder takes two steps. DvRecorder_RestorePrograms() does the second step of initializing the DVR. The structure looks like this:

include/dvr/DvRecorder.h
```
typedef struct Program
{
    const char * name;
    int repeat;
    int channel;
    int startHour;
    int startMinute;
    int durationInMinutes;
```

```
    int priority;
    int preferences;
} Program;

enum {
    ALL_EPISODES, NEW_EPISODES, REPEATED_EPISODES,
    REPEAT, NO_REPEAT,
    LOW_PRIORITY, MEDIUM_PRIORITY, HIGH_PRIORITY
};

typedef struct
{
    int programCount;
    Program programs[100];
    /* etc... */
} DvRecorder;
```

Note how recorder is initialized using memcpy(). If you used the file scope variable recorderData directly, the default data would get overwritten, changing the static data.

The first inclination is to do DvRecorder_RestorePrograms() in setup(), like this:

tests/dvr/DvRecorderTest.cpp
```
static DvRecorder recorderData = {
    4,
    {
        {"Rocky and Bullwinkle", REPEAT, 2, 8, 30, 30, HIGH_PRIORITY, ALL_EPISODES},
        {"Bugs Bunny", REPEAT, 9, 8, 30, 30, HIGH_PRIORITY, ALL_EPISODES},
        {"Dr. Who", REPEAT, 11, 23, 0, 90, HIGH_PRIORITY, REPEATED_EPISODES},
        {"Law and Order", REPEAT, 5, 21, 0, 60, HIGH_PRIORITY, ALL_EPISODES},
        { 0 }
    }
};
TEST_GROUP(DvRecorder)
{
    DvRecorder recorder;
    void setup()
    {
        memcpy(&recorder, &recorderData, sizeof(recorder));
        DvrRecorder_Create();
        DvRecorder_RestorePrograms(&recorder);
    }

    void teardown()
    {
        DvRecorder_Destroy();
    }
};
```

To test different program recording options, you need multiple setup scenarios, many of which are small variations on the default setup. This is a bit of a problem, because if we want to make a small variation in the test data, it's too late—programs have already been restored. To make this work better, we can separate the two stages of the initialization by doing DvRecorder_Create() in setup() but deferring the call to DvRecorder_RestorePrograms() to each test case. Here is the revised setup():

tests/dvr/DvRecorderTest.cpp
```
TEST_GROUP(DvRecorder)
{
    DvRecorder recorder;
    void setup()
    {
        memcpy(&recorder, &recorderData, sizeof(recorder));
        DvrRecorder_Create();
    }
    void teardown()
    {
        DvRecorder_Destroy();
    }
};
TEST(DvRecorder, RestoreSomePrograms)
{
    DvRecorder_RestorePrograms(&recorder);
    //etc...
}
```

Note that some of the tests use the default data. In other tests, some of the statically initialized data is overwritten before the second stage of initialization.

tests/dvr/DvRecorderTest.cpp
```
TEST(DvRecorder, RestoreNoPrograms)
{
    recorder.programCount = 0;
    recorder.programs[0].name = 0;
    DvRecorder_RestorePrograms(&recorder);
    //etc...
}
TEST(DvRecorder, RecordWithRepeat)
{
    DvRecorder_RestorePrograms(&recorder);
    //etc...
}

TEST(DvRecorder, RecordWithNoRepeat)
{
    recorder.programs[0].repeat = NO_REPEAT;
    recorder.programs[1].repeat = NO_REPEAT;
```

```
        recorder.programs[2].repeat = NO_REPEAT;
        DvRecorder_RestorePrograms(&recorder);
        //etc...
}
TEST(DvRecorder, RecordConflictFirstHighPriorityWins)
{
        DvRecorder_RestorePrograms(&recorder);
        //etc...
}
TEST(DvRecorder, RecordConflictHighPriorityWins)
{
        recorder.programs[0].priority = LOW_PRIORITY;
        DvRecorder_RestorePrograms(&recorder);
        //etc...
}
```

This is a fairly simple case here. In legacy code situations, there may be many structures to initialize and wire together and no convenient functions like DvRecorder_RestorePrograms() to help. In the process of applying this idea, you might create some helper functions and discover that they really belong in the production code.

13.6 Crash to Pass

Adding the first test to legacy code is usually the hardest. Knowing what to expect and how to react can ease the process. The *crash to pass* algorithm can help you get through Michael's legacy code change algorithm from Section 13.3, *Legacy Change Algorithm*, on page 255.

Here's the situation. You want to test some existing legacy code. The function to exercise in the test is part of an interwoven mass of C data structures and functions. Just getting this data structure/function call free-for-all compiled in the test harness is a challenge. Getting the code to run in the test harness is enough to make you go for coffee and never come back.

In complex C code, data used by a legacy function may not be obvious. Deciding what to initialize and how to initialize it may again tempt you to give up.

Don't give up; *crash* your way to discover what needs to be initialized to *pass* your tests. The crash-to-pass approach starts with an empty test case and a legacy code function you want to test. The algorithm, expressed in C, looks like this:

```
void addNewLegacyCtest()
{
  makeItCompile();
  makeItLink();
```

```
  while (runCrashes())
  {
    findRuntimeDependency();
    fixRuntimeDependency();
  }
  addMoreLegacyCtests();
}
```

Let's look at each step along the way.

makeItCompile

To call the function under test, you will have to provide data structures and parameters to the function. During makeItCompile(), feel free to use null pointers and simple literal data values. Use memset() to bulk fill data structures with zeros. Later you will have to do more than feed the code under tests meaningless inputs, but by plugging dependencies with null pointers and simple data, you can get to a clean compile sooner.

Initially the test won't even compile. Add #includes to try to get the test file to compile. Add them slowly, one at a time. As you add includes, you are rewarded with a long list of compilation errors. It's best to attack the first error, because it is the likely cause for 101 others. Don't get discouraged.

A shortcut for a really bad dependency mess is to copy the includes from a production code file that calls the target function. You'll get a clean compile but probably a fat include list. Once the test is compiling, try to prune the list of includes.

The less-committed TDDers might get discouraged during this process, resulting in early termination of makeItCompile() via exit(FAILURE). Don't give up; exit(FAILURE) is a last resort. It's also possible that you should start with something that has less baggage.

Once makeItCompile() finishes, makeItLink() starts immediately.

makeItLink

With the includes in place, parameter and global dependencies plugged with null pointers, and other meaningless data, you are ready for your next reward: link errors. makeItLink() can be quite involved. The unresolved externals need to be resolved either by linking in parts of the production code or by providing test doubles. makeItLink() might also result in an exit(FAILURE) for those looking for an excuse to not write their unit tests.

runCrashes

Once the executable test runner is built link-error free, the most likely outcome is for the test runner to crash. The crashes are caused by the uninitialized and improperly initialized data left dangling earlier. You are right on track! Hang in there! The crashes are leading you right to the runtime dependencies.

Stay in the loop as long as runCrashes() is TRUE. In the loop you find and fix the runtime dependencies as you knit together the needed global data and parameters to make the code under test happy. Getting runCrashes() to transition to FALSE is a major breakthrough; the function runs in the test harness! Time to look at the find and fix processes.

findRuntimeDependency

If you have a debugger, fire it up and visit the crash site. Inspecting for clues will likely yield the root cause of the illegal access. If you don't have a debugger, it's time to get one. You can also inspect the input data to find obvious problem initializations. Single-stepping through the code under test can also be revealing.

findRuntimeDependency() leans on the execution environment to help find runtime dependencies.[2] Operating system and hardware support for illegal memory access helps you find runtime dependencies more quickly. When the root cause of the crash is discovered, findRuntimeDependency() returns.

fixRuntimeDependency

With the root cause in focus, the missing initialization is often clear. The cause might be uninitialized global data, a missing function pointer, or some other unexpected value. Figure out what to initialize next and go into a series of makeItCompile() and makeItLink() operations as needed.

Once one runtime dependency is resolved, the most likely outcome is another crash. The good news is that eventually, when all the runtime dependency holes are plugged, the crashes stop. Then new tests come quickly.

addMoreLegacyCtests

You started at nine in the morning, and now it's two in the afternoon. The crashes have stopped, at least temporarily. High-fives are in order. After the celebration, you can add more tests.

---

2. Michael Feathers suggests leaning on the compiler to understand the compile-time impact of a code change.

Let's dig a little deeper into addMoreLegacyCtests(); there are two algorithms to consider. Here is the most common implementation for people new to TDD:

```
void addMoreLegacyCtests()
{
  while (!testsAreSufficientForCurrentNeeds())
  {
    copyPasteTweakTheLastTest();
  }
}
```

You already know that copy and paste without refactoring results in a mess for production code; it's the same for test code. This implementation has problems because there is no refactoring as part of copyPasteTweakTheLastTest(). Here is a better implementation:

```
void addMoreLegacyCtests() //take two
{
  while (!testsAreSufficientForCurrentNeeds())
  {
    copyPasteTweakTheLastTest();
    while (!testDifferencesAreEvident())
    {
      if (setupStepsAreSimilar())
        extractAndParameterizeCommonSetup();
      if (checkStepsAreSimilar())
        extractAndParameterizeCommonAssertions();
      else
        considerStartingANewTestGroup();
    }
  }
}
```

We still use copyPasteTweakTheLastTest(), and we add refactoring steps that extract duplication to make test helpers. The refactoring of the tests has an immediate payback. The helpers make creating new tests easier. Revising tests becomes easier when a revision impacts all the tests; the change can usually be made by modifying just the helper functions. Let's look at each of the steps.

testsAreSufficientForCurrentNeeds

In testsAreSufficientForCurrentNeeds(), you decide if the current tests are adequate to hold the current behavior steady. While deciding, ask the following:

- How should the inputs be varied?
- What should be checked to verify the operation of the code under test?
- What other tests are needed?
- Are there boundary conditions and special cases that need to be checked?

Letting testsAreSufficientForCurrentNeeds() return TRUE is a judgment call. In a legacy code situation, you probably have a production code change in mind. Return TRUE when you judge that the tests are adequate to hold the current behavior steady. Otherwise, return FALSE.

copyPasteTweakTheLastTest

copyPasteTweakTheLastTest() provides a new test case. But the first few times copyPasteTweakTheLastTest() is executed, the resulting test cases are filled with duplication. The valuable tweaks are hidden in the mass of initialization code and a bank of assertions, obscuring the differences between test cases. You are not being paid per line of test code, are you? No! So, clean it up.

Why the big deal about keeping tests clean? Tests have to be kept clean because in a few days (or hours) you or a colleague will look at the test cases again. An easy-to-read and easy-to-modify test case is much more valuable and not much more work. At the time you copyPasteTweakTheLastTest(), the differences are clear to you, but no one else. And they won't be clear to you for long if test cases carry a lot of duplication. So, it is the best time to reduce the duplication and improve the readability of the tests.

Sometimes copyPasteTweakTheLastTest() results in a crash, as you take the code through new execution paths. That kicks you back out to the top with addNewLegacyCtest().

testDifferencesAreEvident

The first time through, testDifferencesAreEvident() almost always results in a FALSE return value. After a few laps around this loop controlled by testDifferencesAreEvident(), the test cases get cleaner as helper functions grow to support the tests. The only way testDifferencesAreEvident() returns TRUE is when the duplication has been refactored into shared test data and helper functions, allowing the tests to be concise and expressive.

setupStepsAreSimilar

Looking over the original test case and its copy, setupStepsAreSimilar() returns TRUE when there is duplication in the setup steps of the test.

extractAndParameterizeCommonSetup

In this activity, common setup is extracted into shared test case variables and helper functions. Tweaked data values often become the parameters of the extracted initialization code. If some of the parameters do not change from test to test, they can go into setup(). setup() should be refactored too. Run the tests after each change.

Sometimes you'll extract initialization code that looks like useful production code. Consider moving that code to the production code and putting it to use, removing duplication, and adding structure.

checkStepsAreSimilar

Looking over the original test case and its copy, checkStepsAreSimilar() returns TRUE when there is duplication in the verify steps of the test cases.

extractAndParameterizeCommonAssertions

This is similar to extractAndParameterizeCommonSetup(). The common assertions will probably depend on the shared test data added during extractAndParameterizeCommonSetup(). Tweaked expected values will become parameters for the extracted helpers.

considerStartingANewTestGroup

You just copied the last test, but the changes to the test setup and check phases are significantly different. It could be time for a new TEST_GROUP(), especially if you envision more tests coming like the new one.

exit(SUCCESS)

Your hard work is rewarded. After several spins through this cycle, copyPasteTweakTheLastTest() won't result in duplication. The differences will be essential differences, and testDifferencesAreEvident() will repeatedly return TRUE.

When the inner loop breaks because tests are well-factored, subsequent loops around copyPasteTweakTheLastTest() usually result in concise and readable test case, requiring no refactoring. Tests get easier to add.

When you've coded enough tests, exit(SUCCESS) with success. If you find you can't get to exit(SUCCESS); choose something that is less difficult to get into the test harness.

13.7 Characterization Tests

One of the problems with legacy code is that you can't be sure of what it is doing. You are going to change some existing function; it is critical that the current desirable behavior is preserved. Capture the current desirable behavior in tests. Michael Feathers calls these *characterization tests*.

Characterization tests really help to understand the code that is being modified. If you understand the code well enough to write a test for it, you probably understand it well enough to modify it. The opposite holds true as well. If you can't write a test for it, you probably should not modify it. Characterization tests also serve as the team's long-term memory.

A mock object can be very helpful in characterization tests. Recall the mock object, MockIO, used in Chapter 10, *The Mock Object*, on page 163. If you had a legacy code driver that you wanted to characterize before modification, you could use MockIO to help see how the driver interacts with the hardware.

The first step when characterizing a driver is to break dependencies with the hardware. You need to replace reads and writes with calls to IO_Read() and IO_Write(). Create a test file and link it with MockIO, which intercepts calls to IO_Read() and IO_Write(), as in the Flash example.

As an example, let's pretend that the Flash driver we created earlier was legacy code and we needed to characterize it. We need a TEST_GROUP() and initial test that looks like this:

tests/IO/LegacyFlashTest.cpp
```
TEST_GROUP(LegacyFlash)
{
    int result;

    void setup()
    {
        MockIO_Create(10);
        Flash_Create();
        result = 0;
    }

    void teardown()
    {
        Flash_Destroy();
        MockIO_Verify_Complete();
        MockIO_Destroy();
    }
};
```

Let's try to characterize the happy path of the Flash_Write(). Have the test case call the production and check its return result:

tests/IO/LegacyFlashTest.cpp
```
TEST(LegacyFlash, FlashProgramSuccess)
{
    result = Flash_Write(0x1000, 0xBEEF);
    LONGS_EQUAL(0, result);
}
```

Because there are no expectations set, the test will fail as soon as the production code makes a call to IO_Read() or IO_Write(). Here's the error:

```
IO/LegacyFlashTest.cpp:39: error: Failure in TEST(LegacyFlash, FlashProgramSuccess)
../mocks/MockIO.c:84: error:
        R/W 1: No more expectations but was IO_Write(0x0, 0x40)
```

MockIO complains there are no more expectations but that IO_Write() was called. We can see that the driver writes a 0x40 to location 0x0. After looking into the production code and finding the symbols for 0x0 and 0x40, add an expectation:

tests/IO/LegacyFlashTest.cpp
```
TEST(LegacyFlash, FlashProgramSuccess)
{
    MockIO_Expect_Write(CommandRegister, ProgramCommand);
    result = Flash_Write(0x1000, 0xBEEF);
    LONGS_EQUAL(0, result);
}
```

Having the first expectation satisfied, now we get a new error:

```
IO/LegacyFlashTest.cpp:39: error: Failure in TEST(LegacyFlash, FlashProgramSuccess)
../mocks/MockIO.c:84: error:
        R/W 2: No more expectations but was IO_Write(0x1000, 0xbeef)
```

Add the expectation for the second interaction with the mock:

tests/IO/LegacyFlashTest.cpp
```
TEST(LegacyFlash, FlashProgramSuccess)
{
    MockIO_Expect_Write(CommandRegister, ProgramCommand);
    MockIO_Expect_Write(0x1000, 0xBEEF);
    result = Flash_Write(0x1000, 0xBEEF);
    LONGS_EQUAL(0, result);
}
```

The failure changes again:

```
IO/LegacyFlashTest.cpp:39: error: Failure in TEST(LegacyFlash, FlashProgramSuccess)
../mocks/MockIO.c:84: error:
        R/W 3: No more expectations but was IO_Read(0x0)
```

Adding expectations for IO_Write() was straightforward, because there was no return result. IO_Read() is a different story; it returns something. To determine the return result, we could consult Flash_Write() or the device spec. (When writing test for legacy code, we might have only the code as the specification.)

src/IO/Flash.c
```
int Flash_Write(ioAddress offset, ioData data)
{
    ioData status = 0;
    IO_Write(CommandRegister, ProgramCommand);
```

```
    IO_Write(offset, data);

    while ((status & ReadyBit) == 0)
        status = IO_Read(StatusRegister);

    if (status != ReadyBit)
    {
        IO_Write(CommandRegister, Reset);

        if (status & VppErrorBit)
            return FLASH_VPP_ERROR;
        else if (status & ProgramErrorBit)
            return FLASH_PROGRAM_ERROR;
        else if (status & BlockProtectionErrorBit)
            return FLASH_PROTECTED_BLOCK_ERROR;
        else
            return FLASH_UNKNOWN_PROGRAM_ERROR;
    }
    IO_Read(address);

    return FLASH_SUCCESS;
}
```

We can see that IO_Read() is part of a loop. If it returns a value with the ReadyBit set, the loop will exit. We could add a few MockIO_Expect_ReadThenReturn() operations so the code takes a spin and then breaks out of the loop.

```
tests/IO/LegacyFlashTest.cpp
TEST(LegacyFlash, FlashProgramSuccess)
{
    MockIO_Expect_Write(CommandRegister, ProgramCommand);
    MockIO_Expect_Write(0x1000, 0xBEEF);
    MockIO_Expect_ReadThenReturn(StatusRegister, 0);
    MockIO_Expect_ReadThenReturn(StatusRegister, 0);
    MockIO_Expect_ReadThenReturn(StatusRegister, ReadyBit);
    result = Flash_Write(0x1000, 0xBEEF);
    LONGS_EQUAL(0, result);
}
```

This would continue until you get through the happy path. After the happy path is tested, make a list of the other scenarios to cover with tests. When all the characterization tests are in place, you can safely refactor the existing driver or start to add new functionality.

13.8 Learning Tests for Third-Party Code

What should a test-driven developer do about tests for third-party code? We should expect that the third-party code is tested, so in general it's not our responsibility to write tests for third-party code.[3] Even though testing the vendor's code is not our responsibility, it does not mean that writing some tests won't help us. Let's talk about the role of tests in an environment where we use off-the-shelf code.

You have an intended use for the third-party code. You could start by integrating it immediately into your application. I recommend against this course because it mixes learning the third-party code with applying the learning in your code.

You must learn the code anyway, so why not learn it by writing tests for the code to exercise it the way you plan to use it? Tests can be controlled experiments that allow you to discover exactly how the code behaves. Once you have learned the package, apply the learning to your product.

A helpful side effect of this approach is that the tests can play an important role in accepting new releases of the vendor's code. If your tests cover how you use the package, then a change in the interface of behavior will show themselves and focus in on the incompatibility.

Here is an example of a learning test my son and I put together.

> **Learning strtok**
>
> My son, Paul, studied computer science at U of I in Chicago. He was taking an operating systems class and had to do some projects in C. (Some things change; some things stay the same.) At the time he had not done much C, so he had some learning to do. I thought I better show him CppUTest. He could use it for a playground to learn some of the subtleties of C, as well as use TDD.
>
> We met for a coffee to set up CppUTest and to start his assignment. His assignment involved parsing a string (char *, that is). His professor suggested they use strtok(). We googled strtok() to read about it.
>
> Here is the signature of strtok():
>
> ```
> char * strtok( char * str1, const char * str2 );
> ```
>
> To see whether we understood strtok(), we wrote this test:
>
> ```
> TEST(Parser, ParseOneElement)
> {
>     char * input = "abc";
>     char * token = strtok(input, "., ");
>
>     STRCMP_EQUAL(input, token);
> }
> ```

---

3. Some of you developing safety-critical systems may have more stringent standards for off-the-shelf code vendors.

The test passed. Feeling confident, we tried a little more interesting test:

```
TEST(Parser, ParseTwoElement)
{
    char * input = "abc,def";
    char * token1 = strtok(input, "., ");
    char * token2 = strtok(0, "., ");

    STRCMP_EQUAL("abc", token1);
    STRCMP_EQUAL("def", token2);
}
```

Much to our surprise, this one crashed. After a little digging, we discovered the error in our ways. strtok() actually changes the string. Now I remember that, but then it was a surprise. The subtlety is right there in its signature. The first parameter of strtok() is a char *, not a const char *. A careful reading of two different strtok() references explains the behavior. It makes sense that giving strtok() a pointer to a literal string causes a segmentation fault when strtok() starts inserting its NUL characters into read-only memory holding the literal string.

Making input a char array fixes the problem:

```
TEST(Parser, ParseTwoElement)
{
    char input[] = "abc,def";
    char* token1 = strtok(input, "., ");
    char* token2 = strtok(0, "., ");

    STRCMP_EQUAL("abc", token1);
    STRCMP_EQUAL("def", token2);
}
```

Finding this subtle behavior in a controlled experiment went quickly...just a few minutes. If our strtok() misuse was in a handful of other lines of code, tracking down the mistake would have been more difficult. This learning test was free, like most of them.

Fast-forward one week. Paul is working on his parser. He could not get the unit test harness going for one reason or another during the week. His main() would grab a line of text and parse it and then print the pieces. He was manually testing the code, and it started crashing.

We dug through his code. With only a little code on top of strtok(), it took a half hour to find the problem. The insight from the previous week's test made the problem evident. Without the tests from the prior week, the debugging would have lasted quite a bit longer.

strtok() is a standard library function. We have an expectation of correctness, although statistically some library functions will have bugs too. In general, we don't need to write tests for library functions to verify the functions. We write the tests for us. We write them so we can learn. What did they cost? Not much, but I think these learning tests have already had a positive ROI. Learning tests are free! Or maybe better than free!

13.9 Test-Driven Bug Fixes

Bug fixes need tests too. The existence of a bug often shows where prior test efforts have failed. If we can write a unit test to reveal the bug, do so. If investigation is needed to track down the bug, do the investigation and capture some of your knowledge in the tests as you go. Once the bug has been located, write a unit test that reveals the bug. Resist the temptation to immediately fix the bug.

You want to make sure you don't give life to new bugs when you kill the bug you were hunting. Also, bugs have been known to nest together. Both of these realities mean you should also write tests to lock in the desired behavior before fixing a bug.

As you noticed in *crash to pass*, the first test in a new area usually has high startup costs. Subsequent tests usually can be written pretty quickly. This will be true when you start adding tests during the bug hunt. Think of the cost of adding a test for the bug as the cost of doing business—as the price to pay down the technical debt. Defects are costly. Fix them right; it's only a fractional cost.

13.10 Add Strategic Tests

Reactively, we add tests to anything that we are changing. Should we proactively add tests? In the beginning, while your skill is building, adding any test is good. You are learning. But that may not be enough. A product team with a legacy code base should consider adding tests proactively to find existing bugs and protect key functionality.

A proactive approach is also called for to help reduce the risk of breaking important features. Consider adding tests that cover the key uses of the system, the things that are the primary reason for the system. Cover the happy path of a usage scenario before the error paths. Look to cover the most bang for the buck, adding tests that help preserve the value of your product. Add tests that reduce safety risks or monetary loss.

You have limited capacity for writing new tests for legacy code, so be strategic.

13.11 Where Are We?

Legacy code, code without tests, is one of the biggest obstacles to adopting TDD. If you plan on continuing to deliver value with your code base, it's best to start today to keep the code from getting worse and, better yet, to start the long road to legacy code improvement.

We've only scratched the surface on legacy code techniques. In a sense, working with legacy code is a mind-set, based on the thought "I'm not going to contribute to the problem; I'm going to make things better." We'll start to pay down some of the principal on the technical debt and reduce the interest payments on future visits to this code.

Some of you will have some very resistant code bases. Don't give up just because you cannot solve the toughest problems right now. Find some important but easier problems to hone your skills. Remember that changing legacy code without adding the needed tests is asking for trouble.

I have a client with a big legacy code problem. I showed the client the techniques you are learning in this book. The client said, "We want to know the fast way to improve our code's design; tell us the fast way," as if I were holding back a secret. I told them, "The careful way is the fast way. Get good at being careful, and you will go faster."

13.12 Put the Knowledge to Work

1. Find a module in your code base that you need to have under test. Work your way through crash to pass. If the code resists your efforts, find something a little easier.

2. Write characterization tests for one of your device drivers using `MockIO`.

3. Fix a bug from your bug list, but add tests first.

4. Make a list of ten critical scenarios your system must handle. Envision how to get the core functionality under tests. Choose one and implement it. Don't pick your biggest challenge first.

Can you clean that up?
> ➣ *Marilee Grenning*

CHAPTER **14**

Test Patterns and Antipatterns

People new to TDD and writing unit tests tend to repeat some of the same mistakes. These common, but counterproductive, patterns are known as *antipatterns*. This chapter will make you familiar with some common antipatterns and the patterns that should replace them.

Most of the antipatterns have their roots in ignoring the Four-Phase Test pattern (described in Section 2.5, *The Four-Phase Test Pattern*, on page 25) and from allowing duplication in your tests. Remember this, and your tests have a chance of being readable and clean.

Let's look at a few common test antipatterns.

14.1 Ramble-on Test Antipattern

A *Ramble-on Test* just does not know when to end. The author either has no knowledge or has no respect for the Four-Phase Test pattern.

```
t0/tests/HomeAutomation/LightSchedulerTest.cpp
TEST(LightScheduler, ScheduleWeekEnd)
{
    LightScheduler_ScheduleTurnOn(3, WEEKEND, 1200);
    FakeTimeService_SetDay(FRIDAY);
    FakeTimeService_SetMinute(1200);
    LightScheduler_WakeUp();
    LONGS_EQUAL(LIGHT_ID_UNKNOWN, LightControllerSpy_GetLastId());
    LONGS_EQUAL(LIGHT_STATE_UNKNOWN, LightControllerSpy_GetLastState());
    FakeTimeService_SetDay(SATURDAY);
    FakeTimeService_SetMinute(1200);
    LightScheduler_WakeUp();
    LONGS_EQUAL(3, LightControllerSpy_GetLastId());
    LONGS_EQUAL(1, LightControllerSpy_GetLastState());
    LightController_TurnOff(3);
    FakeTimeService_SetDay(SUNDAY);
```

```
    FakeTimeService_SetMinute(1200);
    LightScheduler_WakeUp();
    LONGS_EQUAL(3, LightControllerSpy_GetLastId());
    LONGS_EQUAL(1, LightControllerSpy_GetLastState());
    LightController_Create();
    FakeTimeService_SetDay(MONDAY);
    FakeTimeService_SetMinute(1200);
    LightScheduler_WakeUp();
    LONGS_EQUAL(LIGHT_ID_UNKNOWN, LightControllerSpy_GetLastId());
    LONGS_EQUAL(LIGHT_STATE_UNKNOWN, LightControllerSpy_GetLastState());
}
```

The Ramble-on Test can be repaired by applying the Four-Phase Test pattern and extracting some helper functions. The test really wants to be four separate tests, two checking each of the days that are part of the weekend and the two days on either side. I am only glad that example spares us the other three days of the week.

Here are the four tests extracted from the rambling test:

t0/tests/HomeAutomation/LightSchedulerTest.cpp
```
TEST(LightScheduler, ScheduleWeekEndFridayExcluded)
{
    LightScheduler_ScheduleTurnOn(3, WEEKEND, 1200);
    FakeTimeService_SetDay(FRIDAY);
    FakeTimeService_SetMinute(1200);
    LightScheduler_WakeUp();
    LONGS_EQUAL(LIGHT_ID_UNKNOWN, LightControllerSpy_GetLastId());
    LONGS_EQUAL(LIGHT_STATE_UNKNOWN, LightControllerSpy_GetLastState());
}

TEST(LightScheduler, ScheduleWeekEndSaturdayIncluded)
{
    LightScheduler_ScheduleTurnOn(3, WEEKEND, 1200);
    FakeTimeService_SetDay(SATURDAY);
    FakeTimeService_SetMinute(1200);
    LightScheduler_WakeUp();
    LONGS_EQUAL(3, LightControllerSpy_GetLastId());
    LONGS_EQUAL(1, LightControllerSpy_GetLastState());
 }

TEST(LightScheduler, ScheduleWeekEndSundayIncluded)
{
    LightScheduler_ScheduleTurnOn(3, WEEKEND, 1200);
    FakeTimeService_SetDay(SUNDAY);
    FakeTimeService_SetMinute(1200);
    LightScheduler_WakeUp();
    LONGS_EQUAL(3, LightControllerSpy_GetLastId());
    LONGS_EQUAL(1, LightControllerSpy_GetLastState());
}
```

```
TEST(LightScheduler, ScheduleWeekEndMondayExcluded)
{
    LightScheduler_ScheduleTurnOn(3, WEEKEND, 1200);
    FakeTimeService_SetDay(MONDAY);
    FakeTimeService_SetMinute(1200);
    LightScheduler_WakeUp();
    LONGS_EQUAL(LIGHT_ID_UNKNOWN, LightControllerSpy_GetLastId());
    LONGS_EQUAL(LIGHT_STATE_UNKNOWN, LightControllerSpy_GetLastState());
}
```

14.2 Copy-Paste-Tweak-Repeat Antipattern

The satisfaction of getting a test to pass encourages you to get back there again with another passing test. The fastest way to the next passing test is *Copy-Paste-Tweak-Repeat*. Copy-Paste-Tweak-Repeat is not a sustainable practice. It generates a lot of tests quickly from a seed test case, but if refactor is not part of the cycle, a mess follows.

The improved test cases from the Ramble-on Test pattern exhibit the Copy-Paste-Tweak-Repeat symptoms. Numerous tests almost look the same, requiring careful study to see the difference between test cases. The refactored tests minimize the duplication.

t1/tests/HomeAutomation/LightSchedulerTest.cpp
```
TEST(LightScheduler, ScheduleWeekEndFridayExcluded)
{
    LightScheduler_ScheduleTurnOn(lightNumber, WEEKEND, scheduledMinute);
    setTimeTo(FRIDAY, scheduledMinute);
    LightScheduler_WakeUp();
    checkLightState(LIGHT_ID_UNKNOWN, LIGHT_STATE_UNKNOWN);
}

TEST(LightScheduler, ScheduleWeekEndSaturdayIncluded)
{
    LightScheduler_ScheduleTurnOn(lightNumber, WEEKEND, scheduledMinute);
    setTimeTo(SATURDAY, scheduledMinute);
    LightScheduler_WakeUp();
    checkLightState(lightNumber, LIGHT_ON);
}

TEST(LightScheduler, ScheduleWeekEndSundayIncluded)
{
    LightScheduler_ScheduleTurnOn(lightNumber, WEEKEND, scheduledMinute);
    setTimeTo(SUNDAY, scheduledMinute);
    LightScheduler_WakeUp();
    checkLightState(lightNumber, LIGHT_ON);
}
```

```
TEST(LightScheduler, ScheduleWeekEndMondayExcluded)
{
    LightScheduler_ScheduleTurnOn(lightNumber, WEEKEND, scheduledMinute);
    setTimeTo(MONDAY, scheduledMinute);
    LightScheduler_WakeUp();
    checkLightState(LIGHT_ID_UNKNOWN, LIGHT_STATE_UNKNOWN);
}
```

In the refactored test, we used TEST_GROUP variables, lightNumber and scheduledMinute, and extracted setTimeTo() and checkLightState(). Using the TEST_GROUP variables helps illuminate that the day of the week is the input being varied between the tests.

14.3 Sore Thumb Test Cases Antipattern

Sometimes the common setup(), teardown(), and helpers are working for all the test cases, but then you take a turn to a new aspect of the code under test. The new test cases can stick out like a sore thumb, as in these tests for the CircularBuffer_Print():

tests/util/CircularBufferTest.cpp
```
TEST(CircularBuffer, PrintEmpty)
{
    const char* expectedOutput = "Circular buffer content:\n<>\n";
    FormatOutputSpy_Create(100);
    UT_PTR_SET(FormatOutput, FormatOutputSpy);

    CircularBuffer_Print(buffer);

    STRCMP_EQUAL(expectedOutput, FormatOutputSpy_GetOutput());
    FormatOutputSpy_Destroy();
}

TEST(CircularBuffer, PrintAfterOneIsPut)
{
    const char* expectedOutput = "Circular buffer content:\n<17>\n";
    FormatOutputSpy_Create(100);
    UT_PTR_SET(FormatOutput, FormatOutputSpy);

    CircularBuffer_Put(buffer, 17);
    CircularBuffer_Print(buffer);

    STRCMP_EQUAL(expectedOutput, FormatOutputSpy_GetOutput());
    FormatOutputSpy_Destroy();
}
```

None of the other fourteen tests (not shown) is at all concerned with printing. The previous two tests and the others concerned with printing will stick out like a sore thumb because of their different setup(), teardown(), or helper needs. There is also duplication in the tests, and they have steps that are usually in helpers or setup(). When that happens, we should create a new TEST_GROUP.

```
tests/util/CircularBufferPrintTest.cpp
TEST_GROUP(CircularBufferPrint)
{
    CircularBuffer buffer;
    const char * expectedOutput;
    const char * actualOutput;

    void setup()
    {
      UT_PTR_SET(FormatOutput, FormatOutputSpy);
      FormatOutputSpy_Create(100);
      actualOutput = FormatOutputSpy_GetOutput();
      buffer = CircularBuffer_Create(10);
    }

    void teardown()
    {
       CircularBuffer_Destroy(buffer);
       FormatOutputSpy_Destroy();
    }
};
```

You can see that the common printing-related setup and cleanup is in the TEST_GROUP, so tests like this can focus on what is their part.

```
tests/util/CircularBufferPrintTest.cpp
TEST(CircularBufferPrint, PrintNotYetWrappedAndIsFull)
{
    expectedOutput = "Circular buffer content:\n"
                     "<31, 41, 59, 26, 53>\n";

    CircularBuffer b = CircularBuffer_Create(5);
    CircularBuffer_Put(b, 31);
    CircularBuffer_Put(b, 41);
    CircularBuffer_Put(b, 59);
    CircularBuffer_Put(b, 26);
    CircularBuffer_Put(b, 53);

    CircularBuffer_Print(b);

    STRCMP_EQUAL(expectedOutput, actualOutput);
    CircularBuffer_Destroy(b);
}
```

14.4 Duplication Between Test Groups Antipattern

We just saw when it is appropriate to have more than one TEST_GROUP for a module. Graphically, this is the refactoring performed.

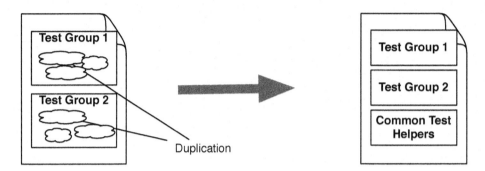

There is nothing that keeps you from having multiple TEST_GROUPs in one file, but I prefer to have one TEST_GROUP per file as represented by this diagram.

If you split files and there are common test helpers in the original TEST_GROUP, you can have duplication. Copying and pasting TEST_GROUP has the potential for the same duplication. Factoring out the helpers into a separate file can reduce the duplication.

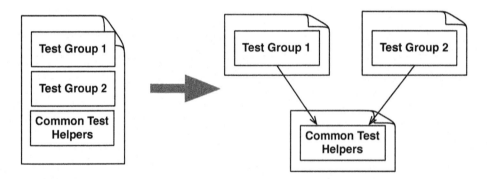

With the helpers moved out of the TEST_GROUP, the test cases no longer have easy access to the TEST_GROUP variables. Consequently, the helpers may need to have more parameters or accessor functions to manage them. The right thing to do is to factor out the helpers and not live with the duplication that comes with cutting and pasting.

14.5 Test Disrespect Antipattern

In teams new to TDD, not all team members will have bought into doing the tests. Those resisting TDD and unit testing exhibit *Test Disrespect*. This behavioral antipattern works like this: you develop functionality using TDD and make it part of the continuous integration build. A teammate makes a change, manually tests it, and checks in their work. Little did they know that their work broke your prior work, but the CI system does not rest. It lets all know about the broken build.

If the respect is low enough, your teammate (if you can call him that after this next move) deletes the rightfully whining test cases. His stuff works after all—he tested it. A less disrespectful teammate just put the tests in IGNORE_TEST() mode and shoots you an email to fix your stuff. Tests fall into disrepair and become irrelevant. In these early stages of TDD adoption, evaluation, and experimentation, you should get a team agreement to respect the tests. The people side of change is often more difficult than the technical.

14.6 Behavior-Driven Development Test Pattern

In this chapter, we looked at some test antipatterns, but now we'll move away from antipatterns and look at another popular testing pattern from Behavior-Driven Development (BDD). Look back at a LightScheduler test after it was refactored:

```
tests/HomeAutomation/LightSchedulerTest.cpp
TEST(LightScheduler, ScheduleWeekEndItsSaturday)
{
    LightScheduler_ScheduleTurnOn(3, WEEKEND, 1200);
    setTimeTo(SATURDAY, 1200);
    LightScheduler_WakeUp();
    checkLightState(3, LIGHT_ON);
}
```

The Four-Phase Test pattern was evident. Now let's look at an equivalent BDD style test.

```
t1/tests/HomeAutomation/LightSchedulerTest.cpp
TEST(LightScheduler, ScheduleWeekEndItsSaturday)
{
    given(lightNumber); isScheduledFor(WEEKEND); toTurnOnAt(scheduledMinute);
    whenTheTimeBecomes(SATURDAY); at(scheduledMinute);
    then(lightNumber); isOn();
}
```

You can see the BDD style test is more declarative and the Four-Phase Test pattern is not as evident. It reads a bit more like a specification rather than a test procedure. This is the BDD style, where the emphasis is on specification rather than testing. BDD-style tests follow this form:

- *Given* some precondition
- *When* something happens
- *Then* something that is dependent on Given and When should be true

Filling in a few more words, you can imagine a specification that reads like this:

- *Given* that a lightNumber is scheduled to turn off on Weekend days at the scheduledMinute
- *When* it becomes Saturday at the scheduledMinute
- *Then* the light with lightNumber should be LIGHT_OFF

The catchy shorthand for this style of test is *GivWenZen*. GivWenZen is another approach to structure tests that may improve test readability.

14.7 Where Are We?

We saw some common ways for tests to go bad. Of course, there are numerous other ways for tests to go bad. You can find more in Gerard Meszaros' catalog of test smells in *xUnit Testing Patterns [Mes07]*. Keeping tests clean and expressive may be more important than keeping the production code clean. Developers with comprehensive well-written tests use tests as the first place to look to understand existing code.

Tests can degrade overtime, because of the same incremental forces applied to any code and because of your own skill growth. As your test-writing skills grow, older tests might not be so easy to decipher. Your sense of smell improves. Smells work their way into the tests just as they work their way into the code, very slowly. Watch for the problems, and fix them right away. This keeps you working smoothly and efficiently when tests need to be revisited, which is often.

14.8 Put the Knowledge to Work

1. Refactor the CircularBufferTest so that there are test groups for the special cases of empty and full.
2. Refactor one of your CircularBufferTest groups to use a BDD test style.

What's the best time to plant a tree?

> ➤ Lee, the landscaper

CHAPTER 15

Closing Thoughts

If you have made it this far, I think you have learned a lot. I know I have through this journey. Through the journey you've seen how TDD guides design by encouraging loose coupling and high cohesion. You've seen how TDD helps catch side effect defects, documents assumptions in detail, and helps track progress.

It's a challenge to learn TDD and make it part of everyday life. When I started doing TDD in 1999, Kent Beck stressed that TDD is about discipline. A couple years later, the story changed. It was about addiction, though without the usual negative connotations. It's an addiction to getting feedback now for code written now. It's an addiction to being productive with less time spent chasing bugs. It's an addiction to fun and a feeling of accomplishment.

I hope through reflection on your own product development experiences, working through this book, and my words of warning that you see that messes in code and the lack of automated tests slow your progress. Visualize the forces at work that lead to software degradation by referring to Figure 31, *The impact of rushing*, on page 286.

With increased schedule pressure, we rush our work and let code quality suffer. We pledge to fix the problems later. But later never comes. We say, "We'll do it right the next time." We don't have time to run through all the manual tests that are really needed, so defects go unnoticed. Soon, the simplest features take surprisingly long to complete, we trip over unknown bugs, and we get into a vicious cycle of test and fix.[1]

You cannot claim you don't know; you've read this far, and you know that messes slow you down. Instead of a slow degrading pace, we can work toward

---

1. The diagrams in this chapter were inspired by Craig Larman and Bas Vodde's book *Scaling Lean and Agile Development [LV09]*.

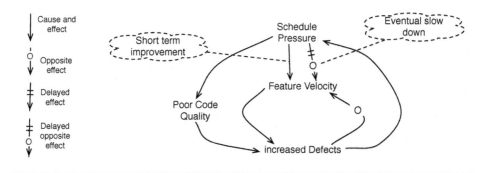

Figure 31— The impact of rushing

a sustainable pace, an improving pace. A development organization cannot maintain a high-quality product and a sustainable development pace with a manual test approach and slowly degrading code base.

As Figure 32, *Slow down to go fast*, on page 287 illustrates, initially your organization will take a productivity hit as you learn the practices of TDD. As you learn, your efforts with TDD improve code and design quality and relieve some of the manual test burden. Like Bob Martin asked in *Clean Code [Mar08]*, "What if code got a little better every time you changed it?" Unfortunately, you can't turn the clock back ten years. But you do have a choice about today and tomorrow.

Back in the 1980s when my wife and I built our home, the grass was coming in well. Lee, our landscaper stopped by; he wanted to sell us some trees. My pockets were empty; I wasn't ready to buy trees. Our conversation went like this:

"What's the best time to plant a tree?" asked Lee.

It was spring. Remembering my dusty bank account, I answered, "Fall."

Lee set the trap: "No, the best time to plant a tree is ten years ago."

I felt puzzled and trapped; I could't do anything about ten years ago, I thought. Lee continued, "What's the second best time to plant a tree?"

After a few seconds waiting for me to solve the apparent riddle, he smiled and said, "Today!"

There was nothing we could do about the past, but we could do something about the present. Within a week we'd bought some trees.

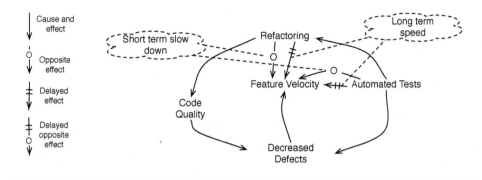

Figure 32— **Slow down to go fast.**

Don't you wish someone would have started writing tests for your code base and refactoring it ten years ago? You can't do anything about that, but you can pick the next best day to start adding tests; that's today.

Part IV

Appendixes

APPENDIX 1

Development System Test Environment

Building for test and building for production are separate operations, likely requiring different tools. This appendix describes some of the tools available, as of the date of publication, for a development system–based test environment.

A1.1 Development System Tool Chain

The examples in this book use GNU Compiler Collection (GCC, http://gcc.gnu.org) for native development system test builds. GCC is free and provides an up-to-date implementation of C and C++. There are a few options for GCC depending upon your development environment.

Development in Linux

Linux by default supports the gcc command to invoke the GNU C compiler. To use CppUTest, you need g++, GNU's C++ compiler. g++ is not installed by default in all Linux distributions. You can load the tools easily enough using the apt-get command. Superuser capabilities are needed, so you would enter this command:

```
sudo apt-get install g++
```

Some Linux distributions have only limited C support and may require you to install *build-essential* using this command:

```
sudo apt-get install build-essential
```

You can also install g++ using graphical package management software like Synaptic[1] or Ubuntu Software Center.[2]

---

1. http://www.nongnu.org/synaptic/
2. https://wiki.ubuntu.com/SoftwareCenter

Development on Apple Macs

Mac OS X's Xcode development environment includes the GNU tool chain. If you have not already done it, install Xcode from the distribution CDs or download it from Apple.

Development in Windows

For Windows development environments, there are a few GNU tool chain choices: Cygwin, MinGW+MSYS, and a virtual machine (VM) running Linux. The easiest to set up is Cygwin, a Unix command-line environment. A virtual machine running Linux is another alternative, but it's more work to set up. Some TDD practitioners have reported that they have a tenfold speed advantage with the Linux VM. So, start with Cygwin or MinGW, but plan on moving to a VM running Linux when test runs become too slow.

Cygwin and MinGW+MSYS offer similar capabilities but with different licensing. Licensing is not an issue for using the tools as a test environment. Aside from the gcc compilation environment, you get a Unix command-line environment, giving you powerful scripting environment for automating repetitive tasks.

Cygwin

Download the installation file.[3] Install the Default packages plus the Devel package. This will use about 500MB on your hard drive and take some time depending upon your download speed. Cygwin is a bit slow, but you can have a development system–based test environment up and running in a morning.

MinGW+MSYS

MinGW+MSYS can be found at http://www.mingw.org/. However, it's easier to install from the distribution at http://nuwen.net/mingw.html. I've had some trouble setting up MinGW+MSYS, so I usually steer people to Cygwin.

Virtual Machine with Linux

For the virtual machine approach on Windows, first you need to install a virtual machine. VirtualBox[4] is open source. Using it you can install a Linux distribution such as Ubuntu.[5] Plan on dedicating a gigabyte of RAM to the virtual machine. You will need to install g++ once you have installed Ubuntu.

---

3. http://www.cygwin.com
4. http://www.virtualbox.org
5. http://www.ubuntu.com

Microsoft Visual Studio

Visual Studio is another option. Make sure your version of Visual Studio supports a command-line build. A command-line build is important so that the build can be automatically run by a continuous integration server, such as Hudson.[6] There are Visual C++ V6 workspace and project files in the code base. CppUTest has additional Microsoft Visual Studio support.

Eclipse IDE

I like Eclipse with CDT (C/C++ Development Tools).[7] It runs on Mac, Linux, and Windows. It's handy for TDD because one key sequence saves all files and triggers a build and test cycle.

Whatever development environment you use, make it easy to run the build and test cycle. If you don't have a single keystroke build, keep a command-line window open so a test run is as simple as the key sequence for the following: save all files, switch windows, run last command.

A1.2 Full Test Build makefile

The makefile for the code examples found in this book provides a good example of how to build for test. The examples use the GNU tool chain for development system test builds. The principles behind the makefile are as follows:

- The makefile must be fast, doing an incremental build based on file dependencies.
- Tests are run with every build.
- Test files override production code.
- No cruft files should be in the directory tree.

The directories are structured to isolate test code from production code. The makefile specifies a list of production code directories. All .c and .cpp files in the production code directories are compiled and put into a library. (That's why the cruft has to be kept out of the source and test directories.) First let's see how the makefile specifies the production code directories:

```
SRC_DIRS = \
  src/IO \
  src/util\
  src/LedDriver \
  src/HomeAutomation
```

---

6. http://hudson-ci.org
7. http://www.eclipse.org/cdt/

The makefile specifies a list of directories containing tests, test doubles, and test helpers; they are compiled but left as object (.o) files. They are specified by directory like this:

```
TEST_SRC_DIRS = \
    tests\
    mocks\
    tests/IO\
    tests/util\
    tests/LedDriver\
    tests/HomeAutomation
```

A special file, usually called AllTests.cpp, is compiled to an object file as well. AllTests.cpp defines the test main(), which calls the test runner to run all the tests.

The test .o files are explicitly included as inputs to the linker along with the test main. Production code is pulled in from the library only if there are unresolved externals.

By explicitly including the test .o files, the link-time test doubles override any production code files in the library, because the test doubles get the first chance to resolve undefined symbols. The linker only brings production code .o files from the library if the .o file is needed to resolve unresolved references.

A1.3 Smaller Test Builds

An alternative approach to including all test .o files in the build is to do a build with a subset of the test files.

To do this with CppUTest, set up a test main file that selects the test cases to include using IMPORT_TEST_GROUP():

```
#include "CppUTest/CommandLineTestRunner.h"

int main(int ac, char ** av)
{
    return RUN_ALL_TESTS(ac, av);
}

IMPORT_TEST_GROUP(Flash);
IMPORT_TEST_GROUP(LedDriver);
IMPORT_TEST_GROUP(CircularBuffer);
```

For this approach, the test files need to be in a library so that only files with associated TEST_GROUP are pulled into the test executable.

You may find that you mix and match the techniques. On a large project, you may need libraries of shared test doubles. A common use would be to stub out the operating system calls so that tests can be run on the development platform.

APPENDIX 2

Unity Quick Reference

This appendix has reference information for Unity. Keep in mind that Unity is open source and likely to evolve. This appendix is in sync with the version of Unity included in the book's source code distribution. You can find out more about Unity and download the latest from the website.[1]

A2.1 Unity Test File

Test cases that belong to a group are put in the same file. The typical name for the file is GroupNameTest.c. The GroupName is usually named after the module under test, such as CircularBuffer. When a module needs more than one TEST_GROUP() to form a group of tests with common setup, introduce another group like CircularBufferPrint for the tests that are concerned with printing a CircularBuffer.

Here is a summary of the elements of a TEST_GROUP that go in a test file:

```
//test harness include
#include "unity_fixture.h"

//#includes for module under test

TEST_GROUP(GroupName);

//Define file scope data accessible to test group members prior to TEST_SETUP.

TEST_SETUP(GroupName)
{
    //initialization steps are executed before each TEST
}
```

---

1. http://unity.sourceforge.net

```
TEST_TEAR_DOWN(GroupName)
{
    //clean up steps are executed after each TEST
}

TEST(GroupName, UniqueTestName)
{
    /*
     * A TEST contains:
     *     TEST specific initializations
     *     operations on the code under test
     *     TEST specific condition checks
     */
}

//There can be many tests in a TEST_GROUP
TEST(GroupName, AnotherUniqueTestName)
{
    /*
     * Some more test statements
     */
}

//Each group has a TEST_GROUP_RUNNER
TEST_GROUP_RUNNER(GroupName)
{
    //Each TEST has a corresponding RUN_TEST_CASE
    RUN_TEST_CASE(GroupName, UniqueTestName);
    RUN_TEST_CASE(GroupName, AnotherUniqueTestName);
}
```

A TEST is a macro used to declare test cases. A TEST_GROUP associates numerous TEST cases with their TEST_SETUP() and TEST_TEAR_DOWN() functions. In the previous code example, the common parameter, GroupName, associates the TEST_GROUP_RUNNER(), TEST_GROUP, TEST_SETUP(), TEST_TEAR_DOWN(), and each of the TEST cases. You could have multiple TEST_GROUPs in a file, but it is more typical to have only one.

- TEST_GROUP(GroupName) defines the test group. Each TEST_GROUP() in your test build must have a unique name.

- TEST_SETUP(GroupName) is run before every TEST() in the TEST_GROUP(). Common initialization for each associated TEST() goes into TEST_SETUP().

- TEST_TEAR_DOWN(GroupName) is run after each TEST() in the TEST_GROUP(), restoring the system to its previous state. Common cleanup code goes into TEST_TEAR_DOWN().

- TEST(GroupName, TestName) defines all the steps of a test case. The GroupName and TestName pairs must be unique in the test build.

- TEST_GROUP_RUNNER(GroupName) is responsible for invoking RUN_TEST_CASE() for each TEST() in the group. If you forget to enter your TEST() here, it won't run. To keep from having to scroll to your TEST_GROUP_RUNNER(), you can put it in a separate file, typically named GroupNameTestRuner.c.

- RUN_TEST_CASE(GroupName, TestName) runs the associated TEST().

It's important to note that the first failure terminates the calling test.

A2.2 Unity Test main

You will have a main() for your production code and one, or more, for your test code. A Unity test main() looks like this:

```
#include "unity_fixture.h"

static void runAllTests()
{
   RUN_TEST_GROUP(GroupName);
   RUN_TEST_GROUP(AnotherGroupName);
   //...
}

int main(int argc, char * argv[])
{
   UnityMain(argc, argv, runAllTests);
}
```

You would define multiple Unity test main() functions and builds when you need to run tests in *chunks*. You would choose to chunk tests when tests run too slowly or when all tests will not fit into the memory of the target system.

A2.3 Unity TEST Condition Checks

Here is a short list of some of the TEST checks supported by Unity. (You can find the complete list of Unity assertion macros in unity.h.) When it comes right down to it, the use of these condition checks are what determines when your code is right or wrong.

- TEST_ASSERT_TRUE(boolean condition): Checks any boolean condition to be true

- TEST_ASSERT_FALSE(boolean condition): Checks any boolean condition to be false

- TEST_ASSERT_EQUAL_STRING(expected, actual): Compares const char* strings for equality
- TEST_ASSERT_EQUAL(expected, actual): Compares two numbers
- TEST_ASSERT_EQUAL_INT(expected, actual): Compares two numbers
- TEST_ASSERT_BYTES_EQUAL(expected, actual): Compares two numbers, eight bits wide
- TEST_ASSERT_POINTERS_EQUAL(expected, actual): Compares two pointers
- TEST_ASSERT_FLOAT_WITHIN(expected, actual, tolerance): Compares two floating point numbers within some tolerance
- TEST_FAIL_MESSAGE(text): Fails test and prints message

The checks are also known as *asserts* or *assertions*. I use these terms interchangeably.

A2.4 Command-Line Options

Option	Meaning
-v	Verbose—announces each test before it runs.
-g testgroup	Selects tests in testgroup using a substring match.
-n testname	Selects tests by testname using a substring match.
-r [count]	Repeats test run count times. The default value is 2. This is helpful for checking for initialization problems and memory leaks that can be attributed to lazy initialization.

A2.5 Unity in Your Target

The only I/O that Unity does is to output characters. By default, Unity uses putchar() for character output. You can send characters to a function of your choosing by providing your own definition of the macro UNITY_OUTPUT_CHAR. Here is how the default is set:

```
#ifndef UNITY_OUTPUT_CHAR
#define UNITY_OUTPUT_CHAR(a) putchar(a)
#endif
```

The function pointer is initialized to point to putchar() like this:

```
int (*outputChar)(int) = putchar;
```

As long as you have a putchar() function, Unity is ready to run in your environment. If your target does not have any way to output a character, you'll have to get creative. For example, *your* putchar() could capture lines of text, see whether the last line begins with "OK", and then drive an output pin to indicate test run status. If your target is this constrained in I/O, running tests off-target becomes really important. You'll probably also want to invest in an eval board that has some way to output characters.

APPENDIX 3

CppUTest Quick Reference

This appendix has reference information for CppUTest. Keep in mind that CppUTest is open source and is likely to evolve. This appendix is in sync with the version of CppUTest included in the book's source code distribution. You can find out more about CppUTest at http://www.cpputest.org and download the latest from http://cpputest.sourceforge.net.

A3.1 The CppUTest Test File

Here's a look at a CppUTest test file. As already mentioned, this is C++ with most of the C++ syntax hidden, making it easy to use for both C and C++ programmers.

```
extern "C"
{
// #includes for things with C linkage
}

// #includes for things with C++ linkage

#include "CppUTest/TestHarness.h"

TEST_GROUP(GroupName)
{
    //Define data accessible to test group members here.
    void setup()
    {
        //initialization steps are executed before each TEST
    }
    void teardown()
    {
        //clean up steps are executed after each TEST
    }
};
```

```
//Many test cases like this can be defined in the test file.
TEST(GroupName, TestCaseName)
{
    /*
     * The test case contains:
     *     test specific initializations
     *     operations on the code under test
     *     test specific condition checks
     */
}
```

As with Unity, the TEST_GROUP and TEST cases are tied together through a common GroupName. Notice there's no TEST_GROUP_RUNNER(). TEST_GROUP_RUNNER() is not needed because each TEST() installs itself into the list of all tests during file scope variable initialization.

Let's see how the test main() is also different.

A3.2 Test Main

A main() is needed to run all the installed tests. It looks like this:

tests/AllTests.cpp
```
#include "CppUTest/CommandLineTestRunner.h"

int main(int argc, char** argv)
{
    return RUN_ALL_TESTS(argc, argv);
}
```

This main() is also missing something—the RUN_TEST_GROUP() invocations. This bit of manual wiring is not needed because each TEST installs itself into the list of all tests.

A3.3 TEST Condition Checks

Here is a list of the TEST condition checks available in CppUTest at the time of this writing. Unity and CppUTest differ in their condition check names. Conceptually they are the same.

- CHECK(boolean condition): Checks any boolean condition
- CHECK_TRUE(boolean condition): Same as CHECK()
- CHECK_FALSE(boolean condition): Passes for a FALSE boolean condition.
- CHECK_EQUAL(expected, actual): Checks for equality between entities using ==
- STRCMP_EQUAL(expected, actual): Compares const char* strings for equality using strcmp()

- LONGS_EQUAL(expected, actual): Compares two numbers
- BYTES_EQUAL(expected, actual): Compares two numbers, eight bits wide
- POINTERS_EQUAL(expected, actual): Compares two pointers
- DOUBLES_EQUAL(expected, actual, tolerance): Compares two doubles within some tolerance
- FAIL(text): Fails test and prints message

The checks are also known as *asserts* or *assertions*. I use these terms interchangeably. It's important to note that the first failed assertion terminates the calling test.

A3.4 Test Execution Order

Tests run backward in CppUTest. Other test harnesses might run in some other order. Test order should not matter, and you should not count on any particular order. Tests should be independent of each other, each one its own little experiment. One test might logically precede another in the design or as documentation, but when it comes time to run them, unit tests must be designed to be independent of each other. Prefer tests that depend only on setup() and teardown().

A3.5 Scripts to Create Starter Files

Included with CppUTest are scripts for generating the header, source, and test files needed for various forms of C modules and C++ classes.

The TDD purist might reject these scripts as not needed. A pragmatist might prefer to eliminate tedious typing and follow one of a few well-defined patterns.

Generating initial versions of the needed LedDriver files is as simple as typing this command:

❮ NewCModule LedDriver

Here's the generated version of LedDriver.h:

include/LedDriver/LedDriver.h
```c
#ifndef D_LedDriver_H
#define D_LedDriver_H

void LedDriver_Create(void);
void LedDriver_Destroy(void);

#endif  /* D_LedDriver_H */
```

Here's the generated LedDriver.c:

src/LedDriver/LedDriver.c
```c
#include "LedDriver.h"

void LedDriver_Create(uint16_t * address)
{
}

void LedDriver_Destroy(void)
{
}
```

Here's the generated TEST_GROUP() in LedDriverTest.cpp:

tests/LedDriver/LedDriverTest.cpp
```cpp
#include "CppUTest/TestHarness.h"

extern "C"
{
#include "LedDriver.h"
}

TEST_GROUP(LedDriver)
{
    void setup()
    {
      LedDriver_Create();
    }

    void teardown()
    {
       LedDriver_Destroy();
    }
};

TEST(LedDriver, Create)
{
  FAIL("Start here");
}
```

A3.6 CppUTest in Your Target

The only I/O that CppUTest does is to output characters with putchar(). As long as you have a putchar() function, CppUTest should be ready to run in your environment.

If your target does not have any way to output a character, you'll have to get creative. For example, *your* putchar() could capture lines of text, see whether the last line begins with "OK", and then drive an output pin to indicate test run status. If your target is this constrained in I/O, running tests off-target becomes really important. You'll probably also want to invest in an eval board that has some way to output characters.

Because embedded C++ compilers and runtime libraries often differ, you may run into portability issues. You'll find all CppUTest's system dependencies in this header file:

    include/CppUTest/PlatformSpecificFunctions.h

There are platform-specific implementations for GCC, Symbian, and Visual C++ in the distribution. The GCC implementation can be found here:

    src/Platforms/Gcc/UTestPlatform.cpp

A3.7 Convert CppUTest Tests to Unity

Look in `CppUTest/scripts/convertToUnity` to see how to convert CppUTest test files to Unity.

APPENDIX 4

LedDriver After Getting Started

This shows the state of the LedDriver at the start of Chapter 4, *Testing Your Way to Done*, on page 49.

A4.1 LedDriver First Few Tests in Unity

```
unity/LedDriver/LedDriverTest.c
TEST_GROUP(LedDriver);
static uint16_t virtualLeds;
TEST_SETUP(LedDriver)
{
    LedDriver_Create(&virtualLeds);
}

TEST_TEAR_DOWN(LedDriver)
{
}

TEST(LedDriver, LedsOffAfterCreate)
{
    uint16_t virtualLeds = 0xffff;
    LedDriver_Create(&virtualLeds);
    TEST_ASSERT_EQUAL_HEX16(0, virtualLeds);
}
TEST(LedDriver, TurnOnLedOne)
{
    LedDriver_TurnOn(1);
    TEST_ASSERT_EQUAL_HEX16(1, virtualLeds);
}
TEST(LedDriver, TurnOffLedOne)
{
    LedDriver_TurnOn(1);
    LedDriver_TurnOff(1);
    TEST_ASSERT_EQUAL_HEX16(0, virtualLeds);
}
```

```
unity/LedDriver/LedDriverTestRunner.c
```
```c
TEST_GROUP_RUNNER(LedDriver)
{
    RUN_TEST_CASE(LedDriver, LedsOffAfterCreate);
    RUN_TEST_CASE(LedDriver, TurnOnLedOne);
    RUN_TEST_CASE(LedDriver, TurnOffLedOne);
}
```

A4.2 LedDriver First Few Tests in CppUTest

```
tests/LedDriver/LedDriverTest.cpp
```
```cpp
TEST_GROUP(LedDriver)
{
    uint16_t virtualLeds;
    void setup()
    {
        LedDriver_Create(&virtualLeds);
    }
    void teardown()
    {
        LedDriver_Destroy();
    }
};

TEST(LedDriver, LedsAreOffAfterCreate)
{
    virtualLeds = 0xffff;
    LedDriver_Create(&virtualLeds);
    LONGS_EQUAL(0, virtualLeds);
}

TEST(LedDriver, TurnOnLedOne)
{
    LedDriver_TurnOn(1);
    LONGS_EQUAL(1, virtualLeds);
}

TEST(LedDriver, TurnOffLedOne)
{
    LedDriver_TurnOn(1);
    LedDriver_TurnOff(1);
    LONGS_EQUAL(0, virtualLeds);
}
```

A4.3 LedDriver Early Interface

```
include/LedDriver/LedDriver.h
```
```c
#ifndef D_LedDriver_H
#define D_LedDriver_H
```

```c
void LedDriver_Create(void);
void LedDriver_Destroy(void);
void LedDriver_TurnOn(int ledNumber);
void LedDriver_TurnOff(int ledNumber);

#endif
```

A4.4 LedDriver Skeletal Implementation

src/LedDriver/LedDriver.c
```c
#include "LedDriver.h"

static uint16_t * ledsAddress;

void LedDriver_Create(uint16_t * address)
{
    ledsAddress = address;
    *ledsAddress = 0;
}

void LedDriver_Destroy(void)
{
}

void LedDriver_TurnOn(int ledNumber)
{
    *ledsAddress = 1;
}

void LedDriver_TurnOff(int ledNumber)
{
    *ledsAddress = 0;
}
```

APPENDIX 5

Example OS Isolation Layer

In Chapter 11, *SOLID, Flexible, and Testable Designs*, on page 189, we looked at the Open Closed Principle (OCP) and Liskov Substitution Principle (LSP). These principles are about creating plug-compatible software. In this appendix, we are going to look at making an operating system isolation layer. The layer is designed to allow your product's core application to run in different operating system environments.

We'll call this OS isolation layer *MyOS*. The layer assures a common interface, as well as plug-compatible behavior across multiple operating systems. We'll talk about one small part of the layer, thread creation, and look at three substitutable implementations to illustrate OCP and LSP.

MyOS must run on Linux and Micrium µC/OS-III.[1] Linux is POSIX compliant; µC/OS-III is proprietary. These two operating systems are important because our product ships in two configurations, one requiring embedded Linux and the other µC/OS-III. For test purposes, it would also be helpful to have MyOS run on Windows.

To illustrate creating layers, we will look at one aspect of the layer, thread creation. Each OS has a unique way of creating a thread. To support an application that can run on any of these operating systems, we need three substitutable implementations. The implementations must provide the same interface as well as preconditions and postconditions surrounding each OS function.

---

1. µC/OS-III is a commercially available RTOS (http://www.micrium.com).

A5.1 Test Cases to Assure Substitutable Behavior

Test cases can help us make MyOS behave the same regardless of the underlying implementation. This is important because we don't want our application to care which OS is under the hood. Before we look at the test cases, let's look at an example MyOS Thread's entry function from our test fixture:

tests/MyOS/ThreadTest.cpp
```
static int threadRan = FALSE;
static void * threadEntry(void * p)
{
    threadRan = TRUE;
    return 0;
}
```

The entry function takes a pointer to anything (void *) as a parameter and also returns a void *. This function sets threadRan to TRUE so the test can check whether the thread is run at the appropriate time. setup() sets threadRan to FALSE (not shown).

This test case assures that a MyOS Thread is not started upon creation.

tests/MyOS/ThreadTest.cpp
```
TEST(Thread, CreateDoesNotStartThread)
{
    thread = Thread_Create(threadEntry, 0);
    Thread_Destroy(thread);
    CHECK(FALSE == threadRan);
}
```

Thread_Create() creates the thread. Thread_Destroy() waits for a Thread to complete; this call may block but not in this case. A Thread that has never been started can be destroyed without blocking. If the threadRan check passes, the thread was not run.

This next test drives us to call the underlying OS functions:

tests/MyOS/ThreadTest.cpp
```
TEST(Thread, StartedThreadRunsBeforeItIsDestroyed)
{
    thread = Thread_Create(threadEntry, 0);
    Thread_Start(thread);
    Thread_Destroy(thread);
    CHECK(TRUE == threadRan);
}
```

Here's the MyOS Thread's interface supporting the first two tests:

include/MyOS/Thread.h
```
typedef struct ThreadStruct * Thread;
typedef void * (*ThreadEntryFunction)(void *);


Thread Thread_Create(ThreadEntryFunction f, void * parameter);
void Thread_Start(Thread);
void Thread_Destroy(Thread);
```

In the next three sections, we'll look at the three compatible implementations.

A5.2 POSIX Implementation

To make this test pass for POSIX, we'll have to use the POSIX pthread functions properly. The POSIX thread create function also starts the thread, so the MyOS Thread creation function can't call pthread_create(). It has to store the parameters, so when Thread_Start() is called, it can create and start the thread. Here is the MyOS data structure used in the POSIX implementation:

src/MyOS/posix/Thread.c
```
typedef struct ThreadStruct
{
    ThreadEntryFunction entry;
    void * parameter;
    pthread_t pthread;
} ThreadStruct;
```

pthread_t is an abstract data type (ADT) from the POSIX API. Here is the POSIX implementation of Thread_Create():

src/MyOS/posix/Thread.c
```
Thread Thread_Create(ThreadEntryFunction f, void * parameter)
{
    Thread self = calloc(1, sizeof(ThreadStruct));
    self->entry = f;
    self->parameter = parameter;
    return self;
}
```

Thread_Create() captures the parameters into the ThreadStruct structure. Thread_Start() uses the parameters to create and start the thread, as shown in the following code:

src/MyOS/posix/Thread.c
```
void Thread_Start(Thread self)
{
    pthread_create(&self->pthread, NULL, self->entry, self->parameter);
}
```

Once a Thread is started, the test must wait for the Thread to complete. If the test does not synchronize with the completion of the running thread, bad things may happen. Here is the POSIX Thread_Destroy() implementation that waits for the thread to end:

src/MyOS/posix/Thread.c
```c
void Thread_Destroy(Thread self)
{
    pthread_join(self->pthread, NULL);
    free(self);
}
```

pthread_join() blocks until the thread exits. The second parameter to pthread_join() allows the caller to capture the thread's return value. The NULL means Thread_Destroy() is not interested in the ThreadEntryFunction() return result.

This test worked fine on my Mac. My continuous integration (CI) build on Linux was not so well behaved. For some reason, joining a pthread that was never started crashed. To protect against this, add the started flag to ThreadStruct, using it like this:

```c
Thread Thread_Create(ThreadEntryFunction f, void * parameter)
{
    Thread self = calloc(1, sizeof(ThreadStruct));
    self->entry = f;
    self->parameter = parameter;
    self->started = FALSE;;
    return self;
}

void Thread_Destroy(Thread self)
{
    if (self->started)
        pthread_join(self->pthread, NULL);
    free(self);
}

void Thread_Start(Thread self)
{
    self->started = TRUE;
    pthread_create(&self->pthread, NULL, self->entry, self->parameter);
}
```

The initial POSIX version passes its tests on Linux and Mac. CI should also build for our embedded Linux environment and push out a test run. There are probably other things we should do to Thread, like setting thread stack size or priority, as well as handling various error conditions, but I think you get the idea.

A5.3 Micrium RTOS Implementation

Let's look at one more implementation using the Micrium μC/OS-III. Micrium's concurrency model is based on tasks that are not allowed to exit, though tasks can be killed. Killing a running task can cause problems, so we'll need to combine a task and a semaphore. We'll use the semaphore to synchronize Thread termination. Here is create:

src/MyOS/Micrium/Thread.c
```
Thread Thread_Create (ThreadEntryFunction entry, void *parameter)
{
    OS_ERR err;

    Thread self = OSMemGet(&AppMemTask, &err);
    self->entry = entry;
    self->parameter = parameter;
    self->started = FALSE;
    OSSemCreate (&(self->Sem), "Test Sem", 0, &err);
    return self;
}
```

Micrium tasks start as soon as they are created too, so we don't create the task in Thread_Create(). We do interact with Micrium functions to get task memory and to create a semaphore.

Here is the ThreadStruct needed for Micrium:

src/MyOS/Micrium/Thread.c
```
typedef struct ThreadStruct
{
    ThreadEntryFunction entry;
    void * parameter;
    BOOL started;
    OS_TCB TCB;
    OS_SEM Sem;
    CPU_STK Stk[APP_TASK_SIMPLE_STK_SIZE];
} ThreadStruct;
```

The struct contains the semaphore and the task data structures. ThreadStruct also contains the task's stack. The stack size is hard-coded in this example, though we'd want to customize that.

Here Thread_Start() creates a Micrium task:

src/MyOS/Micrium/Thread.c
```
void Thread_Start(Thread self)
{
    OS_ERR err;

    self->started = TRUE;
```

```c
    OSTaskCreate(&(self->TCB), "App Task",
                 MicriumTaskShell, (void *)self,
                 APP_TASK_SIMPLE_PRIO,
                 self->Stk, APP_TASK_SIMPLE_STK_SIZE / 10,
                 APP_TASK_SIMPLE_STK_SIZE,
                 0,
                 0,
                 0,
                 (OS_OPT_TASK_STK_CHK | OS_OPT_TASK_STK_CLR),
                 &err);
}
```

As mentioned earlier, Micrium tasks are not allowed to exit. So, we use this extended entry function to get compatible behavior.

src/MyOS/Micrium/Thread.c
```c
static void MicriumTaskShell(void *p_arg)
{
    Thread thread;
    OS_ERR err;

    thread = (Thread) p_arg;
    thread->entry(thread->parameter);
    OSSemPost(&(thread->Sem), OS_OPT_POST_ALL, &err);
    while (DEF_ON)
    {
        OSTimeDlyHMSM(0, 0, 0, 100, OS_OPT_TIME_HMSM_STRICT, &err);
    }
}
```

MicriumTaskShell() calls the thread->entry(). When entry() returns MicriumTaskShell() posts to its semaphore to signal that the task is done. The task enters an infinite loop waiting to be killed. Here, Thread_Destroy() synchronizes with the task's completion signal:

src/MyOS/Micrium/Thread.c
```c
void Thread_Destroy (Thread self)
{
    OS_ERR err;
    OSSemPend(&(self->Sem), 0, OS_OPT_PEND_BLOCKING, 0, &err);
    OSTaskDel(&(self->TCB), &err);
    OSSemDel(&(self->Sem));
    OSMemPut (&AppMemTask, self, &err);
}
```

Once the OSSemPend() returns, Thread_Destroy() kills the task and frees Micrium-controlled resources.

A5.4 Win32 Implementation

Now let's take a look at the equivalent Windows implementation. The Windows implementation sits on top of the Win32 API. Win32 allows thread creation and execution to be a two-step process. So, let's take advantage of that. That would imply that the entry function and parameter do not need to be in the struct. But the Win32 prototype for a thread entry function is somewhat different from MyOS, so we have to store the entry and parameter in the struct after all. Here is the struct:

src/MyOS/Win32/Thread.c
```c
typedef struct ThreadStruct
{
    HANDLE threadHandle;
    ThreadEntryFunction entry;
    void * parameter;
    BOOL started;
} ThreadStruct;
```

Here is the Win32-compatible thread entry function:

src/MyOS/Win32/Thread.c
```c
static DWORD WINAPI Win32ThreadEntry(LPVOID param)
{
    Thread thread = (Thread)param;
    return (UINT)thread->entry(thread->parameter);
}
```

The param passed to the entry function is the Thread pointer. So, the Win32 entry function can pull out the actual thread entry point and parameter from the struct. As a first cut, let's just cast the return type to what Win32 expects. We should start a test list and make sure we check that a pointer can be returned through a Win32 DWORD WINAPI. Thread creation looks like this:

src/MyOS/Win32/Thread.c
```c
Thread Thread_Create(ThreadEntryFunction entry, void * parameter)
{
    DWORD threadId;
    Thread self = calloc(1, sizeof(ThreadStruct));
    self->entry = entry;
    self->parameter = parameter;
    self->threadHandle = CreateThread(0, 0, Win32ThreadEntry, self,
            CREATE_SUSPENDED, &threadId);
    return self;
}
```

Notice the thread is created in the suspended state. The MyOS ThreadEntryFunction() is passed with the ThreadStruct, while the Win32ThreadEntry() is passed to

Win32's CreateThread() function. The threadHandle is stored into the ThreadStruct for later thread controls.

Thread_Start() calls the Win32 function ResumeThread() to get the suspended thread going:

src/MyOS/Win32/Thread.c
```c
void Thread_Start(Thread self)
{
    self->started = TRUE;
    ResumeThread(self->threadHandle);
}
```

Like the other implementations, Thread_Destroy() has to wait for the Win32 thread to complete. That is done with the call to WaitForSingleObject():

src/MyOS/Win32/Thread.c
```c
void Thread_Destroy(Thread self)
{
    if (self->started)
    {
        WaitForSingleObject(self->threadHandle, INFINITE);
        self->started = FALSE;
    }
    CloseHandle(self->threadHandle);
    free(self);
}
```

A5.5 Burden the Layer, Not the Application

Applying the Open-Closed Principle and the Liskov Substitution Principle makes for more flexible designs. High-level application logic can be given a longer useful life by isolating the OS (and other dependencies) using these principles. Test cases, run on each supported platform, assure not only a common interface but a common meaning of all the calls.

APPENDIX 6

Bibliography

[Bec00] Kent Beck. *Extreme Programming Explained: Embrace Change*. Addison-Wesley Longman, Reading, MA, 2000.

[Bec02] Kent Beck. *Test Driven Development: By Example*. Addison-Wesley, Reading, MA, 2002.

[Dij72] Edsger W. Dijkstra. *The Humble Programmer*. Univeristy of Texas at Austin, Austin, TX, 1972.

[FBBO99] Martin Fowler, Kent Beck, John Brant, William Opdyke, and Don Roberts. *Refactoring: Improving the Design of Existing Code*. Addison-Wesley, Reading, MA, 1999.

[Fea04] Michael Feathers. *Working Effectively with Legacy Code*. Prentice Hall, Englewood Cliffs, NJ, 2004.

[GHJV95] Erich Gamma, Richard Helm, Ralph Johnson, and John Vlissides. *Design Patterns: Elements of Reusable Object-Oriented Software*. Addison-Wesley, Reading, MA, 1995.

[Gan00] Jack Ganssle. *The Art of Designing Embedded Systems*. Newnes, Woburn, MA, 2000.

[Gre04] James W. Grenning. Progress Before Hardware. *Agile Times*. 4[1]:74-78, 2004, February.

[Gre07] James W. Grenning. Embedded Test Driven Development Cycle. *Embedded Systems Conference*. Submissions, 2004, 2006, 2007.

[Gre07a] James W. Grenning. Applying Test Driven Development to Embedded Software. *Instrumentation & Measurement Magazine, IEEE*. 10[6]:20-25, 2007, December.

[HT00]   Andrew Hunt and David Thomas. *The Pragmatic Programmer: From Journeyman to Master.* Addison-Wesley, Reading, MA, 2000.

[LV09]   Craig Larman and Bas Vodde. *Scaling Lean and Agile Development.* Addison-Wesley, Reading, MA, 2009.

[Lis74]   Barbara Liskov. Programming with Abstract Data Types. *Proceedings of the ACM SIGPLAN Symposium on Very High Level Languages.* 9[4], 1974, April.

[Lis88]   Barbara Liskov. Data Abstraction and Hierarchy. *SIGPLAN Notices.* 23[5], 1988, May.

[MFC01]   Tim MacKinnon, Steve Freeman, and Philip Craig. Endo-Testing: Unit Testing with Mock Objects. *Extreme Programming Examined.* 1:287-302, 2001.

[Mar02]   Robert C. Martin. *Agile Software Development, Principles, Patterns, and Practices.* Prentice Hall, Englewood Cliffs, NJ, 2002.

[Mar08]   Robert C. Martin. *Clean Code: A Handbook of Agile Software Craftsmanship.* Prentice Hall, Englewood Cliffs, NJ, 2008.

[Mes07]   Gerard Meszaros. *xUnit Test Patterns.* Addison-Wesley, Reading, MA, 2007.

[Mey97]   Bertrand Meyer. *Object-Oriented Software Construction.* Prentice Hall, Englewood Cliffs, NJ, Second, 1997.

[OL11]   Tim Ottinger and Jeff Langr. *Agile in a Flash.* The Pragmatic Bookshelf, Raleigh, NC and Dallas, TX, 2011.

[SM04]   Nancy Van Schooenderwoert and Ron Morsicato. Taming the Embedded Tiger; Agile Test Techniques for Embedded Software. *Proceedings of the 2004 Agile Development Conference.* ADC 2004, 2004, June.

[UNMM07]   Hidetake Uwano, Masahide Nakamura, Akito Monden, and Ken-ichi Matsumoto. Exploiting Eye Movements for Evaluating Reviewer's Performance in Software Review. *IEICE Transactions on Fundamentals.* E90-A, No.10:317-328, 2007, October.

[Wil00]   Stephne Wilbers. *Keys to Great Writing.* Writers Digest Books, Cincinnati, Ohio, 2000.

Index

A
abstract data types, 27–28, 192
adapters, 88
antipatterns
  copy-paste-tweak-repeat, 279
  duplication between test groups, 282
  ramble-on, 277–279
  sore thumb test cases, 280–282
  test disrespect, 283
assertions
  in CppUTest, 304
  in Unity, 299
automated testing
  crashes, 24
  for hardware, 88–89
  importance of, 4
  vs. manual testing, 94
  unit test harnesses, 13–24

B
Behavior-Driven Development (BDD) tests, 283
buffer overruns, 16
build time, 98
BYTES_EQUAL, 305

C
characterization tests, 268–271
CHECK, 304
CHECK_EQUAL, 304
CHECK_FALSE, 304
CHECK_TRUE, 304
CircularBuffer module
  definition, 28
  multiple-instance module in, 194
  verifying printed output, 152–159
CMock, 183–185
code duplication, 69
code smells, 222–232
code structure, 7, 223
code under test, 14
collaborators, 107, 109, 112
commented-out code, 231
comments, 230–231
compiler incompatibility, 81
conditional compilation, 232, 243
continuous integration, 84
CppUMock, 180
CppUTest
  C function declarations, 123
  choice of C++, 101–102
  converting tests to Unity, 102, 307
  examples, 21–23
  function-pointer substitution, 151
  output, 23–24
  quick reference, 303–307
  starter file scripts, 305
  test execution order, 305
crashes, 24
CruiseControl, 84
cyclomatic complexity, 223
Cygwin, 292

D
data encapsulation, 27–28
dead drops, 125
Debug-Later Programming, 5–6
defect prevention, 6, 8, 51
dependencies
  breaking, 108
  dependency graphs, 109
  DOCs and TDOCs, 110
  and legacy code, 256, 265
  in Light Scheduler, 118–120
  and test doubles, 110–113
dependency injection, 33–36
Dependency Inversion Principle (DIP), 192–193
design
  hardware independence, 79
  Rules of Simple Design, 215
  SOLID design principles, 189–195
  and testability, 9, 27–29, 108
design patterns
  0-1-N, 127
  adapter, 88
development cycle
  continuous integration, 84
  embedded TDD, 80–83
  TDD, 6
development environments
  Cygwin, 292
  Eclipse IDE, 293

Linux tool chain, 291
Linux virtual machine, 292
Mac OS X Xcode, 292
Microsoft Visual Studio, 293
MinGW+MSYS, 292
device drivers, 163–180
DOCs (Depended On Components), 110
Don't Burn Bridges, 235
DOUBLES_EQUAL, 305
DRY (Don't Repeat Yourself), 69, 215
DTSTTCPW, 43
dual-targeting
    benefits, 78–80
    risks, 79–80
dummies, 114
duplicate code, 69
dynamic interfaces, 203–214

E

Eclipse IDE, 293
encapsulation, 27–28, 108
evaluation boards, 78, 82
exploding fakes, 114

F

FAIL, 305
failure reporting
    in CppUTest, 24
    in Unity, 20
fakes, 114
feature envy, 228, 244
file scope variables, 27, 39, 194, 230
FIRST (Fast, Isolated, Repeatable, Self-verifying, Timely) tests, 46
flash memory driver
    clock rollover, 179
    design, 163–167
    flowchart, 167
    simulating device time-out, 178–179
    test list, 166
    writing tests, 167–171, 174–180
FormatOutput method, 152–159
FormatOutputSpy class, 153–155
Four-Phase Test pattern, 25, 110
function length, 224–227

function names, 222
function pointer substitution
    FormatOutput method, 152–159
    randomness, testing, 147–152
function-pointer substitution
    CppUTest support for, 151
    defined, 113
    in Light Scheduler, 149–152

H

hardware abstraction layer, 117
hardware issues
    acceptance tests, 89
    build time, 98
    compiler incompatibility, 81
    dependency injection, 33–36
    dual-targeting, 78–80, 100
    evaluation boards, 78, 82
    hardware-dependent code, 79–80, 195–210
    header file incompatibility, 85–88
    impacts on software projects, 77–78
    manual testing, 83
    memory limitations, 83, 99–100
    runtime library issues, 84
    schedule delays, 77–78
hardware testing, 83, 88–91
header file incompatibility, 85–88
Hudson, 84

I

IGNORE_TEST, 63
inline monitors, 258–260
instrumentation, testing with, 90
Interface Segregation Principle (ISP), 191
interface testing, 36

J

JUnit, 9, 23

L

lasagna code, 223
learning tests, 271–273
LED driver
    boundary conditions, 57–63
    dependency injection, 33–36
    interface design, 36–39
    refactoring, 44
    requirements, 29
    test list, 30, 68, 75
    writing tests, 31–39, 41–42, 49–73
legacy code
    Boy Scout principle, 254–255
    characterization tests, 268–271
    code change algorithm, 255–257
    code change policy, 99, 253
    crash to pass, 263–268
    debug output sense points, 258
    inline monitors, 258–260
    sensing variables, 257
    strategic tests, 274
    test points, 257–260
    test-driven bug fixes, 274
    two-stage struct initialization, 260–263
Light Scheduler
    abstracting the clock, 126
    collaborators in, 121
    design, 118–120
    dynamic interfaces in, 203–214
    function-pointer substitution in, 149–152
    hardware variation support, 195–214
    link-time substitution in, 119
    refactoring, 132–134
    single-instance module in, 194
    spies in, 120–122
    stubs in, 126
    test list, 118–119, 131
    vtables in, 211–214
    writing tests, 121–145, 147–152
LightControllerSpy class, 121–145
LightDriverSpy class, 196–210

link seams, 120
link-time substitution, 113, 119
Linux tool chain, 291
Liskov Substitution Principle (LSP), 191, 313
LONGS_EQUAL, 305

M
Mac OS X development environment, 292
makefiles
    full test build, 293–294
    small test build, 294
manual testing, 83, 94
memory corruption, 16
memory limitations, 83, 99–100
Microsoft Visual Studio, 293
MinGW+MSYS, 292
MockIO, 164–168, 171–174, 180, 269–271
mocks
    in characterization tests, 269–271
    defined, 114
    in flash memory driver, 164–168, 171–174
    tools for generating, 183–185
modular design, 27–29
multiple-instance modules, 28, 194

N
names, 222

O
Open Closed Principle (OCP), 190, 313
OS abstraction layer, 117, 313–320

P
pair programming, 61
platform-specific code, 79–80, 85–88
POINTERS_EQUAL, 305
preprocessor substitution, 114
primitive obsession, 227

printed output
    debug output sense points, 258
    verifying with spies, 152–159
production code, 14

Q
quick swap, 243

R
randomness, testing, 147–152
ravioli code, 223
Red-Green-Refactor, 9
refactoring
    benefits, 8, 220
    code duplication, 64–66, 69, 132, 237
    commented-out code, 231
    comments, 230–231
    complex conditionals, 135–138, 227, 241–242
    conditional compilation, 232, 243
    critical skills for, 220–222
    cyclomatic complexity, 224
    deep nesting, 228
    defined, 219
    extracting functions, 225–227
    global data, 230
    initialization functions, 229
    long parameter lists, 229
    names, 222
    performance impact, 249–251
    separating responsibilities, 133
    switch/case statements, 228
    in test cases, 44–45, 134, 277–282
    transforming Light Scheduler code, 232–248
regression testing, 9, 91
RUN_TEST_CASE, 18, 299
RUN_TEST_GROUP, 19
runtime library issues, 84–88

S
seams, 120, 257
sensing variables, 257
setup, 22

Shotgun Surgery, 200
single-instance modules, 28, 194
Single-Responsibility Principle (SRP), 190
software entropy, 220, 286
SOLID design principles
    defined, 189–192
    implementing in C, 193–195
spies
    defined, 114
    and dead drops, 125
    FormatOutputSpy class, 153–155
    header files of, 124
    in Light Scheduler, 120–122
    LightControllerSpy class, 121–145
    LightDriverSpy class, 196–210
    verifying printed output, 152–159
static variables, 230
STRCMP_EQUAL, 304
strstr(), 84
stubs
    defined, 114
    in Light Scheduler, 126

T
TDOCs (Transitively Depended On Components), 110
teardown, 22
test builds
    and development environment, 19
    build time, 98
    makefiles, 293–295
test cases
    antipatterns, 277–283
    Behavior-Driven Development (BDD) tests, 283
    boundary conditions, 57–63
    buffer overruns, 16
    in CppUTest, 21
    defined, 14
    as documentation, 9, 50
    experiments, 59
    ignoring, 63
    interface testing, 36
    randomness, 147–152
    as regression tests, 91
    in Unity, 15–17

test code, 14
test doubles
　defined, 107
　function-pointer substitution, 147–159
　link-time substitution, 119–126
　managing dependencies with, 110–111
　substitution techniques in C, 113–115
　types of, 114
　uses, 112–113
test fixtures
　in CppUTest, 21–23
　defined, 14
　in Unity, 17–18
test lists, 29–31
test points (legacy code), 257–260
Test-After Development, 97
Test-Driven Development (TDD)
　benefits, 6, 8–10, 51, 285
　vs. Debug-Later Programming, 5, 97
　defined, 4–5
　and device drivers, 163–180
　embedded development cycle, 80–83
　"fake it til you make it", 43
　Four-Phase Test, 25
　and legacy code, 253–274
　microcycle, 6
　objections to adopting, 93–101
　physics of, 7
　state machine for, 45–46
　as structured procrastination, 41
　test disrespect, 283
　Three Laws of, 36
　time required, 93–97, 286
TEST_ASSERT_BYTES_EQUAL, 300
TEST_ASSERT_EQUAL, 15, 300
TEST_ASSERT_EQUAL_INT, 300
TEST_ASSERT_EQUAL_STRING, 15, 300
TEST_ASSERT_FALSE, 299
TEST_ASSERT_FLOAT_WITHIN, 300
TEST_ASSERT_POINTERS_EQUAL, 300
TEST_ASSERT_TRUE, 299
TEST_FAIL_MESSAGE, 300
TEST_GROUP, 297–299
　in CppUTest, 22, 138, 303
　in Unity, 17
TEST_GROUP_RUNNER, 18, 299
TEST_SETUP, 17, 298
TEST_TEAR_DOWN, 17, 298
third-party code, 271–273
thread creation
　Micrium, 317
　POSIX, 315
　Win32, 319
Three Laws of TDD, 36
time-dependent code
　abstracting the clock, 126
　clock rollover, 179
　device timeout, 178–179

U

unit test harnesses
　vs. custom test harness, 94
　defined, 13–14
　and legacy code, 263–268
　test execution order, 305
unit tests
　antipatterns, 277–283
　FIRST attributes, 46
　Four-Phase Test pattern, 25, 110
　GivWenZen style, 284
　and legacy code, 256–260
　manual, 94
　vs. other test types, 98
　process-heavy, 95–97
　single-stepping, 95
　small and focused, 43
Unity
　examples, 15–19
　output, 19–21
　quick reference, 297–301

V

virtual function tables (vtables), 211–214

W

Windows development environment, 292–293

Z

Zune bug, 2–4

Long Live the Command Line!

Use tmux and Vim for incredible mouse-free productivity.

Your mouse is slowing you down. The time you spend context switching between your editor and your consoles eats away at your productivity. Take control of your environment with tmux, a terminal multiplexer that you can tailor to your workflow. Learn how to customize, script, and leverage tmux's unique abilities and keep your fingers on your keyboard's home row.

Brian P. Hogan
(88 pages) ISBN: 9781934356968. $16.25
http://pragprog.com/titles/bhtmux

Vim is a fast and efficient text editor that will make you a faster and more efficient developer. It's available on almost every OS—if you master the techniques in this book, you'll never need another text editor. In more than 100 Vim tips, you'll quickly learn the editor's core functionality and tackle your trickiest editing and writing tasks.

Drew Neil
(346 pages) ISBN: 9781934356982. $29
http://pragprog.com/titles/dnvim

Tinker, Tailor, Solder, and DIY!

Get into the DIY spirit with Raspberry Pi or Arduino. What will you build next?

The Raspberry Pi is one of the most successful open source hardware projects ever. For less than $40, you get a full-blown PC, a multimedia center, and a web server—and this book gives you everything you need to get started. You'll learn the basics, progress to controlling the Pi, and then build your own electronics projects. This new edition is revised and updated with two new chapters on adding digital and analog sensors, and creating videos and a burglar alarm with the Pi camera. *Printed in full color.*

Maik Schmidt
(176 pages) ISBN: 9781937785802. $22
http://pragprog.com/titles/msraspi2

Arduino is an open-source platform that makes DIY electronics projects easier than ever. Even if you have no electronics experience, you'll be creating your first gadgets within a few minutes. Step-by-step instructions show you how to build a universal remote, a motion-sensing game controller, and many other fun, useful projects. This book has now been updated for Arduino 1.0, with revised code, examples, and screenshots throughout. We've changed all the book's examples and added new examples showing how to use the Arduino IDE's new features.

Maik Schmidt
(272 pages) ISBN: 9781934356661. $35
http://pragprog.com/titles/msard

Explore TDD in C++ and Node

Expand your TDD skills in C++, and explore what Node has to offer.

If you program in C++ you've been neglected. Test-driven development (TDD) is a modern software development practice that can dramatically reduce the number of defects in systems, produce more maintainable code, and give you the confidence to change your software to meet changing needs. But C++ programmers have been ignored by those promoting TDD—until now. In this book, Jeff Langr gives you hands-on lessons in the challenges and rewards of doing TDD in C++.

Jeff Langr
(380 pages) ISBN: 9781937785482. $40
http://pragprog.com/titles/lotdd

Get to the forefront of server-side JavaScript programming by writing compact, robust, fast, networked Node applications that scale. Ready to take JavaScript beyond the browser, explore dynamic languages features and embrace evented programming? Explore the fun, growing repository of Node modules provided by npm. Work with multiple protocols, load-balanced RESTful web services, express, ØMQ, Redis, CouchDB, and more. Develop production-grade Node applications fast.

Jim R. Wilson
(148 pages) ISBN: 9781937785734. $17
http://pragprog.com/titles/jwnode

The Pragmatic Bookshelf

The Pragmatic Bookshelf features books written by developers for developers. The titles continue the well-known Pragmatic Programmer style and continue to garner awards and rave reviews. As development gets more and more difficult, the Pragmatic Programmers will be there with more titles and products to help you stay on top of your game.

Visit Us Online

This Book's Home Page
http://pragprog.com/titles/jgade
Source code from this book, errata, and other resources. Come give us feedback, too!

Register for Updates
http://pragprog.com/updates
Be notified when updates and new books become available.

Join the Community
http://pragprog.com/community
Read our weblogs, join our online discussions, participate in our mailing list, interact with our wiki, and benefit from the experience of other Pragmatic Programmers.

New and Noteworthy
http://pragprog.com/news
Check out the latest pragmatic developments, new titles and other offerings.

Save on the eBook

Save on the eBook versions of this title. Owning the paper version of this book entitles you to purchase the electronic versions at a terrific discount.

PDFs are great for carrying around on your laptop—they are hyperlinked, have color, and are fully searchable. Most titles are also available for the iPhone and iPod touch, Amazon Kindle, and other popular e-book readers.

Buy now at *http://pragprog.com/coupon*

Contact Us

Online Orders:	*http://pragprog.com/catalog*
Customer Service:	*support@pragprog.com*
International Rights:	*translations@pragprog.com*
Academic Use:	*academic@pragprog.com*
Write for Us:	*http://pragprog.com/write-for-us*
Or Call:	+1 800-699-7764

CPSIA information can be obtained at www.ICGtesting.com
Printed in the USA
BVOW07s1641220715

409930BV00022B/160/P